CHARLES McLEAN ANDREWS

Number 588
COLUMBIA STUDIES IN THE SOCIAL SCIENCES
Edited by the Faculty of Political Science
of Columbia University

Charles M. Andrews.

CHARLES McLEAN ANDREWS

A STUDY IN AMERICAN HISTORICAL WRITING

A. S. EISENSTADT

AMS PRESS
NEW YORK

THE COLUMBIA STUDIES IN THE SOCIAL SCIENCES (formerly the Studies in History, Economics, and Public Law) is a series edited by the Faculty of Political Science of Columbia University and published by Columbia University Press for the purpose of making available scholarly studies produced within the Faculty.

Reprinted with the permission of Columbia University Press
From the edition of 1956, New York
First AMS EDITION published 1968
Manufactured in the United States of America

Library of Congress Catalogue Card Number: 68-54261

AMS PRESS, INC.
New York, N.Y. 10003

TO MY WIFE

ACKNOWLEDGMENTS

I am pleased to record my very great debt to Professor Richard B. Morris, of Columbia University, whose knowledge, counsel, and interest I drew upon at every stage of my work. I also owe much to Professor R. L. Schuyler, with whom I began the study of historiography in general, and to Professor L. W. Labaree, who helped me define the problem with which this volume is concerned in particular. I have been helped considerably by the suggestions and criticisms of Professors Jacques Barzun, Solomon F. Bloom, Jesse D. Clarkson, Thomas P. Furcron, Lawrence Henry Gipson, Samuel J. Hurwitz, Dumas Malone, and Chilton Williamson.

My acknowledgments would hardly be complete without a note of gratitude to those whose assistance went beyond the scholastic: to Professor Herman Ausubel, for his encouragement and friendship; to Mrs. Charles M. Andrews, for her kindness and generosity; to my mother, for her concern and patience; and to my father, for the inspiring example he set, during the course of his life, with his own cultivations in another literary garden.

A. S. EISENSTADT

Brooklyn College
September, 1955

CONTENTS

INTRODUCTION

The proper study of mankind is not merely man. It is man within an historical context, man in relation to the larger currents of his age. And what is true of the study of man in general is no less true of the study of a man in particular. A biography is more than the portrait of an individual, it is something of a mirror to his age as well.

The portrait of Charles McLean Andrews reveals both an age and a distinguished historian. By the time of Andrews' death in 1943, he had made an impressive contribution to American historiography. His published works, containing some twenty volumes, considerably more articles, and several hundred book reviews, constituted a valuable legacy to the world of historical scholarship. The principal element of that legacy, and the one to which he had devoted over forty years of his labor, was his contribution to the field of American colonial history. Indeed, so signal was the contribution that his name became inseparably linked with the study of the early American past.

The writing of history was not the only component of his legacy. Andrews was also a maker of historians, a teacher, the founder of a school of American colonial history. He played an important role as editor, lecturer, and friend and adviser of historians. He served the needs of professional history as champion of the cause of documents and archives, as member of numerous historical societies, as president of the American Historical Association.

At his death, however, he left more than a monumental personal achievement in historiography. He left a monument to the times. By his work, indeed, may we know them. His own career was a summary of that new history [1] which arose in America during the late nineteenth century. Andrews was trained in the 1880's at what was then the foremost center of postgraduate studies in history, the Johns Hopkins University; and his master was Herbert Baxter Adams, the outstanding leader and organizer of the new history. He grew to maturity at the very time that the advanced study, teaching, and writing of history was being organized and shaped into a formal profession. His training at Johns Hopkins brought Andrews into direct contact with the basic ingredients of the new history: the critical use of source materials, the individual research as well as the cooperative enterprise of the seminar, the publication of the findings of research in monographic studies for the benefit of a growing world of historical scholarship. That the world of the new historians was growing, and growing rapidly, there could be little doubt. Other centers of professional historical study were either opening up or expanding at the University of Michigan, at Cornell, at Harvard, at Columbia. University studies were beginning to appear, containing the monographic produce of the rising gild of historians. The rise of the gild was nowhere better signalized than by the organization, in 1884, of the American Historical Association. And when the *American Historical Review* was launched in 1895, it meant that the new history was speaking with a national voice.

But the new history was more than a matter of externals, more than seminars, sources, and societies. It had a standard, a goal to pursue, an ideal. That ideal was best defined by the famous precept of Ranke's that the past had to be presented as it actually was. If the precept had meant, to Ranke, a philologist's ideal for using the sources critically, it came to mean, to the American historian of the late nineteenth century, a scientist's ideal for recapturing the past. The simple motto of Ranke had, in the course of the middle decades of the nineteenth century, been enhanced and transformed by a variety of factors: by the convictions of a world astir with the possibilities of science; by the teachings of Comte, Darwin, Spencer, and Buckle; by the vitality of America's expanding and scientific industry. Consequently, the new historian of late nineteenth-century America was, more than anything else, a man of science, a skilled worker of the most precise methods, a laboratory technician par excellence. And history was a science, a testing for exact information, a probing for incontrovertible fact, a rediscovery of the actuality of the past. This was the ideal which inspired the school in which Andrews belonged. The spirit and method of "historical science" were the very mainsprings of his system of historiography.

It is with that system of historiography—the principles and contents of Andrews' contribution—that the present study is primarily concerned. The study is nowhere designed to be a formal biography, nor does it purport to give a chronological account of his efforts. It is not concerned with his family connections or with his personality, except where they impinge upon the ideas and substance of his historical writings. These writings, indeed, constitute the focus of interest: it was through them that Andrews was known to the world of scholarship and through them that he at once influenced and reflected the new history. That very matter of the relation between the contribution of Andrews and that of the new school of American colonial history provides a second point of stress in this study. Attention is directed not merely to a system of historiography, but to a system of historiography set within the broader context of its times. An attempt is made, in this respect, to understand the achievement of Andrews as a product of the scientific age of American historiography, and to establish the degree to which he represented the school in which he belonged. The study seeks, further, to ascertain to what extent the new colonial history which Andrews helped write was a facet of the social thinking of his age. It seeks, finally, to examine the meaning for the contribution of Andrews of the rise of a newer colonial history during the final decades of his life.

The structure of the present study has been defined by its central theme: the growth and maturation of a great historian's system and the relation of that system to that of his age. Because this theme is treated both topically and chronologically, it is inevitable that there should be a certain amount of repetition of material. The first part of the study deals with the development of Andrews' historiography during his formative years, during the period, that is, when he was concerned principally with European history and before he fully entered upon a study of American colonial history. This part discusses the historiographic legacy he received from Herbert Baxter Adams and Johns Hopkins and presents the system of historiography which he formulated and practiced during his early years as professional historian. The second part examines Andrews' contribution to the field of his major interest, American colonial history. Analyzing the purely substantive elements of his system, the actual contents of his works, this part undertakes to reveal how Andrews came into this area, and what he said about the field of history to which he applied his larger historiographic principles. The third part attempts to see how those historiographic principles were reflected in the writings of his later years, the years he devoted to the study of American colonial history. It also attempts to see how these principles of historiography were reflected in areas other than his historical writings. The final part explores the system of Andrews in relation to that of the school to which he belonged; and, presenting his contribution as the product of a particular era, it indicates how that contribution grew obsolescent in the context of a changing history and of a changing history of history.

Ultimately, the problem is whether a system of historiography may not be merely an aspect of the corporate thinking of an age, bearing upon it a date-stamp, as much subject to change as history itself. And if, indeed, the history of history is essentially social thinking, what then is truth in history? Is it the established actuality of the past, the unalterable fact which the scientific historian so zealously pursued? Or is truth a variable commodity, answering for one age but questionable in the next? If it is, then nearly all our monumental works of history shall one day be colossal wrecks, stones standing in the desert, their epoch stamped on lifeless things.

ANDREWS and HIS AGE
a CHRONOLOGY
1863–1943

Note: Unless otherwise indicated, the author of all the volumes cited is Andrews.

1863 Born February 22, in Wethersfield, Connecticut, to the Reverend William Watson Andrews and his wife Elizabeth Williams.

1869 Charles Kendall Adams introduces a seminar in history at Michigan.

1871 Henry Adams introduces a seminar in history at Harvard.

1876 Opening of the Johns Hopkins University at Baltimore, first institution devoted exclusively to postgraduate study and research. Herbert Baxter Adams appointed fellow in history at the University.

Essays in Anglo-Saxon Law, by Henry Adams and his seminar students at Harvard, among whom was Henry Cabot Lodge.

1880 John Burgess organizes the Faculty of Political Science at Columbia.

1882 Appearance of the first volume of the Johns Hopkins University Studies in Historical and Political Science.

1883 Final edition of George Bancroft's *History of the United States of America* (author's last revision, 6 volumes, 1883–85).

1884 Andrews graduates from Trinity College, Hartford; becomes principal of the West Hartford High School.

Founding of the American Historical Association at Saratoga Springs, N. Y.

First volume of Justin Winsor's *Narrative and Critical History of America* (8 volumes, 1884–89).

1886 Andrews enters graduate study in history at Johns Hopkins.

Political Science Quarterly begins to appear.

1887 Herbert Levi Osgood's article on "England and the Colonies" in the *Political Science Quarterly* signalizes the new approach to American colonial history.

1889 Andrews graduates from Johns Hopkins with Ph.D. degree. Appearance of his doctoral study, *The River Towns of Connecticut.* Receives appointment to Bryn Mawr.
Henry Adams, *History of the United States.* (9 volumes, 1889–91).

1890 Osgood begins to teach at Columbia.

1891 John Fiske, *The American Revolution* (2 volumes).
J. F. Jameson, *A History of Historical Writing in America.* First major study of American historiography.
Death of George Bancroft.

1892 *The Old English Manor.*

1893 Andrews spends summer in England, at the Public Record Office. Had been sent by Frederick D. Stone of the Pennsylvania Historical Society to examine Board of Trade papers. Decides to devote himself to study of American colonial history.
Andrews meets his future wife, Evangeline Walker, a student of English at Bryn Mawr.
G. L. Beer, *The Commercial Policy of England toward the American Colonies.* First major study incorporating the "imperial viewpoint." Beer a student of Osgood's at Columbia.
Frederick Jackson Turner, "The Significance of the Frontier in American History." Address to the American Historical Association.

1895 Andrews is married to Evangeline Walker.
Appearance of the *American Historical Review.*

1896 *The Historical Development of Modern Europe,* Volume I.

1897 Moses C. Tyler, *The Literary History of the American Revolution, 1763–1783* (2 volumes).

1898 Osgood and Andrews address the American Historical Association on "The Study of American Colonial History" and "American Colonial History, 1690–1750," respectively. Constitutes a formal opening of the new study of early America.
The Historical Development of Modern Europe, Volume II.
E. B. Greene, *The Provincial Governor.*

1901 Death of Herbert Baxter Adams.

1902 S. G. Fisher, *The True History of the American Revolution.* C. H. Van Tyne, *The Loyalists in the American Revolution.*

1903 Andrews goes to England to pursue studies in American colonial history. After much correspondence, Andrews undertakes to prepare guides to the British archival materials for the study of American colonial history; project is sponsored and financed by the Carnegie Institution of Washington. Andrews spends the year 1903–4, during which he is on sabbatical leave from Bryn Mawr, doing the basic work on the guides. Recataloguing of the materials at the Public Record Office requires several additional visits during the next decade.

1904 The American Nation Series, constituting the first synthesis of the new American history, begins to appear, under the editorship of A. B. Hart of Harvard. Contains contributions by E. P. Cheyney, E. B. Greene, C. H. Van Tyne, A. C. McLaughlin, and C. M. Andrews. *Colonial Self-Government, 1652–1689* represents Andrews' first major contribution to the field of American colonial history.

Appearance of first two volumes of Osgood's *American Colonies in the Seventeenth Century.*

1905 Edward Channing, *A History of the United States* (6 volumes, 1905–25).

1907 Andrews goes to Johns Hopkins to fill position left vacant by death of Herbert Adams (1901).

G. L. Beer, *British Colonial Policy, 1754–1765.*

1908 *Guide to the Manuscript Materials for the History of the United States to 1783, in the British Museum, in Minor London Archives, and in the Libraries of Oxford and Cambridge* (with Frances G. Davenport).

Conference on research in American colonial and revolutionary history, American Historical Association. Addresses by Osgood, Beer, Andrews, and Van Tyne.

The presidential message of George Burton Adams to the American Historical Association, on "History and the Philosophy of History," defends the scientific ideal and the precepts of Ranke.

1910 Andrews becomes Farnam Professor of American history at Yale University, giving courses exclusively in American colonial history.

1912 *The Colonial Period* (Home University Library).
Guide to the Materials for American History to 1783 in the Public Record Office of Great Britain, Volume I.
Editor of *The Yale Historical Publications* (until 1933).
G. L. Beer, *The Old Colonial System, Part I: 1660–1688* (2 volumes).
James Harvey Robinson, *The New History: Essays Illustrating the Modern Historical Outlook.*

1914 *Guide to the Materials for American History to 1783 in the Public Record Office of Great Britain,* Volume II.

1915 Carl L. Becker, *Beginnings of the American People.*

1917 C. W. Alvord, *The Mississippi Valley in British Politics* (2 volumes).
John S. Bassett, *The Middle Group of American Historians.*

1918 Arthur M. Schlesinger, *The Colonial Merchants and the American Revolution, 1763–1776.*
Death of H. L. Osgood.

1919 *The Fathers of New England.*
Colonial Folkways.
"Present-Day Thoughts on the American Revolution," Phi Beta Kappa address delivered by Andrews, June 18, 1919, at the University of Georgia.

1920 Death of G. L. Beer.

1922 C. H. Van Tyne, *The Causes of the War of Independence.*
R. G. Adams, *Political Ideas of the American Revolution.*
Carl Becker, *Declaration of Independence.*
A. M. Schlesinger, *New Viewpoints in American History.*

1924 *Colonial Background of the American Revolution.*
Andrews becomes acting president of the American Historical Association upon the death of Woodrow Wilson. His address to the Association, "These Forty Years," is one of his major commentaries on his own historiography and that of his age.
H. L. Osgood, *American Colonies in the Eighteenth Century* (4 volumes). Osgood had died in 1918 and the works were published posthumously on a grant from Dwight L. Morrow, a student of Osgood's.

1925 Andrews serves as president of the American Historical Association. His presidential message is on "The American Revolution: An Interpretation."

1926 Andrews and his wife take a trip around the world, 1926–27.
J. F. Jameson, *The American Revolution Considered as a Social Movement.*

1927 A. M. Schlesinger and D. R. Fox, eds., *A History of American Life* (13 volumes, 1927–48). The volumes on the colonial period are: T. J. Wertenbaker, *The First Americans, 1607–1690* (1927); J. T. Adams, *Provincial Society, 1690–1763* (1928); and E. B. Greene, *The Revolutionary Generation, 1763–1790* (1943).
Charles A. and Mary R. Beard, *The Rise of American Civilization.*
Vernon L. Parrington, *Main Currents of American Thought.*

1930 Death of C. H. Van Tyne.

1931 Andrews retires from Yale but continues until 1933 as Director of Historical Publications.
Essays in Colonial History Presented To Charles McLean Andrews by His Students. (The *Festschrift* contains essays by S. M. Pargellis, L. W. Labaree, D. M. Clark, C. P. Gould, L. H. Gipson, as well as an introduction by his most notable student of the Bryn Mawr period, Nellie Neilson.)
The presidential message of Carl Becker to the American Historical Association on "Everyman His Own Historian" sounds the relativist approach to the past.
Death of Edward Channing.

1932 Death of Frederick Jackson Turner.

1933 *Our Earliest Colonial Settlements.*
The presidential message of Charles A. Beard to the American Historical Association on "Written History as an Act of Faith" is a further sounding of the relativist viewpoint.

1934 *The Colonial Period of American History: The Settlements* (Volume I).

1935 Andrews awarded the Pulitzer Prize for the first volume of his *Colonial Period of American History.*

1936 *The Colonial Period of American History: The Settlements* (Volume II).
L. H. Gipson, *The British Empire before the American Revolution* (8 volumes, 1936–54).

1937 *The Colonial Period of American History: The Settlements* (Volume III).
M. Kraus, *A History of American History.*
W. T. Hutchinson, ed., *The Marcus W. Jernegan Essays in American Historiography.*
Andrews awarded gold medal for history and biography by National Institute of Arts and Letters.
Death of J. F. Jameson.

1938 *The Colonial Period of American History: England's Commercial and Colonial Policies* (Volume IV).
Andrews is stricken with illness while Volume IV is in galley.
Carl Bridenbaugh, *Cities in the Wilderness.*
Curtis P. Nettels, *The Roots of American Civilization.*

1943 Death of Andrews, at East Dover, Vermont, September 9.

PART I

THE FORMATIVE YEARS 1886-1903

Chapter 1

THE LEGACY of HERBERT BAXTER ADAMS

If he was destined to make his name in the world of scholarship, the young man of twenty-three who enrolled at Johns Hopkins that fall of 1886 had not as yet given very much evidence of it. As a matter of fact, the evidence concerning the youth from Wethersfield, Connecticut, seemed to run just the other way. Certainly, his first teacher, the tall and acerb New England spinster who taught the elementary grades in Wethersfield, would little have predicted a great success for her mischievous charge. Her own conviction was that he would surely "come to some bad end." [1] Nor did he in any way distinguish himself at the Hartford High School, from which he graduated in 1879. His younger sister recalled that "he was not a specially keen student" and that "he took no prizes and had no honor standing." [2] He could speak well, however, and, at the graduating exercises, elegantly clad in a Prince Albert coat (borrowed for the occasion), the youth of sixteen delivered a self-possessed and graceful oration on Constantinople. At Trinity College, Charles Andrews showed something of his sentiments about things academic in general and things at Trinity in particular by deciding, when he was halfway through his course, that he wanted to abandon his education completely and go into business.[3] Only his mother's persuasion kept him to the end of his course of study. His scholarship at college, reminisced his sister, was no more noteworthy than his scholarship at high school. He managed to keep up with his class, but little more: "he did not distinguish himself as a student, and graduated without any special honors." [4] What evidence he did offer of ability was remarkably confined to fields other than history. He won awards for oratory and for an essay on "The Future of

Astronomy." He was designated Poet of the Class of '84 and spoke at the commencement exercises.[5]

At twenty-one, he was ready to pursue his career, without quite knowing what the career should be. He accepted the principalship of the West Hartford High School only in order to avail himself of an opportunity for further rumination. It was here that the first glimmerings of an affinity between the young man from Connecticut and the world of scholarship became apparent. He discovered soon enough that he liked to teach. What he did not like, however, was the problem of discipline and large classes that seemed to be part of secondary school education.[6] It can be readily understood why, at this critical juncture in his life, Charles Andrews eagerly took up the suggestion of a friend that he go to Johns Hopkins for a Ph.D. If he had a higher degree, he might hope to teach on the college level. Whatever doubts he may have had about his career were thus dispelled. He had saved some money of his own, and generous assistance would be forthcoming from his aunt, whose husband's name he bore.[7] Brimming with a sense of anticipation, and inspired by the prospects of a high position in the teaching profession, Charles Andrews journeyed southward to Baltimore.[8]

Not that other minds and other influences had not encouraged him in a different direction. His Puritan ancestry and the vocation of his forebears should surely have predestined him for the ministry: his father and his uncle had been pastors in the Congregational Church and the foremost leaders of the Catholic Apostolic movement in the United States.[9] "By all the laws of heredity and by all the influences that are brought to bear on youthful and adolescent minds, I ought to have been a minister, for the family tried to make me one."[10] It is not for us to probe just why the predilections of the father were not assumed by the son. Possibly the ministry no longer had the meaning or the appeal it had had in an earlier society. Possibly it was a self-asserting rejection by the son of the wishes of the father. At the very worst, however, teaching—which the young man preferred—was not very far removed from preaching; and if the garments were different, they were both cut from essentially the same cloth. Whatever his private thoughts on the subject may have been in that year of grace 1886, the enthusiastic and spirited young man, casting his eye upon the present and feeling sanguine about the future, decided to throw in his lot with the past.

1. JOHNS HOPKINS AND HERBERT ADAMS

Both history and historians were being made at Baltimore in 1886. The Johns Hopkins University was the most prominent center of the new historical science. Endowed by the rich Baltimore merchant whose name it carried, the university had begun activity in 1876, its purposes being primarily to promote postgraduate work in many fields of study and to afford "specialized training for the preparation of research scholars." [11] The young men who received their training in historical and political science at Johns Hopkins during the 1880's constituted a veritable who's who of the new history: Charles Andrews was but one in a distinguished group that also included John Spencer Bassett, John Dewey, Richard T. Ely, Charles Homer Haskins, John Franklin Jameson, Frederick Jackson Turner, John Martin Vincent, James Albert Woodburn, and Woodrow Wilson. Here could be found, with almost classic exactitude—in one place and at one time—the dramatis personae of the rising historical science. Nor was it lost upon the students of that science that they were attending the genesis of a newer and better firmament, for never were young men so conscious of their task, of their responsibility, of their unique position. Many decades later, Jameson, who had been the first to receive the Ph.D. in history at the new university,[12] recalled that "those were halcyon days of a novel and brilliant educational experiment, when it was a joy to be alive, and when new horizons opened before the eyes of studious youth." [13] Andrews himself characterized these years as "a time of great awakening in the American historical world . . . a time of exhilaration and almost religious fervor among the younger scholars . . . a true renaissance, in which the conception and treatment of history

. . . rose above the level of mere schoolmastering and became creative." [14]

In that "true renaissance," if the patron was the merchant who had given Baltimore its great university, then the Leonardo was surely Herbert Baxter Adams. Perhaps a better view of the latter's achievements was taken by Woodrow Wilson, who called him "a great Captain of Industry, a captain in the field of systematic and organized scholarship." [15] From his postgraduate studies in Germany, Adams had come to Johns Hopkins as a fellow in 1876, the very year the university began its work. His enthusiastic and arduous activities were responsible, in the main, for making Baltimore the capital of advanced historical training. Indeed, for two and a half decades, until his death in 1901, he was the spirit incarnate of the new history.[16] He played an important role in organizing the American Historical Association in 1884 and, as secretary of the Association for sixteen years, helped fashion its policies and guide its progress.[17] From Baltimore he was in constant correspondence with fellow historians throughout the nation, advising them now, being advised then, always fitting the detail into a pattern and organizing the parts into a systematic whole.[18] He spread the dominion of the new history by means of a scholastic "imperialism" upon which he embarked almost at the outset of his professional career. The imperial center at Baltimore served as a school for his young "missi dominici." Having thoroughly trained them, Adams dispatched his ambassadors throughout the American realm, to bring to the provinces the methods and principles of advanced historical research which they had learned at Baltimore.

What were these methods and principles? Imported in their essential features from Germany, where Adams had himself studied, they were designed to make a master historian out of an apprentice. The student was put through an intensive program. He was required to possess a reading acquaintance with French and German authorities in the field of historical and political science. He was to specialize in a particular field, "which though limited shall nevertheless be sufficiently broad to illustrate general truth, the theory being that the way to the general is through that which is special, or *universalia in rebus*."[19] Class work in the different lecture courses might variously demand a knowledge of source materials, oral reports, joint discussions, and the exposition of original texts. The heart and symbol of the new history, however, was the work done in the seminar. Here the primary sources were tested, analyzed, and synthesized; here were fashioned the products of the new historical science. Adams liked to think that "the Baltimore seminaries are laboratories where books are treated like mineralogical specimens, passed about from hand to hand, examined and tested."[20] The seminar might have its own special library of books relating to the general subject under consideration.[21] The seminar groups would be smaller than the usual lecture classes, generally numbering no more than ten; meeting weekly or every fortnight, the students would discuss topics previously assigned them for research.[22] "The natural outgrowth and highest requirement of the above system," ran a list of requirements for the Ph.D. drafted by Adams in 1884, "is a graduating thesis, which must be a positive contribution to special knowledge in the candidate's chosen field."[23] Adams was perceptive enough, moreover, to provide his system with the spur of practical demonstration and rewards. The findings of original research were presented, from time to time, at the Historical and Political Science Association of the university. Meritorious studies might be accepted for publication in the Johns Hopkins University Studies in Historical and Political Science, the first volume of which appeared in 1882. And once they had completed their course of study, the young doctors of philosophy might expect that Professor Adams would undertake to secure their placement in the increasingly more numerous colleges and in the expanding departments of history throughout the country.

It was into this regimen of study that Andrews was introduced when he came to Baltimore in 1886. If, in later years, he was to reminisce pleasurably about "the richness of the early days" at Johns Hopkins and "the flair of enjoyment" which historical enterprise inspired in his classmates and himself,[24] all did not, as a matter of fact, go entirely well with him at the beginning. Indeed, he entertained very serious doubts about the validity of that very principle of advanced historical research which underlay the new history. "There is unfortunately the universal tendency to specialize," he wrote his mother, "to force men into lines requiring special definite work, political, historical, and philological. The desire is to confine the students to one class of work, to require an evidence of interest and practical study in that line in the shape of theses, original work. Too often I think this is done to the detriment of their knowledge of other things, of a broad comprehensive culture." [25]

As the months went by, however, he began to see things differently. Perhaps this was due in measure to the intellectual stimulus of some of the courses he was taking, such as those with Jameson in American history, or with Richard Ely in political economy, or with Woodrow Wilson in administration. The last he found to be "a live subject, treated by a live man." [26] The writer of the brilliant and well-received treatise on *Congressional Government* (1885) impressed Andrews as "an original thinker and a clear lecturer and we feel we are growing under his instruction." [27] Perhaps the "Seminary of History and Politics" conducted by Adams was winning Andrews over to Johns Hopkins and to the new history. It was in this seminar that Andrews was inducted into the rigors and exactitude of historical science, the disciplines of its textual criticisms and of its historical exercises, the ritual of examining documents as though they were laboratory specimens. Perhaps he was enjoying the distinction of having been called upon, in November, 1887, to present his first effort in postgraduate research, "An Historical Sketch of Popular Suffrage in Maryland," before the Historical and Political Science Association of the university.[28] In a subsequent talk, one dealing with the settlement of Wethersfield, he set forth his views on a subject which he would explore more comprehensively in his doctoral dissertation.[29] Whatever the factors may have been that encouraged a change of attitude on his part, it was clear enough that by the time he was well into his second year of study Andrews was thinking differently. "It is wonderful, the influence this University has upon a fellow. I can hardly explain it. It seems to develop the faintest germ of ability and to rouse any latent enthusiasm which a man may have. They do not push nor even urge, they let the atmosphere work its proper course: the growth is slow but it is always in the right direction and the more one knows of the University and its workings the grander its methods become. I am fast becoming a stanch upholder of Johns Hopkins and my basis of authority is what I feel it has done for me and I must add is still doing. It is slowly generating what I need so much, a confidence in myself." [30]

In generating that confidence, Herbert Adams played no small part. It was characteristic of him to take a strong personal interest in the men of his seminar. "I have never seen a man," wrote one of his foremost students, Frederick Jackson Turner, "who could surpass him in inspiring men with enthusiasm for serious historical work and in bringing out the best that was in them." [31] Even at the outset of his studies at Johns Hopkins, Andrews recognized this distinctive quality of Adams, observing that his master's "chief value seems to be in inspiring the members of his class to work." [32] The bond between master and student grew stronger during the three-year program, particularly inasmuch as most of Andrews' courses were taken with Adams. The latter, however, was offering his young charge something more tangible than encouragement. In his last year at the university Andrews was given a fellowship in return for which he was to assist Adams in the seminar and "to have largely the control and ordering of its work." [33] It was reassuring, too, to have Adams accept for publication in the Studies his doctoral dissertation on *The River Towns of Connecticut.* And if the very last step in the course of study was getting a job, here too Adams was helpful. The position of associate in history at Bryn Mawr College, which Andrews received in May, 1889, he felt to be "more than I deserve and I owe the appointment to the efforts of Dr. Gilman [34] and Dr.

Adams, not to any merit of my own." [35] The "great debt" he owed his master Andrews recognized readily enough.[36] The debt went beyond mere encouragements and rewards, however, It involved a system of historiography.

That system was compounded of something more than externals, something more than methods, internal criticism, original sources, and seminar techniques. It contained, too, the basic themes of Herbert Adams' history, the ideas about the past which he had so enthusiastically and convincingly presented to his classes. Integral to these themes and ideas, in one sense at least, were the precepts of Ranke and the whole spirit of "scientific" history. For Adams, as indeed for his generation, Ranke was "the father of historical science" [37] and nothing could be more historically scientific than presenting the past *wie es eigentlich gewesen.* The principle of the great German historian, declared Adams, "was to tell things exactly as they occurred. He held strictly to the facts in the case. He did not attempt to preach a sermon, or point a moral, or adorn a tale, but simply to tell the truth as he understood it." [38] The fact of it was that Ranke had neither argued for nor been able to practice any such principle. And if indeed he was telling the truth *"as he understood it,"* then he was letting in through the backdoor what he was keeping out at the front. At the very least, however, Ranke gave that generation of Americans a slogan for their new history. The meaning of *wie es eigentlich* as a plea for historical-mindedness was for the greater part lost; and the Ranke who was hailed in the preface had long been forgotten by the time of the index. That generation's picture of the past as it actually was could not but reflect the actuality of their own present. No matter what his invocation of the spirit of Ranke, the world of late nineteenth-century America was too much with Herbert Adams for it to be cut out of his view of the past.

That very world was alive with an ideal of science which could not but communicate itself to the gild of historians. Central to the scientific ideal perhaps were the implications of Darwinism. From the greatest natural scientist of their times the new historians had drawn lessons for their own "science."

It was not fortuitous, therefore, that the age of Herbert Adams constantly thought of history in terms of biology. Something of a summary of Adams' whole orientation may be found in his assertion that the United States "will yet be viewed and re-viewed as an organism of historic growth, developing from minute germs, from the very protoplasm of state life." [39] The essence of historical study, to his way of thinking, was the evolution of political institutions, which were best seen organically, and which were to be traced back from their ascendant position in the modern world, through their period of growth, to the originally small institutional germs whence they had sprung.[40]

If Ranke afforded him a moral precept and Darwin proffered a scientific ideal, Adams turned elsewhere for those specific ideas with which he undertook to define the course of recent American history. These ideas he derived from the teaching of his German mentors as well as from his reading among the political scientists and historians of the English school. He fully subscribed to the observation of his foremost master at Heidelberg, Johann Bluntschli, that history was merely a handmaid to politics.[41] Certainly, Adams hoped to use the past to give him further clues to the political present, a present which he saw moving in the direction of centralization and democracy. Surely the recent emergence of the German Empire as well as the outcome of the Civil War would seem to have corroborated this view. The ultimate goal of history, he agreed with Bluntschli, was an ideal world-state.[42]

The view which Adams took of the past also owed something to members of the English school. Edward Augustus Freeman, who had visited the United States in 1881 and who had been invited to speak at Johns Hopkins, furnished Adams with an aphorism, if not too much more. Freeman's assertion that "history is past politics, and politics are present history" was adopted as the motto of the Johns Hopkins Studies in Historical and Political Science. For Adams, the assertion went beyond being simply a commentary as to what field of human activity should constitute the central concern of the historian.[43] It signified too his concurrence with Freeman that all history is a unity, that man's experiences and institutions, as well as man himself, provide the basis for this unity, and that a breakdown of man's story into periods was artificial and historically invalid.[44] Indeed, the age of Tacitus and the age of Gladstone were indissolubly linked, as Adams saw it, for "ancient history was the dawn of a light which is still shining on."[45]

That the dawn's early light which was visible to Adams should be little more than a reflection of the light of his own times was perhaps inevitable. In looking backward and finding the primeval germs of nineteenth-century democracy in the Teutonic forests, he was taking a view which, howsoever utopian and naive, afforded him an explanation both of American democracy and of the affinity which he liked to read into the diplomatic relations of the Anglo-Saxon community of powers —Germany, Great Britain, and the United States. And if, as he believed, history was a unity and continuity, and the larger political forms could be traced to smaller institutional origins, then very much could be said for a close study of American local institutions. His plan for such a study, explained Adams, "was the outgrowth of a special interest in municipal history, first quickened in a seminary at Heidelberg, thence transplanted to Baltimore, where it was fostered by the reading of the writings of Sir Henry Maine, in connection with those of Carl Hegel, Mauer, Nasse, Waitz, Stubbs, and of the Harvard School of Anglo-Saxon law. The continuity of the Germanic village community in New England had originally been suggested to Sir Henry Maine by an article in the *Nation,* communicated by Professor W. F. Allen, of the University of Wisconsin."[46]

The demonstration and proof of this communal continuity became the mainspring of seminar work at Johns Hopkins during the 1880's. Adams accepted as entirely valid the hypothesis that early America was bound by essentially identical institutions to her Teutonic forebears, Old England and primitive Germany:

The science of Biology no longer favors the theory of spontaneous generation. Wherever organic life occurs there must have been some seed for that life. . . . It is just as improbable that *free local*

> *institutions* should spring up without a germ along American shores as that English wheat should have grown here without planting. . . . The town and village life of New England is as truly the reproduction of Old English types as those again are reproductions of the village community system of the ancient Germans. Investigators into American Institutional History will turn as naturally to the mother country as the historians of England turn toward their older home beyond the German Ocean.[47]

The thesis needed proof. To Adams, a captain of historical industry, the American local institutions awaiting "the student pioneer" were veritably "vast tracts . . . almost as untouched as were once the forest of America, her coal measures and prairies." [48] That these institutions had great contemporary significance was eminently clear to Adams, who emphasized their "wholesome conservative power . . . in these days of growing centralization." [49]

Precepts such as these defined their own program of activity for the young historians at Baltimore. American colonial history would naturally draw the attention of a school interested in institutional origins, identities, and survivals. And if within the locality was concentrated so much of world history, it would be well for "the student pioneer" to start his researches inside his own community: history ought to begin at home. From his own community the student might be able to see one end of that chain of continuity which led back to the origin and growth of his state and of his nation, thence to the English mother country and the Germanic fatherland, and finally to the village communities throughout the Aryan world.[50] Accordingly, Adams sent forth the best he bred to study the hamlet, the parish, and the village. Far and wide they ranged, his seminar students, employing for their theoretical end a variety of means, including a study of French parishes for remnants of Canadian feudalism and an interview with the queen of the Montauk Indians on Long Island for an understanding of the history of the common lands in that area.[51] Thus, the doctoral dissertation of Charles Andrews, *The River Towns of Connecticut: A Study of Wethersfield, Hartford, and Windsor,* was designed to afford a footnote to the larger theses of the school of Herbert Adams. And it was a school whose theses dominated the new history, not merely because of the commanding role which Adams played at Johns Hopkins but also because of the central position occupied by Johns Hopkins in American historical writing and study during the last quarter of the nineteenth century.

2. THE THEORY OF THE VILLAGE COMMUNITY

To the historiography of Charles M. Andrews the school of Herbert Adams bequeathed a substantial legacy. That the young associate in history at Bryn Mawr would proceed, in his very first writings, to question some of his master's basic premises ought not obscure the considerable debt which the system of Andrews owed that of Adams. From his master the student had learned all the major components of the new history: the importance and use of primary sources, the spirit and procedure of the seminar, indeed the whole nature and technique of advanced historical research. Moreover, Adams had directed his charge to that concern with institutional history which was to characterize much of Andrews' later work; and it was at Baltimore that Andrews had first been impressed with the vast possibilities for study and writing offered by the field of American colonial history. He had learned something more: that every detail of the past was meaningful only insofar as it could be related to the larger course of history, and that the larger course of history must be related in a meaningful way to the present. If he did not choose to follow Adams through all the devious improbabilities of a theory of institutional germs, he had however followed him a good way up to that point.

What the young historian had made of the legacy of his master could be seen clearly enough in his first contribution, *The River Towns of Connecticut* (1889). His "graduating thesis" fulfilled admirably the condition posed by Adams that such a work should constitute "the natural outgrowth and highest requirement" of the entire scheme of studies at Johns Hopkins. The hundred-page study of the seventeenth-century settlements at Wethersfield, Hartford, and Windsor was a study in institutional origins. Its concern was with local institutions. It was based on a careful study of the documentary materials. And, dealing as it did with an area to which Andrews was native, it clearly satisfied the belief of Adams that history ought to begin at home. However, the dissertation on the Connecticut towns offered its readers more than another bit of that general story of institutional beginnings which was the predominant concern of the school of Adams. True enough, it provided a careful description of the causes and nature of the early settlements; it contained a detailed account of the acquisition and disposal of the land; and it concluded with a survey of the growth of the civil and administrative system that came to characterize the river towns. But it went beyond that. It took up, though somewhat indirectly, a heated controversy which was then going on among several prominent historians, about the nature of the early New England settlements. The controversy touched the very essence of the gospel taught by Adams, inspired by Freeman, and studied by Andrews.

In the compound of the new history, probably the most significant element was the town. Here was the primeval germ of more developed and advanced political forms; here was the earliest cell of Aryan and of Teutonic freedom. Transmitted from the German forests to England in Saxon keels (the keel somehow appeared to be the proper repository for such an institution as the town), it was subsequently carried across the Atlantic to America in similar fashion. Remarkably enough, each time the town was deposited in a new area of settlement, it would regain its pristine individuality and purity. As a matter of fact, argued Professor Alexander Johnston, one of the major protagonists of the theme of the universality of Teutonic experience, the settlement of Connecticut was effected by independent towns, migrating from Massachusetts, in the 1630's. "Since their prototypes, the little *tuns* of the primeval German forest," said Professor Johnston, "there had been no such examples of the perfect capacity of the political cell—the 'town'—for self-government."[52] From this notion of the town as the initial source of political organization, it followed pretty clearly that the state was the creature of the towns and that the towns were "the residuary legatees of political power." It followed, too, that a comparison could validly be drawn between the political history of Connecticut and the political history of the United States. The latter had also been fashioned out of a federation of independent political units (of the non-migrating variety, though), each of which retained powers not expressly delegated to the national government.[53]

Such a relatively uncomplicated view of man's institutional experience as a united and continuous whole was not, however, acceptable to all the historical fraternity. Many could not agree to a view in which the universal village community kept cropping up, with unvaried obstinacy and only under different names, now as the German *tun,* now as the English mark, and now as the American town. Among the dissidents was Charles Andrews, who based his dissidence on his own intensive examination of the records of the early Connecticut settlements. Johnston's views he found untenable. It was only by a vivid use of the imagination, said Andrews, that the early towns could be regarded as "independent republics," as sovereign entities, as possessors of inherent or reserved rights.[54] As a matter of fact, the documents not only denied the thesis of towns federating into a commonwealth but questioned the very existence of towns prior to the formation of the commonwealth. Andrews' central point was that these were no migrating towns which had come to the Connecticut river valley and that it was only after a slow and natural process of evolution that the town organization, in a distinctly political sense, had taken shape.[55] In the settlement of new lands, the concern of the proprietors came ultimately to political matters, after having passed through several earlier stages, wherein agricultural, military, and religious affairs dominated their attention. In his doctoral dissertation as well as in a subsequent article on "The Beginnings of the Connecticut Towns," Andrews asserted that the commonwealth was created by the people and not by the towns,[56] that the supremacy of the General Court was readily accepted and never once contested by the towns,[57] and that any proper consultation of the records could not but end by rejecting completely the theory of the pre-existent sovereignty of the towns.[58] Thus had Andrews, in his very first writings as a member of the school of Herbert Adams, joined in the attack on some of its basic doctrines.

Evidences could of course be found in the novice's writings which indicated that he had been guided to no small degree by the training he had received at Johns Hopkins. Herbert Adams must repeatedly have urged that a sharp lookout be kept for any trace of an earlier Anglo-Saxon age which his young researchers might come upon in their own provincial backyards. Certainly, in his study of the Connecticut river towns, Andrews kept a close record of whatever he found in the form of institutional survivals from the hallowed Teutonic past. These survivals encompassed a variety of matters: the taking possession of land "in good old Teutonic fashion by turf and twig"; [59] the similarity between the position of the lands of the Saxon *haward* and of those "of doubtful characters" in the early Connecticut settlements; [60] the regulation of the common meadow "which has been found to bear such a striking resemblance to certain forms of old English and German land-holding"; [61] and "the ancient right of perambulation, or going the bounds," a custom which "dates back very far in history, and [which] was, in early Saxon times, attended with considerable ceremonial." [62]

But Andrews did not push the theory of the unity of Teutonic history too far. Indeed, no single approach contained the entire truth, he felt, certainly not one so rudimentary and contrived as that of Herbert Adams. Confronted with the problem of tracing the beginnings of the New England town, Andrews early moved to the middle-ground position that was to characterize his views in the entire question of institutional origins. A simplified theory of the village community he found unacceptable. Even in *The River Towns of Connecticut,* he asserted that ostensible identities found in certain phases of New England town life and in the customs of early German tribes might definitely be shown "to have arisen from reasons of economic necessity, and to be nothing more than interesting parallels." [63] Those who traced political institutions back to the simple germ of "our Aryan forefathers" were building their system of survivals and similarities on a basis of imagination rather than historical data. True enough, Andrews did not completely reject the possibility of a transmission of institutions from Germany to England and thence to America. No reasonable scholar, he agreed, would deny that the English village community or the manor contained "many of the foundation principles according to which the German *tun* is supposed to have been built" or that these principles, embodied in customs, were brought by English settlers to America. But this Arcadian political cell must surely have undergone substantial modification in the course of history and could never have been reconstituted in its primordial form in the series of migrations across the North Sea and, much later, across the Atlantic. In evaluating a thesis which depended so much upon institutional identities, noted Andrews, one had to conclude that "there is more that is unidentical than there is that is identical."

While the theory of the village community had been only peripheral to his doctoral dissertation, it constituted the central concern of Andrews in a paper he read before the American Historical Association the very next year, in 1890. The simple formulas of the theory had become so deeply ingrained into the pattern of historical thinking in the United States that, confessed the young man of twenty-seven, "it may seem more bold than discreet to raise the question regarding its soundness." [64] Because they had been so glibly applied to early American history, two premises of the general theory of the village community had to be examined more carefully: first, the belief that the Teutonic village community, the *tun*, had been composed of free tribesmen, possessing an assembly of an essentially democratic nature, and that it was this institution to which the emigrants from England reverted when they landed upon the American shores; and second, the belief that the village community, in Germany, England, and America, was the earliest rudiment of the body politic, and that it was a subsequent amalgamation of such communities into larger and larger forms that resulted in the emergence of the state. Both these premises, which constituted so integral a part of the historical thinking of the new school, Andrews questioned and rejected. If the haze produced by inadequate historical data permitted the application of the theory to the early phases of Germanic and English history, such application to early American history was rendered impossible by the reality of "stubborn facts." To compare the New England town with the German *tun* was to argue a likeness "of the most superficial kind." It was substantially closer to the truth to understand that "the New England town is institutionally as far in advance of the so-called *tun* in the German forest as were the political ideas of the seventeenth century in advance of those of the second." [65] And no careful historical thinker could find any validity in the belief that the New England town was the primordial basis of the state. On the contrary, Andrews asserted once more, "the state is the mother of her towns." [66] All the logic that could be compounded out of Aryan etymology and an enticing theory of historical unity, he felt, could not support the concepts of Freeman, Adams, and their adherents.

As a matter of fact, pursued the young historian, could one seriously support the theory of the village community insofar as its early Germanic and early English phases were concerned? Even here the theory was to be questioned. To begin with, one might argue with greater cogency for the shire as the primordial unit of the state than for the town. And on what ground was the historian to accept the picture of the free village community, whether the democratic *tun* or the liberty-laden mark? What evidence precisely did the scientific historian have of these rustic, idyllic, and self-governing commonwealths? The very existence of a free village community, whether in the German forests or in the English shores, could be "supported by no contemporary historical documents . . . it is the child of . . . much unwarranted dogmatizing and unsympathetic criticism." [67] The truth of it was that the whole theory, in its pristine and unmodified form, could be traced to four principal writers, Kemble, Freeman, Maine, and von Maurer. Of these, Kemble had not a single bit of evidence to support his argument, Freeman built almost entirely on Kemble, Maine spoke in vague and almost contradictory terms, while von Maurer not only qualified his statements to the point of draining the theory of some of its strength but was pursuing the dangerous technique of reading backwards from the actualities of the tenth century to what he supposed had existed in the second.[68]

Integral to the whole critique that Andrews advanced in his paper was not merely the weakness of the theory but also the weakness of the techniques of study that led to the formulation and acceptance of that theory. An accurate portrayal of the economic conditions of England before and during the Anglo-Saxon settlements would, he felt, be far more helpful than endless speculation about German *tuns* and Saxon manors. He argued the need for an exact appreciation of the entire historical environment of that period, the system of landholding, the ways of cultivating the soil, the home life, the structure of politics.[69] On the basis of a more exact and accurate view of English economic history during this critical period, the historicity of the theory of the village community might be fully evaluated and a sounder construction of events might emerge. It is noteworthy that Andrews considered careful method to be indispensable to valid historiography. It is noteworthy, too, that having diagnosed the malady, he undertook himself to provide a remedy.

3. THE OLD ENGLISH MANOR

The venture into English economic history that Andrews essayed in *The Old English Manor* (1892) represented the most original monographic contribution he was to make to historical literature before his full-scale entry into the field of American colonial history. It was of moment not merely in the life of its writer, but in the history of the subject it dealt with as well. The volume revealed a young scholar, not quite thirty, who was proficient in the languages he had to handle (Anglo-Saxon, Latin, French, and German), who could make expert use of documentary sources, and who was rapidly attaining mastery in dealing with the tangled problems of institutional origins. Working with all available original and secondary materials, though concentrating on the evidence found in two well-known contemporary accounts (the *Gerefa* and the *Rectitudines*), Andrews sought to present a comprehensive survey of the Anglo-Saxon manor during the century before the Norman Conquest. The survey brought under close consideration the subjects of manorial lands and landholding, land cultivation, the different social classes in the village community (particularly in their relation to the lord of the manor), and the home life and recreation of the villagers. To this detailed description of the manor, which constituted the bulk of his volume, Andrews added an eighty-page "Introduction," in which he entered boldly upon the question that was being so hotly debated by his older and more learned contemporaries: the nature and origin of the manor.

Several noteworthy points characterized the study. First, the writer had taken great pains to consult all authorities on the subject. Writ large over the manorial survey drawn up by Andrews was the hand of Seebohm, whose *English Village Community* had first appeared some nine years before, in 1883; no less noticeable, though, was the influence of John Earle, whom Andrews had adjudged to be "nearer right than any who have gone before" in the effort to solve the problem of the manor.[70] Based as it was on materials already available, what Andrews had to say could lay claim not to unearthing new evidence but to interpreting the old evidence in a new light. Second, Andrews everywhere conveyed the sense of irresolution and tenuousness with which he had made many of his observations. The reader could not but be impressed by the difficulties of answering many of the questions that faced the study at every turn. The survey fairly teemed with modification of themes, with suggestion rather than fact, with probability and conjecture, with lament that certain problems were "involved in obscurity and as yet the clouds have not sufficiently cleared for us to introduce any satisfactory discussion here,"[71] and with avowal that "regarding this process we know with certainty almost nothing."[72] Third, in proceeding through the maze of problems with which the reconstruction of early institutions was beset, the student of Herbert Adams insisted that argument from analogous institutions was not proof, but illustration;[73] that no uniform process could serve to explain the growth of social and political institutions; and that the uniformity of an institution such as the Anglo-Saxon manor, in all times and in all places, could certainly not be assumed. Fourth, so far as the actual history of the village community was concerned, Andrews joined those historians who had come to see nothing cataclysmic in the effects of the Norman Conquest upon local life: that life remained unchanged and "the village system passed through the shock of conquest uninjured."[74]

If his concern in the larger part of the volume was to present an account of economic and social conditions in the English manor of the period before the Conquest, his concern in the introductory section was to present something of a commentary on the "state of the manor" question as of the year 1892. That question involved several major problems. How could one account for the social structure of the manor—not merely for the free and servile groups, but also for the status of the lord? What was the nature of the relationship between the manorial village community and the tribal society which had preceded it? Was the origin of the English manor to be sought in the Roman villa, as Seebohm and Ashley had suggested, or was it to be sought in Germanic institutions brought by the Angles and Saxons, as Stubbs, Maine, Freeman, and Green had suggested? Had the servile classes originally been a body of kindred freemen or had they before been in a condition of uniform and perhaps even more stringent servility? The social and economic ingredients of the medieval manor had been the subject of much controversy among European historians. It took no small amount of either scholarship or courage to rush in where fools would have been readily discernible.[75] Yet, in a way, his attempt to untie the knotty problem of manorial origins represented the logical end toward which Andrews had been slowly moving, impelled not only by his training at Johns Hopkins but also by his refusal to accept some of the cardinal tenets of that training.

In the summation that the young historian offered were reflected, above all, his sense of moderation, his ability to synthesize, and his understanding of history as a developmental process. Because no one scholar could possibly hope to solve the whole problem, contended Andrews, it was urgent to have cooperation rather than criticism, impartiality rather than dogmatism, a historical spirit rather than a controversial one.[76] One of the main difficulties confronting the historian of the manorial community was the polarity of the views between which he had to choose, the one contending for homogeneous groups of freemen and the other contending for homogeneous groups of men in a servile status. Why was it necessary to postulate so irreconcilable a set of possibilities? A modified view of the theory of the village community afforded a view of institutional beginnings that was more consonant with historical reality. Under this view, the community could be seen to have derived from a subtribal grouping of a composite nature, that is, of a subordinate chieftain leading a kindred group of free clansmen in war. The notion of a mark as the idyllic institution of free Teutons, whether in Germany or England, had no validity. The tribesmen could, accordingly, better be understood as emerging from barbarism than as losing their Teutonic franchises.[77] In conditions of migration and war, the kindred group and their hereditary leader, their chief, settled down on a territorial basis. Arguing for the thesis of a transmutation from clan-community to geographical community, Andrews asserted his certainty that "the local community, the village, was simply the kindred, the sub-clan group, which had become a local habitation." [78] Kemble's argument for an original body of freemen could not be sustained, nor could, for that matter, Seebohm's complete omission of such a group.

> It is for this triple purpose, to do away with the purely artificial origin of the manorial group, to avoid the condition of absolute equality, followed by usurpation and aggression, and to account for the free element which formed the larger part of the Saxon peoples that we have attempted to draw in this introduction a sort of brief in defence of *the composite community group,* which we believe formed one of the starting points for the later manorial growth.[79]

In effect, the key to the problem of the manorial community could be found in the tribe and in the hereditary office of the tribal chieftain.

What Andrews proposed, his colleagues were fairly universally disposed to accept. The American was especially commended by his British brethren. Sir Frederick Pollock deemed it "an opportune and useful piece of work"; [80] Seebohm wrote not only to congratulate Andrews but to explain further his own position; [81] Vinogradoff found the volume "a most important contribution to common studies"; [82] and Maitland, whom Andrews very early came to esteem as the historian par excellence, must surely have warmed the young historian's heart by hailing his effort as an "excellent and important work" and expressing the hope it would not be "the only contribution you will make to legal history." [83]

His reviewers were impressed with the conscious attempt he made to solve the problem by common sense and by taking a middle ground in the whole controversy. Some could not help feeling, however, that the middle ground he had taken was not entirely safe or satisfactory. One reviewer, for example, considered that his solution was a "fusion of contradictories," [84] a view in which Vinogradoff, writing for the *English Historical Review,* concurred. The noted Russian historian made the very telling observation that compromise has not only its credits but its debits, that common sense it not always correct sense: "It would be hardly advisable to seek virtue by toning vice down to a milder form, or to seek truth by averaging opposite errors." [85] Supporting neither an originally servile village community nor one originally free, steering between the Roman Charybdis and the German Scylla, Andrews had somewhat confused moderation with mediation. One could not very well arrive at the truth by adding conflicting opinions and dividing by two.

If the volume was not an entirely acceptable commentary on the state of the manor, it was at the very least a revealing commentary on the state of Andrews. It gave evidence of a craftsman rapidly learning the skills of his trade. Andrews was defining for himself and mastering the whole question of institutional origins. This could be seen not only from *The Old English Manor,* which undertook the answer to a specific historical problem, but also from his essay on "Some Recent Aspects of Institutional Study" (1893), in which Andrews presented a general survey and appraisal of the principal methods that were being used "either in studying primitive institutional history or in discovering the beginnings of institutional changes or transformations in times less remote." [86] Both the volume and the essay revealed that Andrews had long since abandoned the doctrinal simplicities of the creed he had learned from his master; both revealed, moreover, that he was entering the realm of the great medievalists of the English school, men such as Round, Seebohm, Pollock, Vinogradoff, and Maitland. The review of *The Old English Manor* in *The Atheneum* afforded not merely a summary but also an augury when it found that "no more thorough or scholarly piece of work has appeared in the Johns Hopkins University studies than this excellent essay." Indeed, the "excellent essay" was more than a disquisition on past history. It was a disquisition on present historiography, on the system of Andrews and its relation to the system which Herbert Adams was propagating among successive seminars at Johns Hopkins.

4. THE LEGACY OF HERBERT ADAMS

Of the legacy he had received from Johns Hopkins, Andrews made a various disposition. In general, he accepted the method but questioned the creed. Many elements of the new history being taught at Baltimore he deemed entirely valid:

the stress on sources, the conduct of the seminar as a research laboratory, the rejection of earlier historiography as romantic and patriotic, the need for pursuing historical "science." He too saw the historian's concern with the past as a concern with institutional development and above all with institutional origins. He subscribed to Adams' belief, even if Adams did not in practice adhere to it, that institutions were complex matters, reflecting the demands and needs of their particular ages.[87] He accepted his master's assertion that history had laws, that human development revealed a unity and continuity, that institutions were organisms going through an evolution of growth and decline, and that the past could best be understood in terms of an idea of progress.[88] To this degree, the system of Andrews was very much the product of the system of Adams.

What Andrews could not accept, however, was something which he regarded as an unsatisfactory fulfillment of the responsibilities of the historian. It was incumbent upon the latter, after all, to bring to his study both "scientific accuracy and conservative judgment"; he had to have "an open and receptive mind, willing to weigh another's opinion, to investigate another's facts." [89] Especially dismayed was Andrews by the lack of historical-mindedness which had produced that theory of institutional "germs," survivals, and throwbacks which Adams had made his specialty. One ought not, felt Andrews, read into an earlier age the concepts of a later one. Nowhere did he deny of course that the past might be used to give a clue to the present. Nor did he at all doubt that history might yield a philosophy. He simply wanted to be sure of the nature of the philosophy and of the qualifications of the philosopher.

Little wonder, then, that even in his early writings Andrews undertook to combat those doctrines of the new history which he saw being rapidly fashioned into a new orthodoxy. He attacked vigorously what he considered to be the central doctrinal error of the growing gild of historians: "the vague and uncertain generalizations, the questionable theory of reversion in town life to antique models, graphic accounts of the so-called unit of political life, the town meeting, and the whole succession of identities, which have no support save in a superficial likeness." [90] To spare his own mentor at Baltimore, no doubt, for the personal debt of Andrews to Adams was great indeed, he shifted his target to Freeman. Not only had the latter encouraged the institutional studies which were being carried on at Johns Hopkins but he had also furnished Adams with not a little of his orientation. Andrews found very questionable, to say the least, Freeman's presentation of Earl Godwine as an earlier model of Gladstone.[91] The English historian's view of the village community was "nothing more than a revival of the *a priori* theories of Rousseau." [92] Andrews applauded the efforts of Round in dispelling "the democratic and constitutional fog" that Freeman had wrapped about the Saxon period; [93] he hailed Maitland for chilling "the ardor of those who look on the local self-government of the New England town as an institutional retrogression, a kind of revival of a fundamental Anglo-Saxon institution." [94] What distressed Andrews particularly was the larger prepossession of which the teachings of Freeman and Adams were part: that "the Anglo-Saxons are the salt of the earth" and that "without them freedom would never have been." [95] This view the young historian rejected as uncritical and dogmatic. He would have little to do with an orientation which trumpeted "the Anglo-Saxon militant, the Teuton rampant, and the Aryan eternally triumphant." [96]

By his thirtieth year, then, Andrews had fairly well defined his position. He was in the new school which Herbert Adams was helping to build but not entirely of it. He joined his master in proclaiming Ranke's famous dictum and was sorry that Adams had not gone beyond the mere proclaiming. Yet, and this a later age can see, the differences between the two, though substantial, were not much more than differences of degree. One might leave a household, but one could not very well forsake an age. One might question a Founding Father without necessarily giving up the entire Constitution. A single historical context, after all, encompassed both the teacher at Baltimore and the young historian from Connecticut. Herbert Adams and Charles Andrews were both products of a unique and seminal period in American historiography. They sprang from the "village community" of the seminar. They had many more identities than differences. The Connecticut Yankee and the court of Herbert Adams were not actually, when all is said and done, ages apart.

Chapter 2

A PORTRAIT of the HISTORIAN as a YOUNG MAN

Central to the system of Andrews was a scientific ideal. In a way, that ideal summarized the new history which was rising in America and which had already assumed dominion in Western Europe. It imposed upon the historian the rigorous criteria of objectivity and impartiality. If it emphasized that the past was to be recaptured through the sources, it further emphasized that the sources had to be used dispassionately, without prejudice, without any ulterior interest than finding the truth and actuality of the past. Fact by fact, item by item, an earlier age was to be restored, until the whole of it stood forth, as it had really been, *as it actually was.* The ideal which impelled the new historian had more than the promptings of Ranke behind it. Indeed, was not the age itself alive with the discoveries and lessons of the world of science? Comte had already argued the possibility of a science of society, stressing the need for treating social facts like physical phenomena. The findings of Darwin dramatically reenforced the tendency of the times to make the study of man a study of scientific certitude. The ideal which inspired the rising gild of new historians derived, to no small degree, from the teachings of science in general and from those of biological science in particular.[1] Over history now hovered the spirit of the laboratory. The historian was enjoined to submit his material to the most exacting test in order to find out the incontrovertible facts of the past. Most of all, he was to approach the past with scientific objectivity. The facts would speak for themselves. Perhaps they would speak for the past that same message of evolution, optimism, and progress which Herbert Spencer found them speaking for the present. Perhaps the scientific ideal was nothing more than the means which the late nineteenth century was using to "prove" to itself the validity of its own confidence about things as they were. Whatever end it was designed to serve, it was an ideal which governed the new history. And its governance extended beyond the mere confines of Johns Hopkins. Its universality insured this much, that whatever else he may have questioned in his training, Charles Andrews would make the scientific ideal integral to his own system of historiography.

That system was defined early enough in the young historian's career. What he was thinking about history could be found not only in his major works and in his essays but perhaps even more explicitly in his hundreds of book reviews. From these writings emerges a portrait of an historian formulating his views concerning the crucial elements of historiography: What were the nature and use of history? What was the role of the historian? What were the sum and meaning of the past? An appraisal of the system of Andrews during the period from 1889 to 1904 has its special significance. These were the years of his stay at Bryn Mawr, the years before he went to Yale to found a school of American colonial historians. These were the years, moreover, during which he came to a mature understanding of the historian's craft. For the first decade and a half of his professional career, the writings of Andrews were devoted to the history of Europe, medieval and modern; and it was only at the end of this period that he made his full-scale entry into the field of American colonial history. The formative years of Andrews, finally, coincided with the rise and triumph of the new history. It would not be too long after he had fully developed his system and had begun its application to the study of American colonial history that the very principles upon which his system was founded would come under mounting attack. Indeed, the attack was inevitable. A system of historiography, after all, is a juncture of two elements: the historian and his age. But no sooner has the historian defined his system than the age which has shaped his definition has itself passed into history.

1. A PORTRAIT OF THE INDIVIDUAL

There is perhaps no better approach to a system of historiography than through an understanding of the historiographer himself. Nor will it suffice, in attempting to know something about the historiographer, simply to present a portrait of his domestic and nonprofessional pursuits. A figure of such eminent attainments as Andrews poses a double problem: first, to explain what elements of his personality contributed to his success; and second, to explain what elements in particular were responsible for his success *during his era*. That the second aspect of the problem must also be answered is clear enough, for nowhere can it be assumed that greatness is an independent quality which will inevitably demonstrate itself at any time, in any age. It is not a complete accounting to explain why Andrews was a successful historian; it is far more so to explain why he was a successful historian of the scientific school of American historiography.

Perhaps the most important factor in his effective pursuit of the scientific ideal was that he had no strong prejudices about the larger problems of society. He never took up an unalterable view on any major social issue, whether political, religious, or economic. He wondered, with dismay, why there could not "be more catholicity in this world and less of the hard drawn lines of bigotry." [2] The only strong impulse in his immediate environment emanated from his father, a minister, who did not cease either to assert eternal Providence or to clarify the ways of God to his son. This impulse Andrews resisted. "I know I am a little heterodox & papa will probably smile at my arguments," he wrote his mother, in explaining his own views of the nature and importance of church-going.[3] Probably the summary of his sentiment in this crucial area of domestic concern was his "fear that my religious conviction is not strong enough to overcome my desire for rest on Sundays." [4] As a matter of fact, his political conviction ran in something of a similar vein, for not infrequently did he have to be reminded of the need to go out and vote on Election

Day.[5] For the larger part, he refrained from taking a party stand on issues of current political interest. It was not indifference so much as his own moderate view on the course of human events. The scion of a decidedly Republican family, and himself sympathetic to Republican policies, he could however find "no danger of a cataclysm" in the election of Grover Cleveland in 1892. "The general progress of our national affairs is too regular, the inertia too great for four years of even a radical change in theories of rule to alter the course it is pursuing." [6] His moderate outlook toward both present and past were merely two expressions of the same characteristic. And it was a characteristic admirably suited to the ideals of his craft.

Not that scientific history could not be undertaken without catholicity or moderation of temperament. No one, for example, harbored more flagrant prejudices about the different aspects of social experience than Henry Adams, and no one wrote a more excellent piece of scientific history. But the differential between the personality of Henry Adams and the history he wrote was his own painful awareness that a differential did indeed exist. Unlike the greatest historian of his school, Andrews did not have to contend with the strong predispositions deriving from family, social position, or strange turnings of the psyche. The only conviction of strength he had was the desire to succeed, to be an outstanding craftsman at his trade. The desire to be successful only reenforced the tendency to that moderateness of judgment which he deemed to be the essence of sound historiography.[7]

It was not merely that he had no decisive partialities, it was also that he felt he had none. He was free from the doubts which would later beset the historical relativist. Andrews pursued the ultimate truth of the past without ever thinking that he might be an imperfect instrument in attaining that truth, without indeed ever being trammeled by the thought that perhaps truth about the past might not be ultimate. Toward the end of his life he wrote a letter which could serve as something of a credo for the scientific school. He denied emphatically that no one of us can escape the limitations of his surroundings. . . . I was born a northerner, of double-dyed Puritan ancestry, ministerial in many of its members, and ought by all the laws of genetics to have all the prejudices of a Puritan and a New Englander. . . . Yet I have never felt the influences of these limitations upon my freedom of thought or instinctive sense of fair treatment for all. . . . I suppose this balance of mind comes partly as a natural break away from the past, induced by a strongly grounded desire to know the truth of a matter without a leaning one way or another. . . . I have never believed that it was necessary to plead a cause in writing history. All I have wanted was to find out what history is all about.[8]

It may be ventured that, however free he may have been of the values of his immediate environment, Andrews was nowhere free of the values of his age and that he would perforce undertake to plead its cause. He would find out only so much of "what history is all about" as the lights of his times would permit. But herein was the explanation of his success. His attainments and shortcomings were those of the ideal he pursued. This very consonance insured that he would admirably express the purposes of his school. By virtue of his temperament and social outlook, Andrews thus became a fitting agent for the new history.

For the rest, his pursuit of the scientific ideal would depend on his ability for concentrated effort. Here too he had the ingredients for success, for becoming a leader in his school. At the root of it all was the simple and impelling force of ambition. In the very last year of his life he put it this way: "To do something and to be somebody has always been uppermost in my mind." [9] It had been put just a bit differently at the outset of his career, when he wrote his mother about the work he was doing at Johns Hopkins:

I need to rise far higher than I have, to reach the plane of their ideal; the plane reached by their best men, those whose names are spoken of as the lights of the past. Yet I hope in tenderly nourishing my little candle flame, trusting that if it doesn't set the world on fire, it may yet give a little light to the few near it.[10]

That the light got to be considerably brighter than he had

dared hope was at first due perhaps as much to a sense of guilt in not doing work as a sense of contentment in doing it. In the case of Andrews, certainly, both senses were very much related. It would be convenient to ascribe it all to a Puritanical New England upbringing. Whatever it was, letters of Andrews during these early years expressed frequent pangs of conscience about "dissipating," under which censorious title he included such items as hearing the Boston Symphony, going to the theatre or to a party, or simply having a beer and cigar with one of his friends or a visit with his Philadelphia cousins.[11] He hoped he could "develop self-control and work when I don't want to as well as when I do." [12] He feared nothing so much as "growing lazy" and felt certain that such a dire thing might happen "if I don't have enough to keep me scared busy all the time." [13] He was kept busy. Did this mean he was also kept scared? Perhaps the school of Freud will find in all of this the sermonizing of an elderly and imposing reverend father and a son sternly schooled in the simple equation of prayer with work.

If work necessarily meant foregoing the pleasure of company, Andrews was more than willing, particularly so after he settled down to the serious demands of historical scholarship on his coming to Bryn Mawr in 1889. His own view was that his "natural inclination is not that way" and that even "under the most favorable circumstances" he was "not socially inclined." [14] No small part of his disinclination could be attributed to his growing deafness. He was always keenly aware of his disability and hesitated about entering into commitments where it might prove a source of embarrassment.[15] Deafness had its virtues for the ambitious historian, however, for it enabled him "to temporarily retire from the world with great eclat whenever it seems to be beneficial to myself." [16] It was not exactly that he was averse to meeting people. As a matter of fact, he delighted in conversation with fellow historians, particularly the luminaries of his craft, and his correspondence glows with accounts of meetings he had with Maitland, Cunningham, Seebohm, and others.[17] He enjoyed nothing so much as sitting before "the light of a fire on the open hearth," smoking a cigar or a pipe, and talking at great length about problems of interest to him.[18] But as for idling crowds and idle conversation, these held little attraction for Andrews. He was content to have "my work to do and take great comfort in doing it, for if the world looks cold, I can always retire to my room and my books and forget all about it. Past history is always alluring, Clio tempts with many charms, and I am beginning to understand what it is to be wedded to one's work." [19]

It was also felicitous that he was wedded to one who helped his work. He had met Evangeline Walker during the summer of 1893, shortly after her graduation from Bryn Mawr. Her own studies had been in English and Latin. She had never taken courses with the young professor of history, whose enthusiastic teaching and personal attraction were items of well-disseminated information on that entirely feminine campus. The marriage of Charles Andrews to Evangeline Walker in June, 1895, marked the beginning of a long and productive partnership. What an effective and very charming young woman might mean in the life of an historian who aspired "to do something and to be somebody" may have exceeded not only the historian's hopes but also his full awareness. She offered him constant encouragement, "a brave heart," and "a ready cheerfulness that carries me by a good many sober hours." [20] She undertook to school him in the principles of style and exposition. She read and corrected every one of his manuscripts.[21] If Andrews had hoped for a wife who would take care of merely "the little things of life," [22] his hopes had been more than satisfied. "I can see that if she had not got married," he wrote of his wife in 1900, "she would have succeeded admirably as head of a school or of any other organization." [23] He could not at that time have foreseen her independent successes in a variety of administrative enterprises.[24] But that she was even then achieving great success, by means of her part in his own work, had perhaps eluded him. She relieved her husband of most of the details of family responsibility and management. She released him in every way for the pursuit of his work. There is, indeed, something symbolic in the story told of the meeting between Marianne Moore, the poet, then a student at Bryn Mawr, and the seven-year-old son of the historian. When Miss Moore asked the boy to identify himself, he said: "My name is Andrews. My father wrote the history books." It summarized the family life of a great historian. "At our home," said Mrs. Andrews in recalling her son's innocence and perception, "we did nothing else but write the history books." [25]

Andrews had early come to resist any outside interference with writing the history books. This was after all the touchstone of his work, the instrument of his ambition, the sign of his scholastic prowess and leadership. He was perennially glad that "college is closed for the vacation" because it meant "just nothing to do except work on the book, which is continuing to grow." [26] Before his fortieth year he had, one by one, given up those commitments for lecturing and writing which he felt were keeping him from making his contribution to history. During the early years of his marriage he had felt the need for adding to his college salary by turning out some historical surveys and texts. The products of this phase of his career included *The Historical Development of Modern Europe* (2 volumes, 1896–98), *Contemporary Europe, Asia, and Africa* (1902), and *A History of England* (1903). But this sort of enterprise he lamented more than once, resolving that "I shall never take on any more work of the character that I have been doing." [27] He hoped before very long "to turn attention to a different kind of work—my own original studies." [28] His address to the American Historical Association in 1898 indicated that the field of those original studies was to be in American colonial history. It indicated too that the thirty-five-year-old historian was in fact staking out a claim to leadership in the new school. If the time for leadership had come, the time for textbook writing could not be prolonged. "I am too loyal to my scholarly instincts to give myself up to that sort of thing. I do not believe that the two interests can be run side by side and the choice between them has got to be made right here. I am sacrificing a little money in making my choice but I believe that I will gain in the end. I am certainly [gaining] in peace of mind and in reputation, if not in purse." [29]

This indeed was the way his reputation was being fashioned. It arose out of a clear sense of purpose, out of a determination not to have his work intruded upon, out of elemental ambition. He was spurred on by personal circumstances, by his own preference for seclusion, by a growing deafness which either caused or excused that preference, by a wife who both encouraged and assisted. More than personal circumstances, however, made for the possibility of success. The rise of the new history and of the scientific ideal set the stage for a man who was predisposed to nothing but reputation and who was willing to work for it. In that sense, an ideal of labor lay at the root of his contribution. The transcending fact of what Andrews did was the fabulous effort he put into doing it. His brilliance was that of perseverance, his profundity that of building a monument out of the obvious. Nor was it a monument built overnight. He built it patiently, fact by fact, detail by detail, adhering to the scientific ideal of moderation and impartiality, renewing the past *wie es eigentlich gewesen*. His success was a commentary on the inevitability of gradualness, and perhaps here could be found the reason why he published his magnum opus, after more than thirty years of document-hunting and fact-collecting, during the very last decade of his life. As the years wore on, his contribution began to take shape. Cumulatively, it began to grow. By persistence and tremendous effort, the quantitative distinction of his work was transmuted into a qualitative one. At best he was a master craftsman, not a Cellini. But the age did not call for genius, it called for industry. The new history was not for esthetes and romantics, it was for men of cold, sober sense.

2. THE NATURE AND USES OF HISTORY

Wrought out of industry and sobriety, the system of historiography of Andrews reflected the larger patterns of his age and the special convictions of his school. In defining his views about the nature and purpose of "historical science," [30] the young historian subscribed with his colleagues to the belief that the past could be recaptured as it actually was. "The truth is there," he declared, "unalterable, waiting to be known." [31] One had but to seek and one would find. And seeking historical truth was essentially a matter of tracing "the evolution of human ideas and institutions," [32] of answering "the problems of development, of growth, of progress," of bringing to the surface those undercurrents and tendencies that lay deeply hidden in the past.[33] These alone could reveal "the logic of history." [34] And when construed in terms of that logic, the story of human experience represented a unity, an organic whole, a progression of experiences in which the ages were bound in a continuous chain.[35] History, summarized Andrews, "studies the beginning and the end, the cause and the result." [36] In taking this genetic view of the past, and in approaching history as a unity and continuity, the young historian was garnering from many fields: the Baltimore of Adams, the Oxford of Freeman, the Cambridge of Maitland, the Berlin of Ranke.

If history was a unity, then past and present were inseparably bound, and it was this very binding which defined "the final goal" and "highest sense of our [historical] science." In defending the study of recent history, Andrews submitted that the whole purpose of tracing "line by line and sequence by sequence the gradual unfolding of this development of human ideas and human institutions" was to attain a "better understanding of the civilization of the present century, of the present day. . . . We study the past that we may better understand the present." [37] That the young historian took this view of the meaning of the past for the present did not necessarily mean that he was at home in the field of present politics or very happy about discussing it. At the very best, he felt, one could see only "dimly the nature of the problems with which present society is wrestling." One could hardly "determine their proportions" or know with any certainty "the final word that posterity will pronounce upon this period of history." [38]

For which reason, said Andrews, "I rarely discuss current politics in class." [39] He might be persuaded, under great pressure, to lecture on the problem of Cuba, in 1898, or on that of the Philippines, in 1899.[40] For the greater part, however, he kept his distance from the present, both in speech and in writing. It was not from lack of convictions, either. "It does not follow," he felt, that "because one has convictions that he is willing to ventilate them on public occasions." [41] "I do not wish to pose as a writer on modern politics." [42] But if Andrews felt that the light of the past might profitably be thrown upon the present, he deemed a reversal of that process of illumination both erroneous and reprehensible. In the patriotic approach, for example, he saw the past being not so much used as abused. He opposed making history serve the purposes of "the Prussian schoolmaster." [43] For himself, he rejected invitations to speak at patriotic celebrations. "I hate taking any part in such an affair. I haven't the imagination that soars in oratory, and I have too great a love of the truth to say a good many of the things said on such occasions." [44] It is fair to comment, with regard to what Andrews was saying, that there are different loves of different truths and that if his imagination could not now soar in patriotism, it would later rise to great heights on behalf of a cause which, to him at least, was self-evident "truth." [45] Remembering the *Maine,* he could well assert that a proper use of history would "lessen the number of jingoes and of doctrinaires"; [46] afterwards, remembering the *Lusitania,* he would formulate his own proper use of history, supra-patriotic if not jingoistic, indoctrinating if not doctrinaire.

In exploring the meaning of the past for the present, Andrews was voicing sentiments which were being variously voiced by many of the historical gild—by Andrew D. White, John W. Burgess, Henry C. Lea, Albert B. Hart, and William A. Dunning.[47] Nor was Andrews any less in agreement with the prevailing view of the gild that the study of history should encompass the entire range of human experience. There was nothing new in this view concerning the scope of history, as many historians since the days of James Harvey Robinson have delighted in pointing out, not even the declaration that it was new. The intention to remove history from the narrow confines of politics had been proclaimed by Montesquieu, Voltaire, Ranke, Macaulay, Green, and a host of others. Andrews himself continuously took exception to historical writing which did not relate political history to economic currents.[48] He decried accounts which resolved themselves into little more than drum and trumpet views of the past.[49] Seeley was "certainly wrong in limiting history to the growth of political governments,"[50] and no less so was Freeman in asserting that "history is past politics."[51] If he preached a broad pursuit of the past, however, Andrews himself practiced one that was rather limited. In this, no doubt, he was acting in concert with many of his contemporaries. It was nothing unusual to proclaim an alliance of history with the other social sciences and then to proceed in splendid isolation along the familiar path of political and legal institutions and problems.

The ultimate goal of historical study seemed clear enough to Andrews. What else could it be, he asked, but "that philosophical synthesis of history, the summing up of all that history is and history means"?[52] Two fundamental truths were to be uncovered by the student of the past: first, the immediate truth, the accurately construed fact, derived from precise and exact observation; second, the ultimate truth, the philosophy of history, built on the accumulation of the immediate truth, and representing the logic of the past.[53] Regarded in his most crucial capacity, the historian was writing a page of universal history.[54] His governing purpose was "to determine the part that each age has played in producing institutions and ideas destined to shape the civilization of the ages that were to follow."[55]

Fact and philosophy were to be directed toward the achievement of what lay at the heart of the historian's metier: the solution of problems concerning the past. Each institution, each nexus of ideas, each separate age threw up a mass of problems which required, for their solution, the coordinated enterprise of the individual historian and of the gild. Seen in this light, Andrews' most significant single monographic contribution during these decades was his attempt to solve the problem of the nature and origins of the old English manor.[56] Not that he supposed, though the truth was there, waiting to be known, and though the historian's competence was surpassing, that any particular solution would be the final one. The objective in handling an historical problem would be an improvement upon what was already known, a "more accurate rendering of a past movement or series of movements . . . a truer appreciation."[57] That the study of history was essentially an attempt to solve problems concerning the past was certainly impressed upon Andrews at the Johns Hopkins seminar. It was a view of historical study that traced back to the philological *exercationes* that Ranke had worked on in the halcyon German past. It was a view that the activity of the English school, in which Andrews took a very early and intense interest, most certainly confirmed. A summary of all that the young historian construed the study and writing of history to be could perhaps best be found in that famous pronouncement of Stubbs, a pronouncement which virtually served the English school, in typical fashion, as its unwritten constitution.

> The history of institutions [the famous holder of the Chair of Modern History at Oxford had declared] cannot be mastered, can scarcely be approached, without an effort. It has a point of view and a language of its own. It reads the exploits and characters of men by a different light from that shed by the false glare of arms. It holds out small temptation to the mind that requires to be tempted to the study of truth.[58]

The remarkable essay which Andrews had written, before he was quite thirty, on the methods of studying institutional origins, made plainly evident his awareness of the tremendous effort which the history of institutions demanded. He had indeed grasped its point of view, understood its language. The young man knew with exceptional clarity, even as he stood at the very threshold of his life's work, the nature of the study he was entering upon and the way in which he meant to pursue it.

3. THE SCIENTIFIC HISTORIAN

To arrive at a truer conception of the past, to solve the problem of historical movements and ages, to synthesize one's findings into a philosophy: these, then, were the objectives which Andrews set for the study and writing of history. But could one very well think of the conception without the conceiver, the solution without the solver, the philosophy without the philosopher? Crucial to the view that he took of historiography was the role that Andrews defined for the historiographer. Like his colleague in the natural sciences, the historian devoted himself to the search for truth; unlike the natural scientist, however, he was confronted by the difficulties of understanding, weighing, balancing, and sifting tenable conclusions from the variety of human experience. The "judicial sense" that one brought to the complexity of the historiographic process would enable him to arrive at interpretations "which are as near right as human nature is capable of attaining." [59] The historian could not subvert his mission of truth by pleading a cause or sustaining a party.[60] He was "not a lawyer defending a brief," but rather "a judge hearing all the evidence." [61]

Andrews was at one with the precepts of his school in postulating high standards for the writer of history. The latter ought certainly rest his appraisal on the widest survey of sources. Many times did Andrews, in his reviews, remonstrate that "the material upon which this study is based is inadequate"; [62] he regretted, for example, that John Fiske "never used a manuscript or passed beyond the bounds of conventional treatment." [63] For all his documents, however, the student could not effectively proceed unless he were abreast of the very latest literature concerning his subject. John Holland Rose's life of Napoleon received Andrews' commendation for having encompassed the most recent research; [64] B. C.

Barrington's account of Magna Carta, on the other hand, caused the young historian to inquire, with great chagrin, "Where has Mr. Barrington buried himself for the past quarter of a century, that for him [so many historians] have done their work in vain?" [65] Literary polish was of no consequence to Andrews. He lauded the "simple, straightforward" manner of writing,[66] concurring with most of his generation that the truth needed no embellishment. How well he recalled the censure that had been directed toward *The Old English Manor* for its stylistic deficiencies; [67] how well he recalled the severe and successful course in English administered to him by his wife.[68]

Yet sitting in historical judgment depended on something more than mere external attainments. No abundance of materials, no lucidity of style, no contact with the latest research would create that judiciousness and that balance which Andrews made central to the historian's role. The young gildsman appreciated as well as did any relativist that the past was seen "not face to face, but in large measure through that imperfect medium, the human mind." [69] For the very reason that the mind, after all, was the instrumentality through which his judgment of the past was to be obtained, it was imperative to keep the instrument clear and free.[70] By what means? Perhaps it could all be reduced to impartiality.[71] The historian had "to have an open and receptive mind"; [72] his capacity was that of "the judicious investigator," operating "without prejudice, fear, or favor." [73] His greatest obligation was to root out of his mind those "lingering prepossessions which bias the judgment, befog the imagination and weaken the estimate." [74] But while nonpartisanship constituted the primal tenet of the historian's creed, there were other tenets which were no less significant. Andrews argued for cautiousness of judgment, for proportion and perspective in defining the place of an age or a movement in the course of history, for independence of thinking, for seeing both sides of the case and avoiding extreme opinions.[75]

The role of the historian required more than impartiality:

it required imagination.[76] If impartiality was to free the historian from the spirit of the present, imagination was to help him catch the spirit of the past. Nothing was so important in catching that spirit as an awareness that the remembrance of things past could not be achieved in terms of things present. Each historical age had to be understood in its own light, in the light of its own attainments, philosophy, and morality. But historical-mindedness meant more to Andrews than the attempt to avoid anachronism. He believed that a proper understanding of an earlier era could be achieved only if the historian possessed a sympathy for its men and its institutions.[77] Nothing irked him more than the latter-day writer who invoked the achievements of his own era for the condemnation of an earlier one.[78]

Such was the ideal that Andrews had defined for the scientific historian. If he had learned the rudiments of the ideal in the school of Herbert Adams, he had learned its refinements in the school of English historians. Having been led to England by his interest in the problem of the Anglo-Saxon manor, he found there a perfection incarnate of his scientific ideal. For Andrews, the name of this perfection was Frederick William Maitland. "My master was [Maitland] more than anyone else." [79] The English jurist had come into international fame with his edition of *Bracton's Note Book* (1887) and with the successive volumes of original texts edited by him for the Selden Society. For Andrews and indeed for his generation, Maitland represented historical writing at its very best. In later years, Andrews encouraged each of his students never to write "without fancying that someone whom he respected and admired was always looking over his shoulder." [80] For Andrews that someone was Maitland. Nor was it that Andrews had had any close contact with the great professor of the laws of England at Cambridge: indeed, they had met but twice.[81] It was rather that, as Andrews saw it, Maitland was himself leading armies against ignorance on the darkling plain of early institutional history. Andrews hailed his independent thinking, his break with tradition, his tremendous knowledge, his insight and accuracy, his "zeal for the idea underlying the facts, and [his] comprehensive grasp of detail combined with high speculative power." [82] He hailed above all Maitland's respect for the integrity of an age, his ability to understand it from within rather than from without, his unerring and brilliant historical-mindedness. In his review of the English historian's *Domesday Book and Beyond,* Andrews summarized those qualities of a sound historiography which he felt could be insured only by a sound historiographer:

> Professor Maitland has . . . endeavored to interpret every important document beginning with Domesday Book and reaching back to the dooms of Aethelberht and the Burghal Hidage. That he has done this without disturbing at any important point the faith of the reader in the justness of his conclusions is due not only to our confidence in his learning, his unrivalled power of interpretation, and almost unlimited capacity for work, but also to his moderateness and caution in the expressal of any opinion even where the evidence is most conclusive. It is not too much to say that for the first time Domesday as a whole stands revealed . . . that for almost the first time the *terra incognita* of Saxon times has been triangulated and its boundaries ascertained.[83]

No, recapturing the past as it actually had occurred was not a simple thing, and especially difficult (as Stubbs had indicated) was the history of institutions. And yet Maitland had shown to what degree the medium of the historical mind could be perfected, how admirably the gifted historian could solve the great problems of the past. It was with such an example before him that Andrews had stressed the role of the historian. His standards for the historian were far more stringent than those generally practiced by most members of the new school of American history. He looked to the historian's mind and not merely to his method. He examined his views and not only his techniques. A later generation would seriously question whether one could attain that impartial mind and those judicious views which Andrews so earnestly sought. But a later generation would certainly agree with his most important tenet: that the essence of historical science was the historical scientist.

4. THE TENDENCY OF HISTORY

But in a system of historiography, the role of the historiographer was only the means to the actuality of the past, not the end. The end was the quest for the structure and pattern of history, it was "to see the whole, clearly, broadly, philosophically." [84] Few among the prominent contemporaries of Andrews attempted to reduce the past to the dominion of a few laws; but many of them, if unconvinced of a science of history, thought that a scientifically studied history would reveal those tendencies and movements out of which a philosophy could be constituted. If Andrew D. White, the first president of the American Historical Association, sounded the call for "a philosophic synthesis of human affairs," [85] John W. Burgess and Herbert Adams had the syntheses with which to answer the call. A historiography born anew would tend to reflect the newborn spirit of the age. The political revolutions in the West, the findings of Darwin, the advances in medicine and industry, the outcome of the Civil War: these formed a proper background for conjuring up an answer to the general meaning of man's past and the general direction of man's future. And the answer about the past, no less than that about the present, inevitably translated the precisely phrased philosophies of the few into broad colloquialisms for the many. So that words such as progress, evolution, and development entered the vocabulary of historiography as they had entered the vocabulary of every other area of that generation's thought.[86]

That tendency and purpose could be found in the past Andrews never for a moment doubted. It was mental blindness which espoused a theory of chance in history, which saw man as "an aimless actor in an aimless world." [87] History pointed up development and direction: it was governed by forces "which, if not definable as laws in the sense of exact sciences, are close approximations thereto. The truth of a philosophy of history seems to become stronger." [88] Burgess, he felt, had properly assessed the components of the historical view: clearly enough, agreed Andrews, "the highest end and purpose of history is . . . the synthesis of those facts and phases of history that mark the progressive development of the human spirit." [89]

The very word "progressive" carried its own message. The movement of history, Andrews declared, was continuously forward. One could not deny "that the real direction was . . . toward a better social order and a truer freedom." [90] Of course, during periods of transition and crisis, mankind experienced a deterioration of conditions. But the deterioration was only temporary. With the end of the period of crisis it could be discerned that "the real change, the passing to a higher form of social and political order, was for the better." [91] The relationship between the present and the past was clear then. "The heritage bequeathed to us is the sum of the best which the centuries have produced." [92] The good survives, the evil burns itself away; that this was true had been proven over and over again by the great historical struggles and their ultimate results. "Civilization is conquering barbarism, nature and the physical forces have given way before the intellectual forces." [93] Andrews was an unremitting optimist. "It is the study of history which has made me so and I don't believe that any one has a right to hold pessimistic views without a thorough understanding of the present in its relation—not to an ideal—but to the actual past out of which we have sprung." [94] Perhaps his optimism was not so much an outlook which he had gotten from history as one which he had brought to it. And perhaps that outlook had sprung far less from the past than from the bent of his own personality and the spirit of his own age.

It was not a simple calculus, however, with which Andrews computed the sums of historic experience. Though he saw human history being governed by forces "which we may almost call the laws of social progress," [95] he realized only too well the dangers of reducing the varied patterns of the past to a uniform formula. He warned, for example, against "too firm a belief in a law of progress." [96] He rejected the manipulation of historical facts to make them conform to a preconceived pattern. For that reason, the determinisms of Comte,

Buckle, and Draper met with his disapproval.[97] Complex movements could not be simply construed, nor could great events "be traced to a single cause, no matter how important that cause may be." [98] To consider the past only from a psychic or an economic viewpoint, for example, was to subject it to a "dogmatic interpretation" which could not be sustained. Neither would the materialistic approach alone suffice: the historian could not discount religious and political ideals, he could not construe "his faith, his creed . . . his art, and his literature" as "merely the outcome of an economic surplus." [99] Andrews hewed his philosophic line, as he was always wont to, down the middle: the past yielded up neither anarchy nor the strict governance of law.

In effect, the past could be studied philosophically, but not quite with a philosophy; the tendency of history could be determined, but hardly reduced to a determinism. The pattern which Andrews found in the past was not a constant component of his history: it was variously expressed, often in professional addresses, sometimes in book reviews, revealing now one predominant stress, now another. If his history mirrored his sense of pattern, it mirrored more the considerations which Andrews held most important: the search for truth, the complexity and therefore the irreducibility of bygone ages, history as a problem to be solved and historiography as expert judgment in the solution of the problem. Of the three famous Adamses that peopled his generation, there can be little doubt whose views the young historian would have supported: Henry sought a tendency, but his tendency was inflexible, so brilliantly reasoned that it was unreasonable; Herbert Baxter offered not only a tendency but flexibility as well, and all might have been acceptable if only his facts were not so incredibly wrong; George Burton was safer, for he respected the integrity of each age, saw the possibility of a *summa,* but cautioned that it might still be too early to summarize and urged his colleagues to go on establishing the fact of the past *as it actually was.*

5. THE SYSTEM APPLIED—WRITING HISTORY

The system of Andrews found application in his writings: his was a faith justified in all his good works. The outstanding contribution of his formative period, *The Old English Manor* (1892), showed how Andrews put his creed into practice. The study was an attempt to solve a major problem in institutional origins; it sought, by incorporating all the findings of the latest historical research, to achieve a sounder solution and to present a truer picture than had heretofore been achieved and presented; it surveyed the manor in its economic and social aspects, but only insofar as these aspects were defined by prevailing law. Andrews had, moreover, played the role of scientific historian with the greatest care: he was in competent possession of the linguistic knowledge demanded by the subject matter; he was moderate and cautious in his judgments; he respected the integrity and distinctiveness of the later Anglo-Saxon age, taking pains not to read the manor of the year 1000 in any light but its own. Finally, if he did not exactly posit a thesis of progress, he *did* stress the matter of development; elsewhere he was to note that while the emergence of the manor marked a period of decline in Western history, the decline was more apparent than real, for out of it evolved a higher plane of social consciousness and morality.

No less revealing a commentary on the system of the young historian could be found in his two volumes on *The Historical Development of Modern Europe, 1815–1897* (1896–98). Andrews drew the materials for his survey from the courses on the nineteenth century that he had been giving to the undergraduates at Bryn Mawr. His purpose in doing the work was clear enough: "I ought to make enough to add something to my salary." [100] It was Bertha Putnam, a student of Andrews, who had started things off. She had invited her father, a member of the famous publishing firm, to sit in on some of the brilliant and well-attended lectures of her young professor. On the verge as he was of "marrying a wife and building and furnishing a house," the professor was sufficiently persuaded by the assurance of "a good royalty" to undertake casting his lectures into book form.[101]

His survey disclosed readily enough the precepts of Andrews' historiography. He was concerned with tracing "the continuous development of the life and thought of Europe" during the nineteenth century.[102] That he underlined the themes of continuity and development was, of course, not unintentional. He meant to lay bare the inner thread of European experience: to show, for example, "that the events of 1859, 1866, and 1870 were but the logical outcome of those of the earlier period." [103] Whatever breadth of treatment the title of his work implied, Andrews was concerned essentially with international relations and with internal political and constitutional developments in each of the European states. As a matter of fact, his concern extended to only a few of the states, France receiving the longest treatment and England and Russia being virtually absent from the account. The point of it was that Andrews was not merely writing the political and constitutional history which formed the central concern of his school: he was also writing his history with a thesis which formed the prevalent outlook of his age. That thesis—the growth of national unity and individual liberty in Europe—was the principal subject of his work.[104] It explained why France, Italy, and Prussia had been fully dealt with. It also explained the glaring omission of England and Russia. England had earlier attained many of the objectives set by Andrews for the course of European development during the nineteenth century. As for Russia, particularly to an American who had come to know her during the time of Alexander III and Pobiedonostsev, her history seemed to offer little more than autocracy and repression.

His critics were virtually unanimous in their praise for Andrews' impartiality, fairness, and painstaking research.[105] He had indeed, they agreed, written the science of history rather than the drama.[106] "His judgments," said the *Saturday Review,* "are those of the ordinary, fair-minded, reasonable man dealing with matters of common knowledge."[107] Andrews himself noted that he had sought the course between two extremes, that he had not hesitated "to comment upon or interpret events," but could "find no place for personal judgments, which, reflecting merely the sentiments of the writer and based too often on present-day standards, are out of accord with the spirit of modern historical presentation."[108] Perhaps the question of how successfully Andrews satisfied his own standards hinges on the difference of meaning which he meant to draw between "interpretation of events" and "personal judgments" of a present-minded nature. There could be no doubt, however, that he was measuring the events of the nineteenth century against the rod of those principles which he deemed to be the legacy of the French Revolution, that he was weighing the whole course of that age on the scales of national unity and individual liberty. But why was he selecting these particular criteria for evaluating the history of the nineteenth century? Were these criteria eternal or were they meaningful only for the age of Andrews? Could there be any wonder, if they were applied, that Napoleon would be found to have been not the child of the Revolution but its nemesis,[109] that Metternich's conservatism would be visited not with sympathy but with scorn and vilification,[110] that Bismarck's militarism would be condoned because of its "nobler end" and that the Berlin-centered system would be appraised as "better than the old system circling about Vienna"?[111] The past-mindedness of Andrews' preface was thus belied by the present-mindedness of his history. The critics, certainly, had noted his preference for republicanism over monarchy, for liberal constitutions over centralized autocracy.[112] Perhaps the explanation of the difference between what he preached and what he practiced may be found, to some degree, in the fact that he had not worked through the field on his own, but had depended on "the best authorities," with some reference to "material from special monographs and recently printed documents."[113] Perhaps the better explanation is that he was not so much the captive of his materials as of his age.

To what synthesis of history would his age incline him? Democratic and nationalistic strivings seemed to define the direction of Western society. It can be understood, therefore, why Andrews, who had declared that the purpose of his survey was "to study those movements that have made for progress," [114] proceeded to judge the course of European history in terms of progress toward national unity and democracy.[115] His summation of the past had other components. Concerned as it was with underlying tendencies and causes, it saw no incident save in the broader pattern of the evolution of a movement or an idea. It denied "accidental occurrences," throwing up the logic and inevitability of historical development to explain what might superficially seem to be fortuitous.[116] If the individual in history had not quite been reduced to playing the marionette, as one of the reviews complained he had been,[117] he was hardly, to Andrews' way of thinking, a free agent. Any one of the great leaders in nineteenth-century Europe, including such men as Cavour and Bismarck, "would have been powerless to accomplish his object had not the forces making for independence and unity been preparing for half a century." [118] History, then, was moving inevitably toward a certain goal. That none of his reviewers took exception either to the young historian's definition of that goal or to his view of its inevitability only confirmed how admirably Andrews was expressing the larger convictions of his times.

A History of England, a textbook of some five hundred and fifty pages which appeared in 1903, was a comment by Andrews on the three parts into which the new history was divided: study, writing, and teaching. The transition in American historiography during the late nineteenth century had put the writing of history into the hands of the teachers, but all too frequently the teaching reflected little of the newer currents evident in the writing. The Bryn Mawr professor, then in his fortieth year, felt that textbooks ought to be kept abreast of the latest historical scholarship. Not only did he fully document his account with source materials, but he also concluded each chapter with a critical survey of the latest literature on the subject. If he was demonstrating his own expert command of the sources, he was also urging the need for such command upon the teacher of history. In basing his survey of the English past upon the documents and upon the latest literature, Andrews inevitably came up with a view which reflected the moderate and revisionist spirit of the new history. Pollock and Maitland had been consulted on the medieval period, Gairdner and Creighton on the Tudors, Gardiner and Firth on the Stuarts. But no matter whom Andrews consulted, his own approach to the past was readily apparent. Straight narrative was dispensed with, the account being devoted to problems of an institutional nature facing the English nation, and not merely political problems, but economic and religious as well. For having abandoned royal chronicle and for having broadened the scope of his treatment, he was warmly commended by his reviewers.[119] His concern, declared Andrews, would be to get rid of "the stage thunder that passed current for history in the older narratives" and concentrate on those factors that underlie "the true progress of a nation." [120] English history, he later asserted, "gives the amplest opportunity to the pupil to acquire a sense of continuity and historical perspective." [121] Indeed his story of the English past revealed all the essential elements of the system of Andrews. It was a story of problem-solving, of institutional growth, of unity and continuity, of "the true progress of a nation" through asperity to the stars.

Not only in the major writings of his formative years was the system of Andrews expressed: it was expressed in his lesser contributions as well. In his article on "The Connecticut Intestacy Law" (1894),[122] for example, he demonstrated his ability for using a particular historical circumstance as the vantage ground for surveying long-range trends. The particular circumstance involved litigation over the validity of the Connecticut law of 1699 governing the disposal of intestate estates. The basis of the litigation was the difference of Connecticut common law in this matter from English common law, the former providing for equal division of such estates among all the children, with two shares going to the eldest son, the latter providing for inheritance by the eldest son alone. Though the law of Connecticut was disallowed by order in council in 1728, subsequent decisions of the king in council negated the effects of the disallowance and pretty much left the colony to its own devices. In his examination of the Connecticut statute, Andrews revealed not merely his command of the sources, but also his skill in exploiting them. Undertaking to solve a problem in institutional origins and development, he saw legal institutions not as something apart from the rest of American colonial life but rather as something rooted in agrarian and economic activities. A particular law afforded him a point of observation for tracing the growing divergence between the colonies and the mother country, for grasping an historic whole through one of its parts.

In "A Biographical By-Path Through Early New England History" (1893),[123] Andrews used the story of Richard Gildersleeve to cast a wide net upon colonial waters. It was the young historian's familiar device of catching an age through its individuals. Tracing the varied and extensive life and livings of Gildersleeve through Connecticut, New Haven, New Amsterdam, and New York, Andrews found that his subject had "pursued the circle of the colonial systems" [124] and thereby offered "a new point of view from which to study the principles which lay at the foundation of the various forms of colonial government." [125] In his introduction to *Ideal Empires and Republics* (1901), Andrews indicated his belief that an age could also be caught through its aspirations, its plans to perfect itself, its utopias. "Each is . . . a mirror to the prevailing thought of the period in which it is written. . . . To write properly the history of Utopias from the time of Sir Thomas More to the present [1901] is to write the history of the progress of human thought in the last five centuries." [126] Once more were asserted the guiding principles of the young historian: every individual within his age, and every age with its individuality.

In sum, his early contributions, however diversified their themes, were bound together by the principles of his system.

The system was the legacy of his school, the product of his age, the embodiment of his own personality and predilections. During his formative years, the years of his study at Johns Hopkins and of his teaching at Bryn Mawr, he tested and probed his principles. He expressed them in a variety of forms, in long volumes, in essays, in public addresses, in book reviews. He applied those principles to a variety of historical fields, to nineteenth-century Europe, to late Anglo-Saxon England, to early America, to modern Asia and Africa. In a sense, this was for his historiography a period of trial and formulation. Before very long, the heterogeneous elements of his system would settle into a homogeneous whole. Before very long, he would have defined with fair certainty his views on the nature and use of history, on the role of the historian, on the tendency of history. At that juncture of his life, he would seek a vast and hitherto unexplored area of the past to claim for the new history and, more significantly, for his own. For that earlier era he would erect a massive monument fashioned out of the materials of his system. Indeed, in his address to the American Historical Association in 1898, he had already claimed leadership in the field of American colonial history. Here was a field abounding in problems to be solved, in primary materials to be tapped, in eras and tendencies to be defined and explained, in institutions waxing and waning. And the new historical science was demanding of Andrews that he invest all the resources of his craft in bringing forth a truer and sounder evaluation of the American colonial past. The evaluation would inevitably reflect the principles of his system. Inevitably too, since the system was nothing but the creature of its age, the passing of that age would mean the growing obsolescence not only of the system but also of the evaluation it had engendered.

6. THE SYSTEM APPLIED—TEACHING HISTORY

The writing of history was the heart of his contribution and the embodiment of his system. Yet Andrews could not and did not close himself off from other vital areas of the historical profession, areas to which he brought those principles that he had so consciously formulated. He was an active member of the American Historical Association, which, in its early decades, was the very vanguard of the new historical science. Here he served as chairman of the Justin Winsor Prize Committee and as a member of the Public Archives Commission.[127] Here he delivered several addresses, including that famous one in 1898, when he joined Herbert Osgood in formally opening the field of American colonial history to research and reappraisal by the new history. He served his cause and set forth his system in other capacities too: by his active membership in an ever increasing number of local historical societies, by the work he did on the Board of Trade papers for the Pennsylvania Historical Society, by his frequent lecturing before nonprofessional groups.

But archival researches, professional cooperation, membership in historical societies, and popular lectures were never quite so pressing upon the historian as his primary responsibility: that of teaching. In this area too could be found a practical expression of his guiding principles. During the eighteen years that he taught at Bryn Mawr, that very period from 1889 to 1907 which was virtually coeval with the rise of the new history, Andrews brought into the classroom what he was bringing into his books. His lectures ran the gamut "from Adam to McKinley." [128] The elementary courses, meeting five times weekly and given in a three-year sequence, traced the story of civilization from its rise in Asia Minor. The advanced courses, meeting one hour weekly or once fortnightly, dealt with various special subjects, including historical definition, method, and criticism, Roman Law, the English constitution, and continental Europe in the nineteenth century. Particularly proud was Andrews of his seminar, which he first introduced in 1895, and with which he took up the study of the medieval English community.[129] Among the seminarians was his most famous student of the Bryn Mawr days, Nellie Neilson, who later reminisced about "the cramped little seminar room at the top of Taylor [Hall]," where she found her "great love for early English history." [130] It was fortunate for his cause, no doubt, that the young, tall, and handsome professor could captivate his feminine students not only with his principles but with his personality. Andrews was popular on the Bryn Mawr campus. His classes were always well attended, the elementary courses always running over a hundred.[131] After the publication of his *Old English Manor* in 1892 as well as a trip to England during the summer of that year, Andrews was greeted thus by his students on his return to the campus:

> Here's to C.M.A., drink him down, drink him down,
> Here's to C.M.A., does his English Manner pay? [132]

It was a felicitous pun, resting as it did upon the juncture of his personality and his principles. Those principles the young professor always conveyed to his auditors with enthusiasm. He was fully aware of the pedagogic importance of being earnest.

Earnest pedagogy was, for him, designed to attain very significant goals. To insure the attainment of these goals, certainly, the teaching had to be "objective and impartial, free from ethical judgments and free from the bias of ignorance or parochialism, from the whimsicalities of the narrow-minded, and the ill-balanced opinions of those with particular views to impart or doctrines to defend." [133] The study of history itself Andrews regarded as "the best persuader to liberality, sane judgment, and, above all, a habit of fairness." [134] Historical instruction, he contended, ought to encourage the student "to act with reason, with common sense . . . and to draw conclusions which are as near right as human nature is capable of attaining." [135] A course in history was a course in moderation, balance, and perspective, leading its participants to a more optimistic view of life and to a more sanguine "faith in the progress of the human race." [136] In all respects, therefore, whether it touched upon the student's attitude of mind, the smallest detail of his research, or the grand structure of his philosophy, the teaching of Charles Andrews was a reasoned facsimile of his historiographical principles. For him, indeed, the classroom was the day-to-day laboratory in which he might put to work and check upon those elements of his system which he was also exploring in his own researches and writings.

7. THE HISTORIAN VIEWS THE NEW HISTORY

What view did the young historian take of the rise of the new history? How did he himself construe the relation of his own system to the changing currents in American historiography? A portrait of Charles Andrews during his formative years would hardly be complete without some answer to these questions. It was abundantly clear to him, to begin with, that the advent of historical science had marked a term to the patriotic history of the school of Bancroft. It had been the concern of the writers of the mid-nineteenth century, asserted Andrews, to make of their works "little more than huge party pamphlets, written to uphold a cause." [137] It was full of bombast and filiopietism, this history, signifying that Clio had "forgotten the mighty mission of truth that is hers." [138] Perhaps some of it was great literature, very little of it had proven to be great history. How could it be, lacking as it was in "judicial impartiality," revealing at all points its deficiency of perspective as well as its national bias, seeking not truth but "to defend a party . . . to prove, to justify, to defy, to glorify, or to abuse." [139]

The "religious fervor" (as he described it) with which Andrews hailed the new history was no more warm than the jeremiad with which he said farewell to the old. Never had a country so prominent as the United States "been so slow to recognize the importance of historical study"; how lamentable it was to find "so few trained historical scholars," with "so much second-rate and jejune" historical scholarship.[140] But the times were changing and the evidences of change could be multiplied: Winsor's *Narrative and Critical History* afforded "almost the first recognition in this country of history as a science"; the Smithsonian Institution, recently incorporated, would help preserve American historical materials; the revival of interest in local societies would help the national movement; and "a standard of criticism" was being established which would no longer tolerate local prejudices and history with a cause to defend.[141] Andrews hailed "this age of historical iconoclasm," [142] the age of historical science, of "fraternal cooperation" to seek the truth. The trained historian would stand in formidable contrast to the earlier practitioner of history. His work would bespeak "proportion, perspective, historical imagination, historical training, and a knowledge of comparative institutions and historical philosophy" [143]—those very qualities, in effect, out of which the newer history was being fashioned. To Andrews it seemed that the world of American historiography had been wrapped in night. But the night was passing, and there was now morning, a new day.

A new day in historiography had, for that matter, been dawning throughout the Western world. Illumined by a various light, the newer history was composed of a variety of schools. To some degree, the schools formed themselves along national lines. In tracing the institutional origins of the new American school, one would find it to have been the child of the Germans, above all, with some lines of descent deriving from the English. Concerning his own particular place in the historical genealogy, Andrews had little doubt. "I never studied in Germany or looked to any German as guide and model." [144] The young historian little valued the work of Ranke's progeny: it had become so utterly specialized that it was almost antiquarian, it took a patriotic view of the past in order to justify and defend the present.[145] The German school was one of cavilling and carping, of "dullness and pedantry," which the Americans would do well not to imitate.[146] No, he asserted in later years, not from the Teutonic forestlands had he inherited his legacy of freedom to seek historic truth:

> German methods and historiography did not get under my skin. My master was Frederick William Maitland more than anyone else and I was far more influenced by the English school of that day (Gross, Seebohm, Round, Vinogradoff), that represented a reaction from the Freeman-Green-Hallam-Macaulay School, which really at bottom H. B. Adams stood for.[147]

The mastership of Maitland was of course impersonal and symbolic; the English historian was the master not only of Andrews but of his age. As for Herbert Adams, it seemed clear enough to Andrews that he belonged both to the meticulous and pedantic Germans and the Whiggish and pamphleteering English. Seeking survivals and identities, praising Angles and damning Stuarts: it was all of one ilk and Andrews would have little to do with it. In the new age, in the "time of great awakening in the American historical world," what were Freeman and Adams but lost leaders? Ranke was a truer guide. Best of all, Maitland was there, looking over his shoulder.

PART II

THE COLONIAL PERIOD OF AMERICAN HISTORY

Chapter 3

COLONIES, ARCHIVES and GUIDES

A man of Andrews' ambition would seek a practical test of his system, just as a man of his ability would surely be successful in such a test. But what would be the testing-ground? A new age offered many possibilities. Did not the advent of "scientific" history prescribe an epoch of rediscovery? Did not the creed of primary sources, monographic literature, impartiality, iconoclasm, and truth *as it actually was* demand a new orthodoxy? Time had thrown the fields of history back into common and was awaiting the individual claims of the new historian. With so many rich crops to harvest, there would have to be gleaning after no one. It wanted but ambition and ability. Aulard undertook to bring forth a new French Revolution, Maitland a new Domesday, Gardiner a new line of Stuarts. In the United States, the views of Bancroft, which had so long dominated American historiography, were being rejected by the new historical science.[1] The hour for an Andrews was ripe.

1. EARLY AMERICA REVISITED

And Andrews was ripe for the hour. In 1893, at the age of thirty, Andrews went to London to do work on the local institutional history of later medieval England.[2] He also planned doing some work for the Pennsylvania Historical Society on the Board of Trade papers in the Public Record Office. But what had been peripheral to his mission very soon became central. If he had come to study English records for English history, he concluded by discovering English records for American history.

It is rather odd [he wrote his mother] how I have got shunted off from what was my original design, in coming over onto the American work; but it seems decidedly the most available and most important for the present. . . . The volumes are entirely mss. and only a bit here and there has been printed in America, so that I do not see how any one writing upon colonial history can omit consulting them. It gives me a new and necessary point of view, which has not often enough been taken in America and shows the English side of the question. Of course, in the difficulties arising during the colonial period, our sympathies are largely with the colonists; but there is much to be said on the other side, particularly as there was much conscientiousness and legal right in the position of the English officials.[3]

The main elements of his historiographic program were all there. He would spend the next half century implementing them. In American colonial history, he had found an area to test his enterprise and satisfy his ambition.

It was an area indeed which had readily suggested itself to the enterprise of the new school as a whole. The scientific historian, casting an iconoclastic eye over the work of his predecessors, would be enticed by the rich prospects before him: documents by the dozen, new ones to be brought to light, new light to be brought to the old ones; heroes to be understood more judiciously and less reverentially, and therewith made a good deal less heroic; loyalists to be repatriated, patriots to be excoriated, and a balanced via media for the historian to tread, where none but fools had hitherto rushed; political bands, dissolved in the course of human events, which the historian, proclaiming the unity and continuity of history, would seek to restore. Now that the *second* civil war had been concluded, it was high time to resolve the Anglo-American differences about the *first*. The new course of history offered an opportunity to the new course of historiography: those who sat as supreme court on the past followed, as usual, the election returns of the present. At a time when the rest of the nation was making business its history, those studying the past were enjoined to make history a business. With the sobriety, organization, and perhaps even dullness of American business, the new historians were looking for what they deemed the gold of American colonial history rather than its glitter.

With that quest Andrews had, in fact, been concerned from the very outset of his career. He had been trained in the school of Herbert Adams, a school whose predominant interest was in American colonial institutions. His doctoral dissertation, moreover, Andrews had devoted to the problem of local institutional origins in early Connecticut. In an article on "The Beginnings of the Connecticut Towns" (1890), he had sought to challenge the application of a priori notions to early American political history. In 1891, he had recognized that "the lucid, broad-minded history of the colonies has yet to be written." [4] To write such a history became a matter of personal ambition when, in 1893, Andrews first explored the vast materials of the Public Record Office. Mellen Chamberlain, a judge and an historian, must have stirred that ambition not a little in his letter to Andrews the very next year:

> My most ardent desire is to see, before I go, if not the fulfillment, at least the promise of a more original and just account of the beginning and progress of civilization on this continent. . . . I look eagerly to you, and such as you, to do what, from the nature of the case, must remain the dream of an old man. . . . Among the younger men, whose writings I have read, I see no one of whom I have formed so high expectations.[5]

Subsequent articles by Andrews on "The Connecticut Intestacy Law" (1894) and on "The Land System in the American Colonies" (1896) [6] revealed a continuing interest in the same field, an interest further evidenced in several of his book reviews. It was no novice, therefore, who joined Herbert Levi Osgood, in 1898, in formally opening up the American colonial past to the collective effort of the gild. Speaking before the American Historical Association that year, Osgood and Andrews urged that the problem of early American history stood very much in need of solution.

Yet it was not to the entire century and a half from 1607 to 1783 that Andrews directed his attention in that notable address. He was concerned only with the decades from 1690 to

1750, "the middle period between colonization and revolution," a period that had hitherto been "unduly neglected." [7] The importance of those years seemed manifest to him: it was the training time of the men who led the Revolution; it was the time when England was giving her "colonial administration and commercial policy its first systematic form and application," when English wars were leading to coercion of the colonies and a policy of more rigorous control; it was an age when English peace led to increasing conflict with the Americans over questions of trade and government.[8] How had Andrews arrived at this particular interest in the "neglected period" of American history? Largely, no doubt, from having worked among the Board of Trade papers during that summer of 1893: the Board was probably the most significant single agency of British mercantilism and its life was virtually coeval with this "middle period" of American colonial history. Perhaps, to a lesser degree, it was the encouragement of Mellen Chamberlain, who wrote Andrews shortly after the young historian had returned from his first contact with British archival materials. "Sometime," said Chamberlain, "I hope you will turn your attention to the period—say, 1700–1750—and embody the results of your studies in an elaborate work. It seems to me to be a field never much wrought, and even less understood." [9]

If he had had no program before along this line (and there is no evidence that he had), then here it was. For decades afterward, even though he extended his concern to the whole of the colonial period, he continued to see this half century or so as the darkest area on the dark continent of the pre-national era. Constantly, he preached the cause of exploration and enlightenment. He hailed the publication of the papers of Joseph Talcott, governor of the colony of Connecticut from 1724–41, for throwing light "upon an obscure period of our colonial history," a period of "important changes in economic environment and economic ideas." [10] In 1900, he charged his peers with a "neglect of certain periods, such as the era from

1690 to 1750 . . . when the foundations were being laid in government and wealth for the national structure that was to be erected after the Revolution." [11] In 1909, he asserted again that "the day has not come when the history of this troublesome eighteenth century can be written adequately." [12] In 1917, he spoke of growing incursions into "a period not only neglected but largely misunderstood." [13] His plea that this dark age needed light persisted over the greater part of his professional career. The plea was tinged with irony: for when he died, half a century after first contemplating a study of the colonial age, he had not yet, insofar as American institutional development was concerned, published his great synthesis of "the neglected period" of American colonial history.

Yet, Andrews knew, it was not only that especially benighted half century that had suffered a nonsalutary neglect. To his own way of thinking and to that of his school, the entire colonial period stood in need of reinterpretation. Here indeed would be the testing-ground for his system of historiography. He would see the years from 1607 to 1783 as a continuity, seeking the deeper causes of things, concentrating his attention upon institutional origins and growth. He would play the historian's role with utmost care, striving for impartiality, moderation, and sound judgment. Nothing would impress itself more upon his consciousness than his "*duty* to view the colonies as England viewed them" and to grasp "the difference of mental longitude between the seventeenth century and the present time." [14] Ultimately he would be able to attain a "truer colonial history," [15] to understand the place of the colonies "in the progress of civilization," [16] to see the colonial period as part of a philosophic whole.

Reflecting as it did the precepts of the new history, his work would begin with a thorough canvassing of the primary sources. Indeed, urged Andrews in 1900, "accessibility of historical material is the greatest need that confronts the historical workers at the present time." [17] For himself, he could not proceed very far toward his goal without turning to the tremendous and largely unused deposits of the British archives.[18] Locked up within the bundles and the manuscript collections of the Public Record Office, he would find his own version of the new American colonial history.

2. OLD MATERIALS FOR A NEW HISTORY

Perhaps there was nothing so universal in the newer historiography of the Western world as the concentration upon source materials. The new history followed an age that wrote with much spirit and little regard for the documents, just as it ushered in an age that wrote with much regard for the documents and little spirit. Did this regard indicate a sudden awareness on the part of that age of the course of human evolution and a need for documenting the origin of institutions no less than species, the descent of present society no less than man? Perhaps it meant that the national states of the nineteenth century were hoping to enhance their contemporary significance by claiming for themselves an old institutional legacy, a staid medieval lineage. Or was it simply that historians were a race of anchorites, seeking to escape the realities of their own world by putting a documentary footnote to the realities of an earlier one? Whatever may have given rise to the growing concern with source materials, evidences of the concern were everywhere abundant: the *Monumenta Germaniae Historica,* the *Collection de documents inédits,* the *Rolls Series,* and the *Colección de documentos inéditos.*[19] America, too, sought out its national past within the recesses of its documentary sources. The difficulty was, however, that the search could not get very far without going back into the very non-national colonial period. The United States had not much of a history to begin with. And whatever history it had tended only to underline those entangling alliances with foreign archives which vitiated the spirit and purpose of a distinctively national history. As a matter of fact, if the great central collection of national archives of America were sought, would it at all be found within these shores? Would it not indeed be found within England? Here was a paradox which patriots and filiopietists would eventually have to face, that the Monumenta Americae Historica were basically English. In a way, that observation summarizes the contribution of Charles McLean Andrews.

Andrews saw the work of collecting and protecting source materials going on all about him. He was familiar with the pioneering work of Justin Winsor and with the appeals Jameson was making for governmental assistance in the publication of the nation's archives.[20] He knew of the work of the Historical Manuscripts Commission, headed by Jameson, which had been appointed in 1895, by the Executive Council of the American Historical Association, "to edit, index, or collect information in regard to unprinted documents relating to American history." [21] He himself had become a member of the Public Archives Comission of the American Historical Association in 1901, and had with Osgood been appointed a committee of two to plan the transcription of British archival materials.[22] More and more the canvassing of sources would be aided by the grants of the Carnegie Institution of Washington, which had been founded in 1902, and which undertook to publish guides to those materials in the European and Latin American archives that dealt with American history. The work that Andrews did on the British archives, under the auspices of the Carnegie Institution, established his place in American historiography.

Throughout his career, Andrews espoused the cause of the document. In 1891, in one of his earliest reviews, he expressed the hope that pressure could be "brought to bear upon Congress in the interest of preserving our records." [23] Until a National Archives Building was actually built, toward the end of his life, he kept up a continuing demand for one; the indifference of Congress to the entire issue he considered "something of a national disgrace." [24] The interest of the English government in publishing its archives readily served him as a basis for berating the American government for its relative lack of interest in this area.[25] Andrews regularly hailed the publication of local archival materials, whether for early American town or colony, and just as regularly lamented failures to publish such materials as he considered important.[26] During his later years, and particularly in connection with his work on the Legal History Committee (Littleton-Griswold) of the American Historical Association, he encouraged the publication of materials dealing with the higher common-law courts in the colonies, as well as the courts of vice-admiralty, chancery, and exchequer.[27] The special interest he took in early American legal records was, however, only part of a more general interest in all colonial records. The care of manuscript materials was also a matter of the deepest concern to him. Decade after decade he hammered away at the same theme: the mishandling of public archives, the destruction of records by negligence and stupidity, the loss of records as one of the great tragedies of historical science, and the great need for properly handling and housing all manuscript materials.[28]

But the documents, he well appreciated, were only the means to an end. Andrews agreed that the tendency to exaggerate the sources had sometimes attained alarming proportions.[29] He never thought that the alliance between the historian and the past could be reduced to mere scraps of paper; he never confused going into old family boxes with going behind the scenes of history. But the archives of a nation he deemed very important because, he felt, they would reveal the "continuous development and expansion of the functions of its government." [30] And what more important story could there be for an historian such as Andrews, who believed that "the true history of a state and a people" was to be found "in the substantial features of its constitutional and social organization"? [31]

The "true history" of the American colonial past, he submitted, could be found mainly in the British archives. The road to the colonies was the royal road through Whitehall. This was the theme he sounded throughout his professional career, beginning with his address before the American Historical Association in 1898, in which he detailed the materials that were available for laying bare the period 1690–1750. Item by item, the tapping of the British archives was proceeding: in the great *Calendar of State Papers* dealing with America and the

West Indies; in the *Calendar of Treasury Papers*; in the *Calendar of Home Office Papers*; with the publication of the *Acts of the Privy Council* dealing with the colonies and of the *Proceedings and Debates of the British Parliaments respecting North America.* Hitherto, felt Andrews, historians had failed to see British administration as the only element of unity in a world of colonial diversities; they had "groped in the dark as far as the fundamental principles of British policy were concerned." [32] But through the archives one could apprehend "the true inwardness of the British position." [33] Taking one's stand within the different administrative departments, whether the Privy Council, the Board of Trade, the Treasury, the vice-admiralty courts, to name some of the more important ones, one might "begin to see some aspects of colonial history in a new light." [34] The historian could not continue to believe, for example, that colonial management in England during the first half of the eighteenth century had been inefficient or that Burke's comment on the "salutary neglect" of this period was in strict consonance with the actual facts.[35] In evaluating what the calendaring of the state papers, colonial, would mean for the new history of eighteenth-century America, Andrews felt "there is not a treatise or monograph now written that will not need entire revision eventually." [36] Could this possibly explain why the colonial house that Andrews built was started late and never finished?

3. GUIDES TO EARLY AMERICA

It was the spirit of the time, certainly, which prescribed that the solution of the problem of American colonial history could be achieved only by viewing that history from the English standpoint and only by going to the English archives in order to really know that standpoint. But it would be extending the governance of the time-spirit too far to suppose that Charles McLean Andrews was destined for the herculean task of drawing up the guides to the English archives for materials dealing with early American history. The story of how Andrews came to undertake the job, which is adequately recounted elsewhere,[37] need not long detain us. His interest in the English archives as repositories of American history dated back to 1893, when he first examined the Board of Trade papers in the Public Record Office. "From that time—when I discovered the material in the P. R. O.—I was committed to Colonial history, as a life work." [38] At about the time that Andrews was calling upon the American Historical Association to explore the British materials, Jameson began to plan, in conjunction with the American Antiquarian Society, for a guide to British records dealing with American history. Andrews indicated he would be willing to do the work, and when the Carnegie Institution of Washington offered to finance it, the American Antiquarian Society, which felt it did not have enough funds for the project, withdrew. The minor archives in London and elsewhere were canvassed by Andrews with the assistance of Frances G. Davenport, of the Department of Historical Research in the Carnegie Institution; but the massive labor on the great Public Record Office he did entirely alone.

He was to have spent on this "preliminary" task only the year from the summer of 1903 through that of 1904, which he had taken as a sabbatical leave from Bryn Mawr. Having begun by contemplating a year, he concluded by spending more than a decade. Several summers were devoted to an enterprise whose dimensions had not only been underestimated, but which grew enormously and was long delayed when the Public Record Office instituted a new system of classification of some of the largest manuscript collections with which Andrews was concerned, particularly the Colonial Office papers. "If I had known that instead of working one year and issuing one volume, I would work ten years and issue three, I would never have undertaken the job. Probably it was one of the luckiest things that ever happened that I didn't know what I was in for." [39]

The monumental labor was contained in two major works: a one-volume *Guide to the Manuscript Materials for the History of the United States to 1783, in the British Museum, in Minor London Archives, and in the Libraries of Oxford and*

Cambridge (1908), and a two-volume *Guide to the Materials for American History, to 1783, in the Public Record Office of Great Britain* (1912–14). Whether the materials were arranged according to a larger over-all plan, as they were in the case of the Record Office manuscripts, or whether they conformed to no such intelligible pattern, as was true of the manuscript collections of the British Museum, the *Guides* offered succinct descriptions of the records involved. In many instances, particularly where the documents were deemed to be of special importance to the student of American colonial history, the descriptive comments were considerably amplified. The *Guides* noted those documents which were duplicates, gave cross-references to related materials elsewhere, specified (wherever pertinent) the fuller descriptions cited in the Calendars concerning some of the records, and indicated too which of the records had been printed. Aids to the researcher abounded: the excellent index that each volume contained; the list of volumes and documents in the Public Record Office, the British Museum, and the Bodleian Library at Oxford that had been transcribed for the Library of Congress at Washington, D.C.; and the key indicating, to those who had been using such materials, the old reference numbers of the recently reclassified Colonial Office papers. In addition to this, the volumes on the Public Record Office contained extensive introductory comments of an historical and descriptive nature concerning the departments whose materials they canvassed. The *Guides,* said Andrews, were to be "something more than a mere catalogue of entries." He hoped that they "might serve as an introduction to the system of British administration, particularly in the eighteenth century" and "would make it possible for the student to approach the documents with an understanding already quickened regarding their place in the British administrative routine." [40]

The *Guides* are a portrait of the man. They are among the best works deriving from his system. In his own estimate, they represent "my chief contribution in the field." [41] The four-volume summation of *The Colonial Period of American History* which he wrote in his final decade would, he felt, in time be superseded. But "if my name lives, it is because I was the author of [the] Guides." [42] More than his notable contemporaries Osgood and Beer, he was devoted to the task of making the Record Office public. More than they, he was loath to proceed to the center of the story, the British system of trade and administration, until the documentary roads leading to the center were fully revealed. As he saw it, getting to the sources meant getting to the solution of the problem. When, in 1898, he first addressed the American Historical Association on the subject of the colonial period, he submitted that "it is not essential that we should know what subjects to study beforehand, but rather it is important that we should know what material is available, and let that guide our thoughts." [43] If Osgood imposed the severity of historical logic upon the materials, Andrews permitted the materials to impose their own logical severity upon history. Within the British archives could be found the rationale of the colonial period, and within the *Guides* could be found the rationale of the British archives.

It was not merely that these were *Guides* for the perplexed, it was that they were also volumes with a philosophy. The philosophy, based as it was on the premise of solving problems through manuscript materials, naturally tended to define itself in terms of those manuscript materials that were uncovered. If Andrews had come to believe that there was no better way of studying a government than through its archives,[44] it meant that he had also set the scope and limit of his historiography. Equating the rediscovery of an earlier age with the rediscovery of a vast body of a particular type of materials determined, moreover, the nature of the work and research that would have to be done for the next few decades. Here was the reason, for example, why it became almost a sine qua non for those who belonged to the school of Andrews to make a pilgrimage to the British materials. Here too was the reason why that *summa* of early American history which he had contemplated when he was forty would not be made until he was past seventy. One need not wonder that he always "resisted the impulse to write the larger work early in life"; one can readily understand that he "knew he was not ready." [45] Andrews himself had laid bare the staggering proportions of the work to be done to solve the problem of the American colonial past. The inner workings of that British system of which the American colonies were part would be revealed slowly and painfully, by hard work, bundle by bundle, volume by volume, folio by folio. The historian would have to make his way tediously through those items that constituted the brick and mortar of the monumental *Guides*: the addresses, journals, maps, petitions, instructions, acts, minute-books, patents, entry-books, ships' logs, lists, accounts, charts, and extensive correspondences. It would take years of active pioneering at the Public Record Office.[46] To solve the problems of American history that awaited solution, one would have to do "a great deal of arduous grubbing."[47] One could not very well win the battle of the archives by being simply an armchair historian.

Unearthing materials became a way of life, affecting every facet of the historian's activities. The library of Andrews revealed his intense and abiding concern with sources pertaining to the British commercial and colonial system of the seventeenth and eighteenth centuries.[48] Records, guides, calendars, reports of the Historical Manuscripts Commission, statutes at large, proceedings and debates, state archival collections: they all sounded the same note. It was a note again audible in extensive lists that Andrews prepared for publication in various annual reports of the American Historical Association. The lists were concerned with a diversity of items: the journals and acts of the councils and assemblies of the thirteen original colonies; the commissions and instructions which had been issued to royal governors and others in America; and the reports and representations of several of the British councils and boards concerned with the American plantations. Yet whatever their diversity, the lists, each running a hundred or more pages, contained essentially the same message: that the documents specified were "among the most important constitutional documents of our colonial history,"[49] that they "contained, when studied chronologically, a complete exposition of British policy,"[50] that they would help "the student of colonial history to find out, with greater certainty than has yet been attained, the motives which underlay the colonial policy of the British government and the part taken by the various advisory boards in originating that policy and giving it shape." [51]

It can be understood why his interest and his knowledge led him to guide the transcription of important bodies of documentary material contained in the British archives. The transcripts, a logical concomitant of the *Guides,* were designed to offer at home, in the Library of Congress, what the student of American colonial history would ordinarily have to seek abroad. Working for some time with Osgood, and under the general direction of Herbert Putnam, the librarian of the Library of Congress, Andrews devoted, on and off, a quarter-century's work to the task of supervising the transcription of important British archival materials.[52] The same abiding interest could be seen in his own manuscript materials.[53] Each of his vast number of notebooks and folders, brimming with the painstakingly written and well-organized details of the records he was surveying, indicates that an earlier Anglo-American world was being explored. The same message is conveyed by the hundreds of letters he sent and received. To his personal and exhaustive knowledge of the British archives, Andrews added a similar knowledge of every major manuscript collection up and down the Eastern seaboard, as well as elsewhere in the United States. Because of his command of the materials, he was increasingly consulted by his colleagues as the years went on.[54] Reliving with Andrews the particulars contained in his correspondence, or going through with him the details of the collections he was canvassing, his biographer may sometimes wonder about the overwhelming abundance of minutiae. Yet the point of it is precisely this, that the historiography of Andrews was a historiography of minutiae. Andrews did not, however, lose the total view for the individual manuscript. Indeed, it was through the individual manuscript that he gained it.

The importance of the *Guides* was at once recognized. Jameson averred that it would "do more to promote scholarly study of American history before 1783 than any one book ever previously published," [55] that it marked an era in the study of its subject, putting that subject "at once on a new and higher basis."[56] W. T. Root, whose study of the *Relations of Pennsylvania with the British Government, 1696–1765* (1912) had led him to a close examination of British archival materials, well understood the historiographical significance of the *Guides.* They meant, said Root, that no longer would American history be written as though it had been "unaffected by and unconnected with the main currents of the world's history"; historians were now "coming to a study of the past with a new vision"; and the new vision was being achieved by a growing knowledge "of the nature, the scope, and the spirit of British imperial policies and of the relations of the colonies to the parent country."[57] The *Guides* revealed clearly enough the effort it would take to solve the historical problems with which they dealt. The new structure of American colonial history, Root felt, could be erected only after "years of diligent labor by pioneer investigators" whose task would be "to blaze the trail and push back the frontier in preparation for the master historical builder."[58] It probably did not enter Root's reckoning of the future, as it must have Andrews', that the trail-blazer might become the house-builder. The appraisal set upon the *Guides* by Osgood must have reminded Andrews of what he himself had earlier said of the work of Maitland:

> It is a chart of an hitherto imperfectly discovered country. . . . The explorers . . . have hitherto touched the shore of the continent or penetrated a little distance inland. Historical students will now have in their possession a chart which indicates in sufficient outline the entire territory which they have to explore, with its chief natural features and artificial divisions. . . . The publication of the *Guides,* therefore, is one among many signs that we have entered upon a new epoch in the study of American history. It is the outgrowth of a demand for a more thorough and exhaustive investigation of the sources. It implies and will be followed by a more comprehensive and scientific treatment of the period as a whole than hitherto has been possible or even imagined. The era of partial views and isolated efforts, whether in the collection of materials or the writing of history, is passing away.[59]

In achieving that "more comprehensive and scientific treatment of the period as a whole," Andrews would be no mere onlooker. To be sure, he thoroughly approved of the work Osgood and Beer were engaged in; and the efforts of many younger historians, such as Dickerson, Root, and Mary P. Clarke (the latter a student of his own), were, to his mind, properly redrawing the early American scene.[60] But if his manuals on the British archives meant that he had written a guide for his age, they also meant that he had, far more important, written one for himself. The central idea of the *Guides,* that "the only scientific approach to American colonial history" was through the British system of administration,[61] demanded a full exposition. The *Guides,* as he told Jameson after a decade of labors on them, were the instrument without which he could not have proceeded to shape out the newer forms of the past: "The simple truth of it is, as you know, that I have spent all this time on this work not . . . out of interest in the Carnegie [Institution] or out of a desire to do something for the profession but also because it represents a task that I needed to do for myself." [62] What he hoped to do for himself he had confided to Jameson even before undertaking work on the *Guides*: "I am on the war-path with a magnum opus, which I mean to pursue till captured." [63] It is not too often that an historian writes one magnum opus in order to write another.

When, after the completion of the *Guides,* Jameson congratulated him for having reared, "just as a by-product of a greater work, a 'monumentum aere perennius,' " [64] Andrews ventured to reflect upon that "greater work." Feeling that perhaps he was about to embark on more than he could hope to accomplish, he knew, at the very least, that "I shall spend at least the next fifteen or twenty years upon this undertaking." [65] He was to spend considerably more time than he had imagined. The delay was not without its significance. It meant that Andrews would come to build a synthesis based on the principles of his system at a time when the very foundations of that system were beginning to deteriorate. But was this not actually the essence of the greatest *summae,* that they could appear only when the intellectual ages they summarized were indeed at an end?

Chapter 4

MAJOR THEMES

The contribution of Andrews was that of a new American colonial history. He devoted the years of his maturity to re-writing the story of early America. If the new viewpoint he was presenting had been spurred by his own ambition, it reflected at every turn the principles of his school. He construed his great undertaking as an attempt, together with his age, to solve the problem of an earlier period. He had equipped himself with the precise and carefully fashioned instruments of historical science. The newer technology would produce a sounder historiographical product. Iconoclasm, to Andrews and his generation, was not the same thing as nihilism: the false views had to be smashed and cleared away, the past had to be reconstructed. For that reconstruction, Andrews was drawing his own plans. He set them forth in addresses before the American Historical Association on "American Colonial History, 1690–1750" (1898) and before the New Jersey Historical Society on "Some Neglected Aspects of Colonial History" (1900). The distinctiveness of his own plans and dimensions for the new house of American colonial history carried its own message. It meant that before very long the master planner might turn his interest to master building.

The house that Andrews built was not, to say the least, entirely uniform. Some forty years in the building, it could not but reveal a changing use of materials and patterns of construction. What Andrews had to say, however, was essentially well-knit, essentially consistent. Some critics, indeed, would later find it a basis for reproval that views which he announced in 1900 were still being reiterated several decades later. Three works, above all, contained the core of his contribution: *The Colonial Period* (1912), *The Colonial Background of the American Revolution* (1924), and the four volumes on *The*

Colonial Period of American History (1934–38). Different aspects of the same central view were treated in the great number of lesser works, including *Colonial Self-Government 1652–1689* (1904), *The Fathers of New England* (1919), *Our Earliest Colonial Settlements* (1933), as well as his very many addresses, articles, and book reviews. Year after year, he restated the major themes of the new American colonial history. More than any of his great contemporaries, he spread the newer views. More than any of them, he made the heterodoxy of the 1900's the orthodoxy of the decades that followed.

1. SOME POSTULATES FOR A NEW HISTORY

To solve the problem of the American colonial past, one had to begin, as Andrews saw it, with several larger observations. Used in some measure by other members of his school, and deriving from the newer orientation of the age, these observations were, however, so distinctively formulated by Andrews and so rigorously applied that they became peculiarly his own contribution. To him, they were virtually truths a priori, truths which one could not but hold to be self-evident.

It was clear, to begin with, that the past had to be freed from the prepossessions of the present. This would alter the whole traditional approach to the colonial period. The years from Jamestown to Yorktown would be freed from the hindsight of the Revolution: the century and a half might then become less a matter of the inevitable emergence of United States and more one of the progress and development of only partially united colonies. The movement of the story would be constantly forward, following a natural course, and "disregarding all preconceptions based on later events." [1] It was sounder to view the events of 1776 as something of a finale to the colonial period, than to view the colonial period as mere prelude to 1776.[2] The simple metathesis meant a basic change of outlook.

It meant, as Andrews aptly summarized his lifelong program, that he was trying to put back the "colonial" into American colonial history.[3] How could that entire century and a half be understood unless it was first understood that the colonies were indeed colonies, and not independent communities?[4] In all his work, Andrews undertook "to show that in the colonial relationship with Great Britain was to be found the key to the problem."[5] This relationship gave the entire period its tone, its rationale, its unity. The historian of early America had perforce to reckon with the interdependence between Great Britain and her colonies, an interdependence which clearly defined the three underlying factors of prenational history: "the mother country, the colonies, and the relations between them."[6]

Putting the "colonial" back into colonial history meant giving up the colonies as a vantage point and shifting that vantage point to the mother country. The colonies were best viewed "not from within, as is commonly done, but from without . . . for this purpose I have approached the subject from the English end, from the land whence the colonists came and of which they were always legally a part."[7] The common denominator of all of American colonial history was, after all, precisely this: that the colonies were part of a great empire, that the center of this empire was at Whitehall.[8] A study of the colonies from the vantage ground of the land of their origin would restore balance and perspective to the historian's picture of early America.[9]

From the axiom that England alone was the proper point for observing the colonial world as it actually was *at that time,* several significant corollaries were to be derived. First, by taking one's stand in the mother country, one necessarily looked out upon a wider scene than the continental colonies. The unifying force in that heterogeneous colonial world was Britain alone, and British policies affected all the colonies, not merely the notable thirteen.[10] The colonists on the Atlantic seaboard, Andrews recalled to his readers, lived and traded in a world larger and less parochial than that subsequently fashioned for them by patriotic historians.[11] It violated any sense of history to remove artificially from the integrated commercial empire, composed of some thirty colonies, those thirteen that were later to break off from British dominion. "That some of those colonies remained British while others became American does not, historically speaking, enter in as a determining factor." [12] Second, if England was the center of the American colonial world, then it was patent that English policies and English history must be understood.[13] Every change in English government, policy, and purpose found its reflection in the colonies.[14] It was the purpose of Andrews to discover not merely the nature of English commercial and colonial policies but, equally significant, to relate those policies to the broad currents of English national life from which they had derived. Third, the story of England and of the English colonial empire had little meaning apart from developments within the Western world during the early modern era. The age was one in which the European powers were pushing beyond their boundaries and establishing a great western frontier overseas across the Atlantic.[15] They were engaged in a world-wide colonizing movement, one designed to fill their treasuries and finance their wars.[16] The colonies which these powers were planting in America could be correctly understood only when related to the goals of the national economies to which they were linked. Whatever a later age might think of it, the governing principle of that age was that a colony ought to serve "to the advantage of the state under whose aegis it had been established." [17] In sum, the "wider and deeper significance" of American colonial history could be grasped only by bringing it back into the mainstream of English and European developments.[18]

A product of the Rankean ideal, and very much in consonance with the principles of the new age in American historiography, the colonial world of Andrews was fashioned out of the conviction that the past had to be understood "in the light of its own age and of the ages that have preceded it." [19] Pursuing that conviction led Andrews to find, in the prenational period, not so much an American past as one that was Anglo-American.[20] The thesis which dominated more than forty years of his own historiography might be the epitaph of the older historiography that he was putting to rest: "The years from 1607 to 1783 were colonial before they were American or national, and our Revolution is a colonial and not an American problem. During the colonial period, the dependence and interdependence of mother country and colonies were ever-present realities to the settlers in America and determined to no small extent the attitude and policy of mother country and colonies alike. To ignore this relationship, or to misjudge it . . . is to leave the problem still unsolved." [21]

2. THE SETTLEMENTS

In solving the problem of American colonial history, the very first step would be to survey and explain the settlement of the English colonies during the seventeenth century. It was consonant with his theme that Andrews should stress the central role of England in the process of settlement. To his way of thinking, America at that time was nothing so much as an English frontier, an open expanse into which English ideas and institutions were being poured. What happened in England during the age of the Stuarts determined, moreover, everything of moment that was happening in America.

If the settlement of America was to be understood as a phase of English expansion, that expansion was in turn to be understood as a phase of the expansion of western Europe. Andrews drew his canvas wide enough to encompass major developments within the great maritime powers along the Atlantic: the emergence of monarchies in conflict, the increased volume of trade, the quest for new routes and new lands.[22] England, like the continent, was astir with change. "Commercial expansion was the order of the day." [23] Having no outlet for rapidly accumulating capital, England emulated other Western monarchies in seeking to build up her economy by planting colonies. The English colonial idea was motivated by more than trade or profit and thus differed from the idea governing the colonizing activities of her rivals.[24] The further motives included the desire for land, the lure of excitement, and, of no little importance, the search for a religious refuge. Discontent with one's lot in England was a strong stimulant to emigration.

Although England's expansion overseas was an "outworking"

of domestic influences, these influences did not involve a majority of the English people. The religious and commercial purposes that gave rise to the planting of Virginia and New England affected, relatively speaking, but few in the mother country. It was only when the possession of land became the principal motive for emigration and began to dominate the setting up of colonies that more fundamental currents in English life were tapped.[25] Herein lay the significance of Maryland. An exception during the first period of colonization, it was to become the rule during the second.

An English vantage ground afforded Andrews a basis for relating to each other the different forces that entered the colonizing movement of the early seventeenth century. Through it all he saw a unity that could be traced "to the cooperative activity of the mercantile and capitalist classes." [26] Through it all he saw the hand of the joint-stock companies, which "were behind every important material advance that accompanied the expansion of the island kingdom across the oceans into the eastern and western world." [27] The principal agencies of colonization during this first phase of expansion, these companies had been financed with funds accumulated during the Elizabethan age by the capitalist leaders of southern and southwestern England.[28] It was these capitalist leaders, intent, well organized, seeking profit wherever they could, who pushed the English domain westward to the North American mainland, to Bermuda, and to the West Indies.[29]

Standing in England and looking for central forces in the settlement of America was at best, for Andrews, a formula for understanding history, a formula that ought not be too inflexibly applied. It had to be emphasized, for one thing, that the process of settlement was far from being homogeneous and continuous. Two distinct periods of English expansion comprised the seventeenth century: the first beginning with Jamestown and ending with the settlement of St. Mary's in 1634, the second beginning with the conquest of Jamaica and ending with the founding of Pennsylvania in 1682. It also had to be emphasized that each settlement had its own distinctive characteristics, due largely to the fact that English colonization was a matter of private enterprise, "promoted by individuals or groups of individuals for purposes of their own." [30] Reflecting a variety of commercial, religious, and political developments in the English scene, the settlements "reproduced . . . the complex activities of a confused and changing era." [31] For that reason, concluded Andrews, "any attempt at a synthetic or synoptic treatment of them in this early period of our history is clearly impossible." [32]

Each colony had its own problems, its own character, its own significance. Virginia distinguished itself as "England's first permanent colony, the seat of the first experiment in Anglo-Saxon colonization in the New World." [33] Fitting in admirably with England's economic expansion and needs, and adhering very closely to the basic patterns of English law and government, it had all the aspects of a "normal" colony.[34] More than that, within its political experience was developed the principle of self-government, a principle which became the heritage of the other colonial settlements.[35] Massachusetts, of little economic value to England, was more a commonwealth than a colony, its tone set by "a single purpose—the erection of a City of God in the wilderness, in which God alone was to be served." [36] Governed by this purpose, its basic problem in the seventeenth century was how to expand the trading company's charter by which the Massachusetts Bay Company had been created into a constitution suitable to the needs of a growing commonwealth.[37] Rhode Island, which grew out of the discontent of many with the Puritan rule of thorough at Massachusetts Bay, achieved historical significance as "the home of soul liberty." Composed as it was of separate, independent, and conflicting communities, the little colony was beset with the difficulty of fashioning one commonwealth out of several.[38] If Massachusetts had law but not liberty, Rhode Island had liberty but not law.[39] Connecticut represented an overflow from the Bay colony, a settlement stimulated more by the promised land of the Connecticut River valley than by anything else.[40] Its tone was that of an isolated agricultural community, its conviction that of a Puritan land of steady habits, its aim that of maintaining a strict discipline in religious and political ideas.[41]

Maryland was unique in having been a place of refuge for English Roman Catholics. It was unique too in the wide prerogative of its proprietor and the great revenues that his domain afforded him, circumstances which stamped Maryland as "the most singular and striking proprietary province in the English portion of the New World." [42] Barbados, a West Indian island planted by merchants under a proprietary letters patent, developed along the lines of a "normal" colony of the Virginia variety. Known eventually as "Little England," the sugar island revealed the extent of England's dominion overseas and the role of the West Indies in shaping English commercial policies.[43] Barbados served Andrews' purposes admirably. It drew attention to the larger colonial world of which the thirteen mainland colonies were but a part; and, in its own distinctive blending of institutions—proprietary, mercantile, and political—it again emphasized the heterogeneity of the English colonial experience.

The second period of English colonization in America began with the capture of Jamaica in 1655. Before this, said Andrews, the spirit of the age had been religious and political, intolerant, taking its cue from the past; the principal agent of colonization had been the chartered company.[44] The new age of expansion was more worldly and opportunist than the first, more concerned with material prosperity, more tolerant of differences in religious conviction: it looked to the future and broke with the past.[45] The significance of Jamaica was great. It enlarged English territory and expanded English commerce; it underlined the value of America and the West Indies; it threw up the need for a more reliable method of colonial administration and marked the beginnings of a change in English colonial policy.[46] Though permitting the colonizing agents to pursue their activities with little governmental interference, England was "rough shaping" a policy of control in this transitional era.[47] The agencies of colonization during this age were proprietary in character, and the proprietors were, by and large, men linked to the court of Charles II, hopeful of restoring in the new world the money they had lost or the ideals they could no longer pursue in the old.[48] Nowhere did Andrews better demonstrate his thesis of seeking the mainsprings of American colonization within the structure of English domestic conditions than in that famous introductory chapter to the proprieties.[49] He found his clues to the proprietary settlements in the English land system and in the effect of a changing economy upon the security and status of the English squirearchy.

In the proprietary settlements Andrews perceived both a similarity and diversity of characteristics. The diversity stemmed from geographical differences, the terms and clarity of the charters, the personality and intentions of the proprietor or group of proprietors, the nature of the settlers, economic conditions within the colony, and commercial and political relations with England. Thus, the history of the Carolinas was in no small measure determined by their proximity to French and Spanish areas, while the history of the Jerseys was largely determined by the Duke of York's casual, almost haphazard grant to Berkeley and Carteret.[50] New York was fashioned by the strong will and the financial aspirations of its proprietor,[51] just as the "Holy Experiment" in the province of Pennsylvania was not a little shaped by the hopes of William Penn and his ability, or lack of it, to reconcile ideal with reality. For all their diversity, however, the proprieties presented many similarities. These stemmed, to some degree, from the fact that they arose, nearly all, in the short space from 1662 to 1664, that they reflected the return to power of a Stuart king and his friends, that they contained certain legal principles concerning the jurisdiction of the king over ungranted land in the new world, and that they, in effect, summarized the "sudden transition from republicanism to monarchy" which had been brought about by the Restoration.[52] There was yet a larger historical trend which unified the proprieties. They were unsuitable to the American environment, not only because of the political strivings of the settlers against proprietary rule but also because of growing problems of trade and defense. In every one of the proprieties attacks were launched against the prerogatives of the owners.[53] In virtually every one, moreover, it was becoming apparent that the private policies of the proprietor were running counter to the public interests of the mother country in matters of trade, defense, and international relations.[54] England was beginning to find that merely "rough shaping" a policy was not enough. With the introduction of a more closely defined colonial system, from 1688 and on, the end of proprietary rule was in sight.

To the subject of the settlements, a subject which he had earlier treated in less imposing though not less decided a manner, Andrews devoted three extensive volumes of his major work. For all the welter of details, for all the paraphernalia of scrupulous scholarship, he had clearly sounded his major themes. He had restored the colonies to England. He had written their story as a phase of English expansion. He had seen America as a frontier region. Taking his stand in England, he had considered that his "first duty" was "to discover the place that each group of settlers occupied in this great colonizing adventure and to determine the exact character of the ideas and purposes of the founders in relation to the similar ideas and purposes that were influencing men at the same time in England." [55] He had underlined the variety of pattern and tone in each colonial settlement. He had brought his account, which he did not pretend to be either geographically or chronologically complete,[56] to the point where a policy of commercial and colonial management was being more clearly and decisively formulated at Westminster, Whitehall, and the Plantation Office.

One point he had made eminently clear, and it was a point which bound together that whole transit of civilization across the Atlantic which he had so painstakingly described: "The world of the colonies in the seventeenth century was an English world." [57] If settlement overseas necessarily meant "a continuous process of adaptation of English ways and institutions to an unfamiliar environment," [58] it had to be understood that these ways and institutions underwent little change during the first century.[59] In the first three volumes of his great tetralogy, as well as elsewhere, Andrews documented this theme with numerous examples. The England of Raleigh was "a manorial and monarchical England and his America would have been a manorial and monarchical America likewise." [60] In the establishment of the proprieties in America could be found "a reproduction . . . of the time-honored and familiar customs and incidents of the seignorial and manorial life in England." [61] The colony of Virginia "followed English custom very closely, in its land law and law of descent, in its ecclesiastical organization, in the procedure and practice of its assembly, and even in the form of its legislative chamber." [62] The popular assembly's desire for control in Pennsylvania "represented the liberalizing trend that characterized the vigorous political trend of Charles II's England. The settlers in Pennsylvania . . . considered themselves part of the English scene, as it were." [63] In fine, the colonial world of the seventeenth century could not be understood, as Andrews saw it, without reference to the world of the mother country. In their basic patterns, the American ways were but reproductions of the English originals. It was not until the eighteenth century that one could discern "the gradual transformation of that which was English into something we can begin to call American." [64] It was not until then, too, that the colonial policy of the mother country, several decades in the shaping, emerged in full and clear definition.

3. ENGLAND'S COMMERCIAL AND COLONIAL POLICIES

To understand American colonial history, felt Andrews, one had also to understand England's commercial and colonial policies. The colonies were, after all, parts of a greater dominion and were "subordinate both as a matter of law and as a matter of policy to the higher sovereign power across the sea at Whitehall and Westminster." [65] They could not be seen properly, argued Andrews to Turner, unless they were seen "from the side of the mother country," and unless one kept "the idea of a colonial connection constantly in the foreground." [66] Andrews achieved the final and most comprehensive statement of this viewpoint in the fourth volume, the very last, of *The Colonial Period of American History.* Here he restored the colonies to England and England to the larger Western world of those centuries. Here he set up indissoluble ties between American colonial history and the British system of colonial management.[67] Here he asserted and undertook to prove his basic contention that "the problems of our early history were British colonial problems first and American problems afterward." [68]

Jamaica had marked a turning point in English colonial policy. Decentralization was abandoned in favor of a program of regulation and control; indeed, the regulation and control were inevitable.[69] A promised land appeared to be opening up for English capitalists, Puritan and otherwise, who had been wandering about in an economic desert for several years. Seeing the great possibilities for trade, shipping, and the merchant marine afforded by an expanding colonial area, they urged the government to adopt a definite commercial and colonial program.[70] The acts of trade and navigation constituted a response not only to the mercantile demand, however, but also to the government's need for revenue and financial solvency.[71] Underlying every specific purpose and detail of the new system of control, moreover, was the general "necessity of winning commercial and colonial leadership among the maritime powers of Europe." [72] The emerging policy of central regulation thus aimed at using the far-flung colonial world which was taking shape to meet the problem of England's growing competition with her European rivals.

It was this competition which fashioned the policies adopted by England after the Glorious Revolution. If the colonial system of the late seventeenth century had been defined in no small measure by the difficulties of Anglo-Dutch relations, that of the early eighteenth century was largely the product of English rivalry with the French. If the earlier system had "sought to wrest from the Dutch their control of sea-borne trade," [73] the later system was concerned with establishing a "self-sufficing empire" in order to meet the challenge of the Bourbon monarchy. Rapid French expansion, both colonial and commercial, posed a serious threat to England, causing her to turn more and more to the resources of her plantations.[74] English policy became colonial as well as commercial; [75] an imperial concept began to emerge.[76] The colonies were called upon to furnish men and supplies in times of war on colonial soil; [77] moreover, they were expected to provide the mother state with whatever raw materials would aid it in the world contest for commercial and colonial supremacy.[78] When the rapid growth of colonial population impressed itself upon the British official mind, halfway through the eighteenth century, attention began to center on using the colonies as markets both for British manufactures and for foreign goods shipped through British ports.[79] Changes though there were in a situation which was in no wise static, "the interests of the colonists were inescapably tied up with the international aspects of a self-contained commercial world of which they were an integral and necessary part." [80]

The view which Andrews took of England's colonial policies was characterized by a few basic ideas. To begin with: these colonial policies, which later came to be known as mercantilism, were practical expedients, constituting "a *modus operandi* for the purpose of meeting the needs of a growing and expanding state." [81] Mercantilism was not a theory but a condition, not an exact system but one changing with the times and more characterized by diversity of opinion than by orthodoxy.[82] Second: working on the universal premise that outlying plantations were to be fitted to the needs of the mother country, England formulated policies that primarily served the purposes of the realm. Mercantile rather than colonial, these policies involved the development of no special administrative machinery; what satisfied for the trade problems of the realm was also used for the control of the colonies.[83] Officials appointed for colonial purposes exclusively were exceptional; instead, "by enlargement and adjustment the prevailing system was adapted to meet the new demands." [84] Third: England's mercantilistic practices were motivated by self-interest, not by a "desire to tyrannize or even to meddle." [85] Whatever a later age might think, these practices represented the best thought of the eighteenth century, were entirely defensible from the English viewpoint, and had indeed gained England her supremacy on the seas and in the colonial worlds.[86] Fourth: Andrews was not entirely convinced that a policy of self-interest for the metropolis necessarily meant a policy of deprivation for its plantations. The colonies came to accept as "unquestioned fact that . . . the acts of trade affected but little either their commercial activities or their financial prosperity." [87] The injurious effects of the famous acts concerning manufacturing in the colonies had, to Andrews' way of thinking, been much exaggerated. He doubted whether any of them had "materially hampered the progress of colonial industry." [88] Viewing the old colonial system as a whole, he concluded that it "did not at any time before 1764 seriously interfere with the growth or prosperity of the colonies." [89]

Not that Andrews could not understand why conflict might develop between the mother country and her colonies or failed to perceive weakness in the old colonial system. The essence of the weakness was the inability of the British administration to adapt itself to the changing conditions of colonial life.[90] In matters touching the colonies, the administration was slow and ineffective, its attitude indifferent and, in fact, irresponsible.[91] There was little cooperation among the various executive departments; [92] efficient teamwork was lacking.[93] The desire of the growing imperial state to centralize control was bound to clash with the desire of the growing colonial settlements to be free from that control. Difficulties were further enhanced by the refusal of Parliament to lend statutory support to the English administration in dealing with the colonies, fearing that it might thereby strengthen the arm of the executive to the detriment of the legislative.[94] The "salutary neglect" which seemed to characterize Britain's management of the colonies when the popular assemblies in America were making their greatest strides toward self-government could thus be attributed in large measure to an impasse between Parliament and the agencies of the Crown.[95] By 1763, the breach between British and American purposes had become so great that parliamentary intervention into the system of colonial management became imperative. By 1763, however, it was far too late to do anything much about it.

4. THE REVOLUTION

The history of the American Revolution had particular significance for Andrews and the school in which he belonged. It was a question, for them, of redefining national ideals, of feeling that the Civil War had insured the national union which the War of Independence had first achieved, of removing from the Anglo-American scene of 1776 an animus which was no longer valid in the Anglo-American scene of 1876, of revaluating the age when America was a colony for an age of nascent American colonialism, of looking at the secession from an irate Great Britain in the light of changing relations with a friendlier Little England, of substituting for the romantic patriotism of the early nineteenth-century historian the sober industry of his late nineteenth-century follower, of bringing the luminous spirit of contemporary science to shine into the darker corner of an earlier world, of converting ancestral demigods into partisan businessmen, of rescuing American adults from George Bancroft and American children from Parson Weems. For Andrews, the problem of the Revolution was above all a problem of explaining why the colonial relationship came to an end, why the Anglo-American community was torn asunder. Standing as he was at Whitehall and Westminster, he was interested in understanding why and how the British system of management had failed to meet the challenge of altered conditions within the colonial situation. Finding that looking backward from latter-day prepossessions was better for patriotic utopians and myth-makers than for historians, Andrews undertook rather to move forward, from decade to decade, noting everything, predicting nothing. The Revolution took on its fullest meaning, for him, not as the beginning of independence but rather as the end of interdependence. "Our Revolution," he did not cease to argue, "is a colonial and not an American problem." [96]

Andrews sought the causes of the Revolution in the deeper recesses of the colonial period. Revolutions were always long in the making,[97] and the separation from Great Britain was "not achieved at a single stroke by war or otherwise." [98] It was, rather, a century-long process, a silent and peaceful revolution, without dates and without boundaries.[99] In its very essence, the Revolution was the slow emergence of ideas and institutions that were more distinctively American. To Andrews, the outstanding feature of the eighteenth century was the process whereby "that which was English was gradually transforming itself into that which was American." [100] And seeking those purely American ideas that were taking shape, he discovered them in the new concepts of the franchise, of landed property, of representation, of public service, and of society itself. What stood out particularly was the new idea that a colony was "a self-governing dominion, the members of which were competent to develop along their own lines, while working together with the mother country as parts of a common state." [101] It was an idea which took tangible form in the growth to maturity of the colonial assemblies.[102] The rise of the assemblies summarized the rapidly growing divergence between the institutional patterns and ideals of the mother country and those of the colonies.

That divergence could not but be reflected in sharpening clashes of interest. The British official class, concerned with Britain's maritime and commercial fate, was intent upon more centralized control.[103] The selfishness of British policy and the ineptitude of British statesmanship aroused the colonies, which were themselves "growing in self-consciousness, population, and the complexity of their social and economic needs." [104] If the colonies did not seriously question royal or parliamentary authority before 1763, they could not, however, accept the British view of their assemblies, a view which reduced those bodies to the subordinate position of provincial councils.[105] Andrews wondered at "the official blindness of the British authorities" to this most conspicuous aspect of eighteenth-century colonial life, that is, to "the rise of the colonial assembly with its growth to self-conscious activity and *de facto* independence of royal control." [106] The differences on this issue between metropolis and colony were irreconcilable.

These differences had to be understood, Andrews felt, in the widest possible terms, in terms that encompassed not merely English bureaucrats and American assemblies but two nations and two states of mind as well. An aristocratic and feudal tradition governed the mother country. Her rulers were landlords and lords of money, men who venerated their constitution and their law and deprecated the need for reform at home or freedom for their plantations.[107] "In contrast to this highly conventionalized social class, with its stereotyped, unprogressive system of thought and government, stood the American colonies, in large part an agricultural frontier, with an environment that was favorable to the development of man as an individual rather than as a member of society." [108] The resistance of the frontier to the "old, well settled, highly organized land" across the ocean evidenced itself increasingly throughout the eighteenth century. The spirit of colonial independence grew by questioning and rejecting British authority in a variety of matters: in refusing to pay quit-rents, in limiting the power of the royal governor and his control of finances, in objecting to the disallowance of colonial laws, in refusing to permit the unlimited extension of English common and statute law into the colonies, and in evading acts of parliament affecting colonial economic life.[109]

Self-control became the breath of their life. . . . Hundreds of such efforts in the direction of independence, expended during a period of a century and a half, were creating, line upon line, a situation in which independence of outside control was becoming the most conspicuous feature of their history. In this way was colonial independence won, before a single American leader had dared to deny his allegiance, to raise his voice in behalf of separation, or to take up arms in a military struggle for the severing of the legal ties which bound him to the mother country.[110]

Inevitably and gradually the conflict had grown. It was in every wise irrepressible.

Yet if Andrews plumbed the depth of a century and more in order to set the Revolution in deeper perspective, he nowhere failed to stress the importance, in precipitating the conflict, of what transpired in 1763. Britain's victory over France brought with it problems of territorial administration which taxed both the ingenuity of the British and the purse of the Americans. The colonial relationship, hitherto concerned largely with matters of trade, now took on a form that was distinctly territorial and political.[111] An empire not merely of commerce but also of land began to emerge, aggravating a situation already fraught with danger. Applying old thought to new problems, a mediocre, short-sighted, and unimaginative British statesmanship undertook to strengthen its control over the colonies and to tax them in order to meet the expense of empire.[112] If Andrews was convinced that it was imperialism and not mercantilism which was the first cause of the open split between Britain and America, he was equally convinced that it was the issue of finance, posed by the whole matter of territorial and administrative control, which "proved in the end to be the rock upon which the British system foundered." [113] At the very time that Britain's acquisition of Canada had freed them from a fear of the French and from dependence on the military aid of the mother country, "the colonists were being called upon almost without warning to face an exasperating tightening of the bonds." [114]

With diligence and care, Andrews explored the decade before Lexington and Concord, intent upon understanding how the larger issues were actually expressed from year to year in specific events and by specific personalities on both sides of the Atlantic. At times he permitted himself to ruminate that "a little more yielding, a little more of the spirit of friendliness and compromise, and a little less of British ignorance, stubbornness, and prejudice, would have calmed the troubled waters and stilled the storm that was brewing." [115] On the whole, however, he tended to the conviction that the waters had long been troubled and could not be calmed, that the storm had long been brewing and could not be stilled. Ultimately, the conflict between the imperial view of the colonies and the colonial view of the empire would shatter the Anglo-American relationship. Ultimately, the moderates on both sides would lose out and leadership would pass to intractable ministers on the one hand and to intractable radicals, "many of whom did their thinking in their muscles," on the other.

As the radicals in America persisted in their demands, as they advanced from arguments about trade to arguments about the civil rights of British subjects, and from these to arguments about inherent and self-evident rights according to nature, Englishmen in authority hardened their hearts, because in their minds recognition of the radical claim meant not only the wrecking of what they deemed their greatest asset in America, their profits from colonial trade, but more serious still the abrogation of their own constitutional system.[116]

The tea issue raised by Lord North and his cabinet Andrews deemed "an irretrievable blunder." Where ministerial forbearance was necessary, ministerial indiscretion prevailed. The crisis which had been impending for a decade could no longer be averted. For the first time, the moderates in America were thrust into an alliance with the radicals, and the radicals proceeded to throw down the gauntlet to Great Britain, in December, 1773, at Boston harbor. "On both sides of the water, the extremists were in command, grim and unyielding." [117] The final break came because the mother country could not fathom the changes that had occurred within her colonies, because her colonial policy was inflexible, because she saw fit to apply coercion rather than understanding.[118]

Casting the Revolution into relief, distilling the generality out of the welter of details, Andrews found it to have been "a mighty cosmic event," a world movement of the greatest importance.[119] Fundamentally, it was not to be explained in terms of economics or of tyrannical monarchs. Not bread alone, nor acts of trade, nor even the obdurate Hanoverian who had been told to "be a king," had produced the separation.

Rather, it was an uprising against a state of mind, a state of mind which had refused a new role to the full-grown colonies, one moreover which had even failed to recognize that the colonies were indeed full-grown.[120] Ultimately, the issue centered in the colonial demand for political freedom; [121] ultimately, it simmered down to "that most fundamental of all issues, the status of the colonies and their political and legal relations with the mother country." [122] For a century, both partners of the Anglo-American relationship had been moving toward opposite poles, and in mutually contradictory directions: the mother country toward empire, the colonies toward greater self-government.[123] The separation from Great Britain summarized this polarization; it summarized indeed the eternal conflict between the conservative and the radical influences in history.[124] In his presidential address to the American Historical Association, in December, 1925, Andrews reduced the Revolution to basic terms:

> Primarily, the American Revolution was a political and constitutional movement and only secondarily one that was either financial, commercial, or social. At bottom the fundamental issue was the political independence of the colonies, and in the last analysis the conflict lay between the British Parliament and the colonial assemblies.[125]

The Revolution was ultimately concerned neither with mercantilistic restriction nor imperial authority, but rather with "the very constitution of the British empire." [126] The essence of the decline and fall of the first British empire was that a *re*constitution could not be achieved. That colonial relationship which Andrews underscored as the central theme of American history from Jamestown to the Peace of Paris had now run its inevitable course, and had come clattering down in ruin.

5. THE CONTRIBUTION OF ANDREWS

The contribution of Andrews to American historiography was, in large measure, the contribution of a new outlook toward the colonial period. Dedicated to the proposition that all English colonies overseas had to be considered equally, and equally considered from the English vantage ground, this outlook bound together four decades of his labor and the preponderance of his efforts. Into the nebulous system of thirteen colonial bodies he had introduced the order, the direction, and the central pull exerted by the metropolis. He had argued the need for remembering that there were two sides to the colonial equation rather than one. It had been unthinkable to him that one might talk of progeny without knowing the progenitor, that one might analyze the colonial environment without first analyzing the English heritage. This had been his lifelong thesis, one which, as Henry Steele Commager suggested,[127] ranked in significance with Turner's view of the frontier or Beard's economic interpretation of the constitution. And if the thesis had also been espoused by others, it was one which Andrews had, by monumental proof and constant application, made virtually his own.

As the proof and application emerged in each successive volume, the reviewers sounded their approval.[128] Andrews was hailed for having brought into clearer focus than ever before those English conditions and movements which formed the basis of early American history. His *Colonial Self-Government* (1904), for example, the first of his contributions (apart from his doctoral dissertation) on American colonial history, contained the earliest attempt to describe English policy and administration as it affected the plantations and to integrate these elements into an account of colonial development. His tracing of the role of the trading companies and of the transition in English agriculture was especially lauded. No one before him had made so clear, step by step, detail by detail, the transit of English civilization across the ocean during the seventeenth century. If his chapter on the English land system was praised for having furnished a clue to the nature of the colonial proprieties, his chapters on the Board of Trade, the customs service, and the vice-admiralty courts were equally praised for furnishing a superb portrait of the British system of management at work, for being administrative history at its very best.

He moved from area to area, all parts of the larger domain he had mapped out for himself, bringing wide knowledge to a variety of subjects: to the question of Anglo-French commercial rivalry during the first half of the eighteenth century, to the role of individual colonial leaders, to the problem of colonial law. Especially outstanding was the work he did, throughout his lifetime, on the history of each of the colonies, particularly on that of Connecticut, to which he was bound by birth and by family ties reaching back to those very centuries which were his concern. With Connecticut, as with all of the colonies, his central problem was so to place the individual tiles as to bring out the mosaic. With a sweeping glance over the mass of colonial histories whose particularism he wished to correct, Andrews found that in order to become the historian of all the colonies he had to become the historian of each of them. No small part of his effort was taken up with breaking down this historiographic provincialism, setting each colony within its proper place in the larger context, evaluating its role relative to the other colonies, relating its position to that of the mother country. The fabulous mastery of detail which this effort required he deemed eminently worthwhile. For was not his thesis essentially that the colonial whole was far greater than the sum of its parts?

Whatever limitations there were to the contribution of Andrews were limitations inherent in his premises or in his ability to satisfy those premises. He had argued, for example, that to know the colonies one had perforce to know England. Evarts Greene questioned the accuracy of Andrews' knowledge of England. He disputed the simple view that Andrews took of the effects of the Glorious Revolution on English constitutional development; he disputed, too, a favorite thesis of Andrews'—that royal prerogative, during the eighteenth century, was declining at home while remaining fully in force in the colonies.[129] Lawrence Harper doubted whether Andrews was correct in his assertion that the Navigation Acts had not worked to the disadvantage of the colonies. Having read the galleys of the last volume of the magnum opus, Harper, who had devoted more than a decade to the study of this subject, wrote Andrews conclusively on behalf of the opposite view.

Conceding that the English, in adopting the acts, were not unfair, judged by contemporary standards, and that they were not unfair when one considers the protection and other advantages the colonies received, I think that the laws did interfere with the development and prosperity of the colonies . . . it seems only reasonable to conclude that the colonists would have been more prosperous if they had been free to sell in the highest market and to purchase in the cheapest. Also, I believe that the effects of the regulation of colonial industry have been underestimated. . . . Last but not least, it seems to me that the acts of trade had a very detrimental effect upon the colonial monetary supply.[130]

Part of the criticism against Andrews was that he had drawn his picture too sharp and had made his theses too sweeping. This could be seen, certainly, in his description of the English landed classes during the seventeenth and eighteenth centuries, wherein he hoped to afford a basis for understanding the proprietary mind that was at work in America. The questionable element was this, that he tended to reduce the landed classes to the mentality and outlook of a Squire Western, and that the colonial proprietors were implicitly cast in a similar mental mold. What was equally questionable was the monolithic view that Andrews took of English society and politics during the eighteenth century. He saw an England of "placid waters," ruled by "a highly conventionalized and social class, with its stereotyped, unprogressive system of thought and government." [131] Andrews formed his outlook before the great researches of Lewis Namier broke up the uniformity, conventionality, and dullness that had hitherto been eighteenth-century England. For all that, Andrews might have exercised caution and avoided anything that suggested a rigidity either of social structure or of politics. That it had been a necessary thesis to him can be readily understood. Seeing the American Revolution as a conflict between two national patterns, he set against the pressure of a mobile frontier society that of an immobile society of landed gentry. Perhaps he had seen too plain; perhaps he was reducing to integers an historic situation that were best left with fractions, unintegrated.

The most telling criticism of his work was leveled, as one might have expected, against his major premises. Taking the vantage ground of England, seeing the colonies from without rather than within, finding an English world overseas during the seventeenth century rather than an American one, perceiving no democratic elements within that world, putting the "colonial" back into American colonial history: each of these solved a problem for Andrews but raised one for his reviewers. Could one, for instance, subscribe to the view that "the seventeenth century shows us an English world in America, with but little in it that can strictly be called American"? Said Marcus Jernegan:

> I am afraid I cannot agree with that statement. How about land, labor, education (New England school system), the system or representation (territorial—*not class*), plantations, the frontier influence, Indian influences on the colonists, agriculture, headright system, town meeting. It seems to me that in many aspects of these topics there is much that can be called "American" as contrasted with the "English world in America." I think this could be carried further too, in the realm of ideas, particularly on the frontiers of the colonies—as they were in 1700 at least.[132]

Had there, as Andrews asserted, been no democratic tendencies in the American colonial world? In a distinct sense, the issue was related to the previous one, and Jernegan was no less doubtful of Andrews' contentions. Of course, much of the question hinged on a definition of democracy, and Jernegan agreed that there was a danger of reading latter-day concepts back into the earlier period. But it was just as dangerous, he argued, to set up a twentieth-century concept of democracy, calculated almost entirely in terms of universal manhood suffrage, and to deny any trace of democracy to the past because everybody did not vote.[133] If universal manhood suffrage was lacking, other "democratic elements" could certainly be found in abundance: the extension of the suffrage in various colonies, the ease of becoming a freeholder, the trend toward greater religious toleration, the educational legislation of the New England colonies, and the existence of the frontier as a democratizing force.[134]

As a matter of fact, the observation point taken up by Andrews led him to a view that was exclusive rather than comprehensive, a view that could, moreover, easily become distorted. Looking out from England, and not so much from England as from London, he was inclined to see America as little more than a receptacle for English ideas and institutions. He made little or no accommodation for the infusion of other national elements into the process of American settlement and development. Far more significant, concerned as he was with the agencies of settlement and with the central control emanating from London, he tended to see American development largely as the institution of forms of political authority. His vantage point and his controlling theses defined the lacunae of his work. And the lacunae, as Jernegan correctly indicated, consisted of those ways of living, social, economic, religious, and political, which were palpably American, which took their outstanding characteristics from the very fact of a new environment.

Much too inflexibly had Andrews pursued his thesis of the transit of English civilization overseas. He tended to see merely the top layers of authority under whose guidance and surveillance the transit had been effected; he tended to ignore those more numerous substrata, the emigrants, the disaffected, the generations born on American soil, whose very migration, disaffection, and American birth meant that one crucial feature of American development would be its differentiation from things English. Taking the view he did, he would find it difficult to account for the emergence of things American during the course of the eighteenth century. Baffled by the whole problem of social history, and having cut himself off from the possibility of an increasingly American world during the seventeenth century, Andrews fairly equated the distinctively American character of colonial life with the rise, during the early Hanoverian period, of new political institutions in general and of the colonial assembly in particular. He would not have been driven, as Jernegan jested, to saying that essentially American history began on New Year's day, 1701; but that he had been victimized by his own formula there could be no doubt. Probably the best commentary on this was the fact that, though he had begun his career in American colonial history with the avowed purpose of reconstituting the "neglected period" of the early eighteenth century, he never anywhere arrived at an adequate exposition of its inner meaning and structure. What he wrote on that period was at best a statement of intentions rather than a fulfillment of them. By far the larger part of his contribution was taken up with the seventeenth century. Within the great system of his works on the colonial period, the "neglected period" was left, in all too many respects, neglected.

Perhaps the crux of the criticism was that Andrews had freed himself from the limitations of an essentially American orientation only to bind himself by the limitations of one that was essentially English. Carl Bridenbaugh, one of the outstanding historians of the American colonial period in recent years, reminded the readers of Andrews that "there is another side of the picture to be studied—that of the colonial outlook on its own problems and towards England."[135] He questioned whether a view of the colonies taken principally from London was entirely correct.

Mr. Andrews' almost exclusive emphasis on the British point of view implies a misleading neglect of the colonial aspects of the problem. While British policy shifted to meet the needs and conditions of the eighteenth century, the colonies themselves underwent a marked transformation. The clash of British with colonial interests can be understood only in the light of the remarkable growth of the latter. Mr. Andrews touches only briefly on the growth, and his own undoubted awareness of it is not always made clear to the reader. His insistence upon colonial particularism, which appears to me to have been largely political, seems to blind him to the very considerable development of cooperation and even unity in social and economic spheres. His statement that "contact by land was infrequent" seems to overlook the great inter-colonial migrations, the circulation of ideas and information via the colonial post and press, and the increasing amount of land travel. . . . Nor am I able to agree that the colonies were "as far apart mentally as they were geographically." Extensive study of colonial culture seems to reveal more uniformity than diversity, its differences those of detail rather than of fundamentals. . . . More consideration of the centripetal forces in colonial society would, I believe, lead to a reassessment of the relative importance of the centrifugal influences of politics.[136]

The dialectics of historiographical movement are such perhaps that the corrective to the extremes of an older view itself involves extremes. For that colonial parochialism against which he was inveighing Andrews had substituted something of an English parochialism of his own. The effect was inevitable. In putting the "colonial" back into American colonial history, he had removed no little of the "American."

But that his contribution was, apart from that of Osgood, the greatest one made by any member of the modern school cannot seriously be questioned. Like Osgood, he translated a formula into a monumental work; like Osgood, again, he used a formula which could throw a total light on merely a partial field. Despite the tenuousness of some of his theses, the sheer mass of knowledge he brought into his writing could not but constitute a major achievement. Scientific historian par excellence, he had been a veritable pioneer in the factual reclamation of large segments of the colonial area. No one had ever given so clear, detailed, and integrated a presentation of what the English system of control meant for the Anglo-American community of the seventeenth and eighteenth centuries. His chef d'oeuvre had the limitations of its formula, but that it was indeed a chef d'oeuvre there could not be the slightest doubt.

PART III

THE LATER YEARS 1903-1943

Chapter 5

SUMMA HISTORICA
1903–1943

The contribution of Andrews was no random thing. His portrait of colonial America was the product not only of a system of themes and contents but of a system of historiographical principles as well. Each aspect of his contribution was of course inseparable from the other. If Andrews is remembered for what he said about American colonial history, it should not be forgotten that what he said was fashioned by how he thought. It should not be forgotten, too, that his thinking comprised a historiographical *summa* and that the *summa* was largely a product of the age in which Andrews had grown to maturity.

It is perhaps somewhat artificial to divide, for purposes of analysis, a man's professional work into two segments that are conveniently labeled "earlier" and "later." Yet if the division is made, in the instance of Andrews, at 1903 or 1904, it has more than a modicum of validity. For it was then that he entered completely upon an active career in American colonial history. In 1903 he had gone to London to begin his great work on the *Guides.* He was, at that time, formulating his first major contribution to the field: the volume on *Colonial Self-Government, 1652–1689,* part of the American Nation Series, appeared in 1904. In 1907 he was called from Bryn Mawr to assume the chair of his late master, Herbert Baxter Adams, at the Johns Hopkins University; and in 1910, he was called to Yale University, to devote himself to leading graduate research in American colonial history. His primacy in the field, apart from that of Osgood, was now generally recognized. From 1903 on, in effect, Andrews abandoned the larger frame of European history that had hitherto been his concern and turned his efforts to the early history of his own country.

For other reasons too, a survey of his system of historiography during the later years of his life has its validity. He had attained the fullness of his powers; he had perfected his craftsmanship. His principles had settled into a comprehensive pattern. His *summa* encompassed a resolution of the basic problems facing the historiographer: the nature, scope, and uses of history, the role of the historian, the tendency of history. For the last four decades of his life Andrews was to apply his principles in a finite area of history. For four decades he was to practice his own ideal of scientific history in the realm of the American colonial past.

If the matter of his history was changing at the turn of the century, could the same be said of his art? Actually, the system of Andrews was nowhere radically altered. It is true enough that before 1903 his predominant concern had been with the principle, just as thereafter it would be with the fact supporting the principle. It is also true that there were shifts in stress and tone from one decade to the next. Certainly, after 1903, in conjunction with changing currents in American diplomacy, Andrews was to relate his views on the past to the problems of the present in a more tangible, explicit, and purposeful way than had hitherto been his wont. Yet, in the larger sense, his system of historiography was not substantially different. The new hand may have seemed to imply a difference, but the voice, after all, was still the voice of Andrews.

1. THE NATURE AND USES OF HISTORY

Born of an age that saw clear and plain, untrammeled by the suspicion that history was more social thinking than objective reality, Andrews defined the historian's goal as the attainment of truth. He never wavered from the belief that the truth was there, unalterable, waiting to be found.[1] A bald statement of the Rankean creed, it was a belief that summarized both the history and the historians of late nineteenth-century America, a generation which knew, as none has quite known since, exactly where it was going. The governing precept, so "obvious" to Andrews, was that "history must be true and that the truth of history should be the only end sought."[2] But since our knowledge of the past was always in the making, no rendering of history could be deemed complete or final.[3] The concern of the historian was, rather, with "a near approach to the truth"; and, building upon the contribution of its predecessor, every age approached nearer than before to an understanding of the past.[4] For that reason, Andrews argued for a "truer colonial history" and "a truer comprehension" of the place of the colonies in the history of America and of the world.[5] For that reason, too, Andrews recognized his own work as a step in a certain direction rather than something fully arrived. Concluding his outstanding essay on *The Colonial Background of the American Revolution,* he insisted that he had "made no attempt to discover with any finality" the causes of the Revolution.[6] He was aware of the "tentative character of many of its conclusions." [7] That is not to say that Andrews subscribed to an ideal of historical relativism. If his suggestions were tentative, it was because the facts had not yet been thoroughly canvassed or brought to light. Andrews did not argue a change of historiographic outlook with each historical age. He argued, rather, a constantly growing accuracy in the prevailing historiographic outlook.

The historian, for Andrews, had a more definite objective than that of going out and seeking truth. The objective was to understand the underlying influences that had produced the modern world.[8] In discovering "what history is all about," the historian, like the scientist, ought be concerned not only with *how* things had happened but also with *why* they had happened.[9] Andrews agreed with Beer that history was not a narrative, but "a science of the origins, connections, developments, and transformations of policies and systems." [10] The historian, therefore, could not be content with merely garnering facts. He had to understand their significance, he had to grasp the pattern of historical development.[11] He would then better see the unity and continuity of history, the waxing and waning of social ideas and institutions; and he would then better understand the relative importance of his own subject.[12] The history that Andrews wrote adhered indeed to the principles he was pronouncing. If it noted the fact, it underlined the trend.

His history also adhered to the principle that the group was more important than the individual.[13] The American colonial past, he felt, could hardly be approached from the standpoint of biography alone.[14] Not that Andrews denied the tremendous influence of certain men in shaping the course of early American history. The leaders of colonization, particularly the proprietors, towered over the scenes of his magnum opus. Yet he subordinated them to the trend of the times. He related them to "the organized life of groups of men" in which alone the historian might touch "the hopes, aspirations, and progress of a people." [15] The historian was to encompass not only all men: he was to encompass all their activities as well.[16] It was a narrow history which limited itself to past politics, to the biography of states, to diplomacy and war.[17] Weighed in the scales of the newer historiography, Freeman, Fiske, and Palfrey were found wanting.[18] Andrews had words of praise for those newer historians, such as E. B. Greene, who had woven economic patterns into their historical fabric. Indeed, said Andrews, the historian who would mind the structure of politics had to compass a wide range of subjects: he had to know "the circumstances under which the mass of people shared their lives, earned their living, met their wants, and developed their aspirations." [19]

To what degree did Andrews achieve the breadth of treatment that he prescribed to others? The truth was that he was talking about a larger garden than he ever cultivated. Social history, as a comprehensive and synthetic way of tracing the progress of a people, remained something of an enigma for him.[20] His only noteworthy effort in this field, *Colonial Folkways,* he himself would probably have recognized as a catch-all, an "*omnium gatherum* of everything not political, institutional, or military." [21] Insofar as economic history was concerned, there could be no denying his contribution. The courses he gave contained a vast amount of descriptive materials on basic institutions in colonial economic life: tobacco, land, currency, and commerce.[22] His writings, moreover, showed full awareness of the importance of trade and traders in the Anglo-American world of the seventeenth and eighteenth centuries. It should be noted, for example, that Andrews' monograph on the Boston merchants during the pre-Revolutionary decade, covering a far wider area than its title indicated, preceded by more than a year the more familiar and style-setting one of Schlesinger's. For all that, his economic history remained little more than an adjunct of his political history. In an ultimate sense, the scope of his work was defined both by the interest of his school and by the thesis he had undertaken to prove. If the one inclined him to a study of institutions, the other delimited the study to the relations between mother country and colonies. The key to these relations Andrews sought in the Public Record Office, whose materials, strewn throughout the pages of his writings, yielded up precisely the type of history that one would expect to find growing out of a dominant interest in state papers.

What Andrews wrote was an historiography of the legal processes of settlement and of the institution and course of government. It was an historiography of patents and charters, land-titles and political agencies. He was concerned above all with the agencies of settlement, with their legal rights, with the problems arising out of conflicting land-titles, and with the issues involved in setting up the different forms of colonial government. The dominant theme of his history was the emergence of central British control. The theme was sounded most clearly in the last volume of his *Colonial Period of American History*. Here indeed was the best of the kind of institutional history that Andrews wrote. Revealing a highly skilled use of materials, peopled with living men and women, judicious in its appraisals, it was surely the product of a master craftsman. Yet it was institutional history in a very limited sense, a history of policy and administration, of statutes on the one hand and of agencies charged with their enforcement on the other.[23]

The process of historiography ought not, felt Andrews, be haphazard. His feeling was not a fortuitous one: if the age of Ranke had defined the goal for the historian, the age of Darwin had defined the means. The historian that Andrews saw was an expert scholar, doing his work according to definite principles, "pursuing his experiments just as does the investigator in the scientific laboratory."[24] Like his brethren in the field of science, moreover, the historian was working cooperatively with other members of the fraternity, in America and abroad. And nothing signalized the cooperative venture so much as the monograph, which closely corresponded "to the experiment in the laboratory, where the investigator is at all times in touch with the problems and workers in the field and is able to make his results known to his brother scientists."[25] In his own writings, it is true, Andrews acknowledged all too little debt to the contribution of his great contemporaries, Osgood especially. From the footnotes of the magnum opus one might infer that American colonial history had become the private demesne of the Yale paterfamilias and of his students and friends throughout America. However that may have been, the spirit of the laboratory, of a defined area for experimentation and "scientific" techniques of procedure pervaded much of his work, whether he was concerned with English administration of the colonies during the seventeenth century, the Boston merchants on the eve of the American Revolution, or the vice-admiralty courts in the colonies.[26] His was a literature of monographs, of limited experiments. For all that, Andrews consistently had before him the larger purpose of which the monograph was part. Unlike the great majority of his fraternity, Andrews made not only the small analyses but the great syntheses as well. Thus, if he was concerned with proprietary difficulties in New Jersey, it was to relate them to English colonization and settlement, and to place the whole into the context of Western history.

To say that Andrews regarded historiography as a series of monographic "experiments" is also to say that it was for him not so much a narrative to be written as a problem to be solved.[27] Why did the proprietary system encounter difficulties in the colonies, what were the characteristics of early seventeenth-century colonization, why did the New Haven colony fall, why did the American Revolution take place, what accounted for the provisions of the Navigation Act of 1660, what was the meaning of the term "current Lawful money of New England," how were the acts of trade enforced, why was the Board of Trade established, what was the nature of American colonial history: each was a problem facing the historian and each, as Andrews well demonstrated in all his writings,[28] demanded a thorough, critical, and impartial use of the materials in order to arrive at a "scientific" solution. More than the course of historiography was construed as problem-solving: the course of human events was similarly construed. History as problem-solving was a view which encompassed all of American colonial history: "Within its own environment, each colony, settled at different times and under different circumstances, was working out its own destiny . . . each had its own problems to solve."[29] In a distinct sense, the central theme of *The Colonial Period of American History* was "the problem of settlement" with which each colony was concerned.[30] The problem of early Massachusetts was "to stretch the terms of a trading company's charter to meet the needs of a growing commonwealth";[31] and the essence of "Rhode Island's colonial problem was . . . how to create a single commonwealth out of . . . multifarious and discordant elements."[32] It reflected the orientation of the historian, of course, that the problems his subjects were solving were essentially political; it reflected his orientation, moreover, that his subjects were problem-solvers to begin with. But was not this view inherent in the new history? The historical gild had turned with sobriety from the romantic literature of its predecessors. It had incorporated the spirit of enterprise and science. The history it formulated had been comprised, in fairly equal parts, of bookkeeping and Bunsen burners.

The solution of historical problems could not proceed without adequate documentary materials. For the historian of colonial America they were indispensable. The sources would yield "a better understanding of our colonial relations with the mother country,"[33] a new version, indeed, of the entire period from Jamestown to the Peace of Paris. And if the problem was to be solved through the documents, then it was to be solved through the widest possible range of documents, for "the modern scholar considers as grist to his mill anything whatever that represents man's activities on earth."[34] Andrews criticized Beer for depending largely "on the records that accumulated in the hands of the various governmental departments and boards in England" and therefore giving an account that did not sufficiently consider the social and economic conditions in the colonies.[35] The criticism was equally applicable to himself. If Andrews had thoroughly canvassed the Public Record Office, he had not done very much more. It was achievement enough. The four volumes of his major work were a monument to his fabulous knowledge of these sources. With them he wove into his text the flavor and tone of the past.

In this historiography of sources, skill, and scientific problem-solving, style was of no great consequence. It might almost be said that to write well was suspect. The generation of the new history had disclaimed the Macaulays and the Carlyles, feeling that "what these men have left us is often great literature rather than great history."[36] It was not that Andrews denied that the historian had to be capable of properly expressing his ideas. His own writings, certainly, were masterpieces of exposition; whether he was addressing the public at large or the limited membership of his gild, his language was a model of lucidity and extremely well adapted to his varying purposes. For all that, he felt that a historian who was too much concerned with style might be too little concerned with truth. It impressed him that "the readability of a history is no guaranty of its artistic or intrinsic worth."[37] The dictum of "historical science" was more matter, with less art. Together with his age, Andrews wrote for the minds of mature men rather than for the tables of young ladies.

And the minds of mature men demanded of the historian that he use the past for sound purposes. It was misuse of the past, said Andrews, that had characterized the earlier historiography. History had been political propaganda, religious pamphleteering, tracts on democratic progress, hoping both to entertain the reader with dramatic narrative and to instruct him in specific ideas.[38] Even the present had not overcome the desire to color the past with its own needs and prejudices. "We shall always have history written in terms of race and ethnology . . . in terms of excessive patriotism and dynastic loyalty . . . and in terms of sectional animosity." [39] Andrews perennially despaired of Goldwin Smith, for example, who impressed him as having written historical morality rather than objective history.[40]

Yet it was clear, Andrews felt, that a newer orientation was emerging toward the past and its use by the present. The essence of the newer orientation was that modern and personal standards could not justifiably be applied to the past, that the goal of historical study was understanding, not preaching or condemnation.[41] The purpose of the historian was "to study history for its own sake and not primarily for the sake of interesting or benefiting society." [42] Not that Andrews construed the study of the past as merely antiquarian or denied that it might very well benefit society. History revealed the lines of human progress, it afforded that insight into reality which made the past "instructive to living men." [43] If these insights and revelations were interred beneath the scholastic paraphernalia of Andrews' monographs and of his magnum opus, they emerged clear in his more popular writings. In these, particularly in his comments on the American Revolution, he undertook to apply the lessons of the past to the problems of the present. The historian, he felt, could not permit so crucial a study to be abused by "the propagandist, the hero-worshipper, or the patriotic partisan." [44] Andrews would hardly have agreed that *his* interpretation was its own propaganda or partisanship. He was fully aware, however, that reflection upon the past was also a reflection upon one's self. "A nation's attitude toward its own history," Andrews believed, "is like a window into its own soul and the men and women of such a nation cannot be expected to meet the great obligations of the present if they refuse to exhibit honesty, charity, openmindedness, and a free and growing intelligence toward the past that has made them what they are." [45]

2. THE ROLE OF THE HISTORIAN

It was an ideal of science that dominated the school in which Andrews belonged, an ideal compounded from the precepts of Ranke and the findings of Darwin. And if history was a science, then the historian was a scientist. True enough, there could be found a wide variety of views concerning the scientific nature of both history and the historian. But that the latter was indeed a scientist, that he too "should have the quiet observatory and the tranquil laboratory," [46] Andrews always believed. This concept he had learned during the years of his apprenticeship in the seminar of Herbert Baxter Adams. The scientific historian, to Andrews, was one who had been well trained, who was expert in his craft, who studied history for its own sake, who sought "the nobility of hard work." [47] The historian was to aim not only at ascertaining the facts of the matter but also at interpreting them. In his interpretation of "what history is all about," [48] he would reveal the degree of his mastery and genius.[49]

To Andrews, the heart of scientific history was the scientific historian. Science, after all, was merely a method of acquiring knowledge.[50] Much depended on who was using the method and on the way he used it. In this whole issue could be found the difference between the ideal to which Andrews adhered and the view of historiography later set forth by the historical relativists. To the latter, the historian was the captive of his age, writing in somewhat unconscious conformity to the "controlling assumptions" of that age. That is not to say that Andrews and the school in which he belonged had reckoned their history without their historian or had denied that the historian was, after all, the refracting medium through which the past was seen. Their conviction, however, was that the error of refraction could be much reduced. They would agree that history was thought about the past, but they would deny that the thought must necessarily change from age to age. To them, the important thing was to insure that he who was doing the thinking about the past was conscious of his own individuality as an element in his historiography, that he would strive "by moderation and restraint" to achieve objective truth.[51] This was the creed of the school of which Andrews was a member, the school of Maitland, Stubbs, Gardiner, Tout, Osgood, Lea, G. B. Adams, and McIlwain. It was a creed which, as Andrews saw it, constituted the principal contribution of his own era to the study of history. Addressing the American Historical Association in 1924, a decade before the relativist critique was to be more widely sounded in the historical gild, Andrews hailed the advances in historiography that had been made during "these forty years," the years, that was to say, since the organization of the Association in 1884. The essence of the advance was the growth of "an historical state of mind," the state of mind of the scientific historian.[52]

What were the ingredients of this "historical state of mind"? The primary ingredient, certainly, was impartiality. The historian could not use the past to plead some special cause.[53] He could not come to his subject with a preconceived idea. He could come to it only with balance and perspective, with sound understanding, with "an instinctive sense of fair treatment for all."[54] Maitland's work represented to Andrews the finest of scientific history, revealing as it did an "unrivalled power of interpretation" and "moderateness and caution in the expressal of any opinion even where the evidence is most conclusive."[55] Beer too had written excellent history. He had studied the past with "a trained and judicial mind," he had analyzed it with thoroughness, candor, impartiality, and scientific accuracy.[56] Andrews found few such qualities in the "writers of the older generations," whose attitude toward their subjects he considered antagonistic and critical.[57] Especially reprehensible was the school of Bancroft, the school of patriots, perfectionists, pietists, and hero-worshippers.[58] Governed by ignorance and national bias, historians of this variety had perpetuated a tradition of historiography which was "nothing less than a crime against historical truth."[59]

What Andrews prescribed to his peers, he applied to himself. His basic premise was that both sides of the colonial story had to be understood, the English as well as the American. He hoped "to eliminate those patriotic and nationalistic obsessions" that had distorted earlier appraisals of the American colonial past.[60] Nowhere did he better demonstrate this element of his historiography than in his writings on the American Revolution. He sought to understand the British mind and social structure no less than the American. He argued for the repatriation of those who had remained loyal to the mother country. One could not forever deny a hearing to the conservative side, one could not condemn, almost unheard, the cause that was lost. "The established order, then as to-day, has a right to defend itself . . . it is the duty of the scholar in history to present its claims." [61]

In issues of lesser moment, too, Andrews tried to bring sound judgment to wide knowledge. Evaluating the case of Andros versus Massachusetts Bay Colony, for example, Andrews felt that much could be said for the Governor-General of the Dominion of New England. Andros was a person of honesty and loyalty, and he did not use his office for purposes of gain.[62] If he was self-willed, imperious, and peremptory, on the one hand, then the Puritan leaders were obstructive and disputatious on the other.[63] Whether he was trying the case of Andros and the Bay Colony, Claiborne and the Calverts, or the Americans and the British, Andrews always wore the robes of his office. Even those of his reviewers who wondered about his Jovian footnotes (in which he often rendered a summary verdict upon the mortals of history) would agree that his attitude was indeed Olympian. They hailed the balanced and masterly summation, the calm appraisal, the judicious and tolerant attitude, the impartiality.[64]

This did not mean, of course, that no criticism was entered against some of Andrews' judgments on American colonial history. One reviewer believed that Andrews had unjustifiably condemned Sir Edwin Sandys and condoned James I in the matter of the downfall of the Virginia Company.[65] Another noted that some of Andrews' generalizations "about the cultural and intellectual life of early Massachusetts are debatable."[66] The most serious of the charges that could be advanced against him was that presenting the British side sometimes became equivalent to espousing it. His thesis, after all, was that in order to see the colony better one had to take up the vantage ground of the metropolis. Preoccupied as he was with the theme of emerging centralized control, Andrews became too much the Londoner, too much the bureaucrat at the imperial table.

To some degree, then, it may justifiably be asserted that Andrews came to see colonial life through Tory-colored glasses.[67] Certainly, as the Anglo-American relations in his own day began to improve it seemed as though his own attitude toward their earlier relations was growing more sympathetic.[68] Yet this is not to say that he uniformly condoned the conduct of British colonial policy during the eighteenth century, much as he insisted that it be understood without recourse to modern standards. Of British administration on the eve of the Revolution he had nothing favorable to say: it was short-sighted, inept, confused, ill-informed.[69] And as for the Americans, what more favorable judgment could he pronounce than that "the colonists were justified in their revolt"?[70] Justified or not, insisted Andrews, their cause could not be validly understood unless the British cause had also been understood. This the historian had to do. At the bar of history, he was not a disputant, but a judge.

But he was to be more than a judge. The age of Andrews also saw the historian as a challenger of tradition, a crusader advancing to new conquests.[71] A whole terrain of infidel history lay before him: the history of the patriots and the filiopietists, the history of the Whigs, the history of Bancroft and his idolatrous followers. And what was to be the armor of the new historian? Inquisitive skepticism, historical doubting, the eternal question mark. These constituted the beginning of wisdom, these provided "the motor power that makes for progress in the writing of history."[72] It was true enough that the public at large would be quite "content to continue reading the same old story" about the past.[73] It was very much, said Andrews, as Anatole France had put it:

Si vous avez une vue nouvelle, une idée originale, si vous présentez les hommes et les choses sous un aspect inattendu, vous surprendrez le lecteur. Et le lecteur n'aime pas à être surpris. Il ne cherche jamais dans une histoire que les sottises qu'il sait déjà. . . . Un historien original est l'objet de la défiance, du mépris et du dégoût universels.[74]

Yet these ought not deter the historian. He could not in conscience accept that there was anything either orthodox or infallible about historical interpretation.[75] The historian's purpose ought clearly be "to effect a wholesome revision of historical judgments that have overlong possessed the popular mind in America."[76]

The work of Andrews was, of course, dedicated to precisely such a purpose. Inveighing against the "writers of the older generation," it undertook to give "to the colonial period of our history a new aspect and a new perspective."[77] The novelty of the viewpoint that Andrews was proposing consisted in shifting the vantage ground for observing colonial development. Constantly he reiterated the underlying tenets of his revisionist creed: that the settlement of the colonies was a phase of English expansion, that a unilaterally American approach to the colonial period would destroy a historical reality which involved not merely colonies but a mother country as well. Seeing things from England would mean understanding English purposes in a new way. It would mean, for example, that the Stuarts would be given a fair hearing. Andrews felt that earlier views, which had argued a Stuart despotism, were "even more arbitrary and prejudiced than anything charged against the Stuarts themselves."[78] If Andrews could never quite bring himself to a state of kind regard for the purposes of the Duke of York, he took pains to note that the future James II "was not unjust and he had good advisers."[79] As for the downfall of the Virginia Company, nowhere was it a question of Stuart tyranny versus popular government. James I "acted with a strict regard for the rights of the company."[80] The investigation he ordered was conducted with "the utmost fairness."[81] Andrews regarded a political interpretation of the whole incident of the company's downfall as "merely another instance of the survival of the Whig tradition that has done so much to misrepresent and falsify American colonial history."[82]

No small part of destroying the Whig tradition was a reconstitution of English colonial policy. It was his conviction that, in the long run, the Navigation Acts little interfered with colonial trade, that they constituted no serious restriction upon the commercial growth of the colonies.[83] On the industrial side, he was equally dubious that the famous acts of 1699, 1732, and 1750 had hampered colonial progress.[84] He challenged the traditional outlook toward the vice-admiralty courts:

> The part which the vice-admiralty court played in the history of the colonies has been over-stressed on the coercive and oppressive sides, and insufficient attention has been paid to its great usefulness as the guardian of the rights of the seamen and a very ready help in time of trouble for all whose life lay upon the sea or who were dependent upon it for their maintenance and prosperity. In none of the leading ports, particularly on the continent but probably scarcely less so in the West Indies, could commerce have been carried on without the aid of these courts and in none of them did there exist agencies which pursued their humanitarian work with more regard for justice and fair dealing than did the judges of vice admiralty. . . . I have yet to find an instance of manifest partisanship or injustice on the part of a colonial judge of vice-admiralty.[85]

The light of reappraisal that Andrews threw upon American colonial history served not only to restore the English from villainy but also to remove the Americans from heroism. It was inevitable that the myth-blasting should center largely in the land of the Pilgrims' and Puritans' pride. Andrews was quite insistent that "by no stretch of the imagination can the political conditions in any of the New England colonies be called popular or democratic."[86] The great colonial charters of "liberty and progress" were revealed to be neither modern constitutions, nor radical innovations, nor documents of early democracy.[87] No single group stirred Andrews to "historical doubting" as much as the Puritan leaders of Massachusetts Bay. The fact of their having been persecuted, he felt, had been greatly exaggerated. The treatment they received in England was nothing as severe as that which they themselves meted out to their political and religious antagonists in Massachusetts.[88] They were men burdened "by the weight of their convictions and narrowed by their own dwarfed and cramped outlook on life." [89] They constituted a self-interested, oligarchical clique, none of whom "would have subscribed to our American doctrines regarding church and state, popular government, or religious freedom." [90] Andrews hoped that those pursuing the colonial past might be a good deal less than kin to the subjects of their histories, a good deal more than kind to historical truth.

Andrews cast his historian in various molds and dimensions. He made of him a scientist, a judge, a doubting Thomas. Yet the summary of it all could only be the degree to which the historian had recaptured the past, the degree to which he was able to reconstruct the earlier age *as it actually was*. He could prove his mastership, his critical use of the sources as well as his qualities of skepticism and judiciousness, by imaginatively recreating the spirit and tone of the past. Here was the very essence of the Rankean ideal, of *Historismus,* of the teachings and perfection of Maitland. More than the majority of his school, Andrews was seized with this as the ultimate attainment in historical writing. The historian had to be able to measure the difference in mental longitude between the past and the present. Inasmuch as human conditions were relative rather than absolute, it was the duty of the writer of history "to understand the past in the light of its own age and of the ages that have preceded it." [91] He had to be aware that the men and women of an earlier period were responding to their own problems and could not be judged by responses that a later period would make.[92] Pursuing the ideal of Ranke and Maitland to its fullest implications, Andrews urged that the historian seek to "attain to a state of more or less complete absorption in the life of the age to which he is giving his attention, and be so far at home with the spirit and thought of a people as intuitively to avoid anachronisms and misreadings of the data at his disposal." [93]

The theme of historical-mindedness gave unity to the works of Andrews. Projecting himself into the Anglo-American world of the seventeenth and eighteenth centuries, he saturated himself with the historical literature of the period: his own writings, deftly woven from a vast knowledge of the sources, breathed the very spirit and tone of the times. His "original source" was more than documentary: it was topographical as well. The historian of the colonial period, felt Andrews, had to have an intimate picture of the London of the later Stuarts and early Hanoverians, a tangible and material picture, one that embraced "the administrative organization in all its aspects, the men and the rooms, the buildings and the streets, the physical conditions under which the work was performed." [94] To this important frame of knowledge the historian had to add an even more important frame of mind. He had to become a loyal subject of England, he had to see the colonies the way England saw them.[95]

From his premise that the historian's sense of time ought not be out of joint came the newer colonial history of Andrews. Colonies they were, and not independent states, and thirty odd in number, not thirteen. Moreover, they were restored to a larger English system of control and the vantage ground for observing that system was taken up in London. The colonial world of the seventeenth century was an English world and not an American one. One would do wrong to read back into that age any concepts of manifest destiny, rugged individualism, or democracy triumphant.[96] The British colonial system grew out of the needs of the times; whether injurious to the colonies or no, it was fundamentally right to the Englishmen of that day.[97] It ought not be condemned "in the light of what we conceive to be the more rational standards of the nineteenth and twentieth centuries." [98] As for 1776: the colonists were *not* daily awaiting the signature of the Declaration of Independence, nor did they regard themselves as ripened fruit ready to fall from the parental tree.[99] The summary of it all, said Andrews, is that "those who study the colonies merely as preliminary to what is to come are not studying colonial history properly so called":[100] they are looking, rather, for American origins in an Anglo-American world.

If Andrews was for the greater part successful in seeing the past in its own light, there were some conspicuous instances where he was not. An element of paradox could be found, for example, in his preaching fairness to past history and practicing gross unfairness to past historians. The predecessors of the "modern" school were charged with being "credulous, careless and childish," with misusing and abusing history.[101] Bancroft especially was condemned, with reference to little else, in fact, than the latter-day standards of scientific historiography. His ex post facto view of earlier historiography Andrews sometimes carried into his view of earlier history. The Puritans in Massachusetts Bay, he argued, did not grasp the meaning of England's new colonial policy; [102] they were unable to foresee the inevitable consequences; [103] their religious deeds were governed by "a mistaken sense of religious duty." [104] Another Andrews would have justifiably inquired: can we blame the Puritans for consequences they could not have seen, and are we justified in arguing the inevitability of these consequences? According to the standards of *which* age, and in the light of *whose* personal judgment, was theirs a "mistaken sense of religious duty"? Andrews' treatment of the American Revolution was, again, far from being historical-minded. His premise had been, of course, that the colonial past had been seen too much through the looking glass of 1776, that what took place afterwards was all too often read back into what took place before. Curiously enough, however, one can find evidences in all of his major works, particularly in his *Colonial Period of American History*, of that very orientation against which he inveighed. The Revolution is lurking in every phase of British policy and American development; the political and institutional paths from Jamestown all seem to be converging on Philadelphia. The truth of it was that Andrews never really managed to declare his independence from the year 1776, even though this declaration was one of the major goals of his work.

Deviating from a principle of historical-mindedness was one thing; using the principle erroneously was another. So intent was Andrews upon correcting the extremes of a present-minded approach to the colonial period that, in some respects, his own approach went to the opposite extreme. Not wishing to impute to the past the modern meaning of a historical development or institution, he sometimes concluded by denying that development or institution altogether. His contention, for example, that "there was no 'proletariat' in colonial times," was challenged by Michael Kraus.[105] A more serious challenge was entered against Andrews' refusal to apply the concept of "empire" to England's relations with her colonies before 1763. Taken to task by Andrews for precisely such an application, James Truslow Adams, in a long correspondence, demonstrated that the word and the concept had been extensively used prior to that year, in contemporary literature, and that no latter-day misreading of England's colonial relations was being committed by speaking of "empire" during that period.[106]

Andrews became the victim of his own thesis on the question of whether seventeenth-century America had had any elements of democracy. Probe as we might into this earlier world, he said in 1936, "we shall find nowhere any manifestation of democracy or even the suspicions of democracy in any form, any aspirations that anticipated future political ideals, any beginnings anywhere of an American mind." [107] The paradox of it was that Andrews was using a twentieth-century barometer for seventeenth-century weather: finding no universal manhood suffrage, he tended to find no democracy at all. Marcus Jernegan cautioned that a serious semantic problem was involved, that the concept of democracy had evolved and changed through the centuries, and that Andrews ought to insure against *"reading back into this period later ideas of democracy."* [108] Perhaps it was adding insult to injury to remind Andrews, as Jernegan repeatedly did, that he was guilty of gross inconsistency, for in his earlier volume on *The Colonial Period* (1912) Andrews had not infrequently noted the growth of democratic institutions and ideas in colonial America.[109] An emphasis upon limitations in the suffrage in the various colonies, wrote Henry Steele Commager, obscured that more crucial principle to which Andrews had himself referred: that "the source of authority was below and within and not above and without." Here after all was the signal contribution of American colonial development; here was the root of the democratic idea, an idea which grew and was extended. Commager wondered whether Andrews, in his anxiety to correct historical astigmatism, had not tended to *over*correct it.[110] That Andrews sometimes put on the wrong lenses ought not obscure the fact that most of the time they were properly fitted—indeed, that the prescription was after all his own.

Andrews had imposed strict demands on the historian, far more strict indeed than those generally imposed by the school in which Andrews belonged. The new history of the late nineteenth century had canonized Ranke and prescribed a ritual of science for his worship: all too frequently, however, the worshippers were pronouncing a decalogue with their lips and making graven images with their hands. But the historian that Andrews had conjured up was practicing to perfection the elements of his creed. In a way, Maitland summarized the practice brought to perfection. His craftsmanship added art to scientific methodology. It was an art compounded of self-consciousness, fabulous knowledge, consummate use of the sources, and imaginative projection into the very heart and spirit of the past. To Andrews written history was not so much an act of faith as an act of learning, discretion, judgment. Everyman might very well be his own historian, but it was the duty of the scientific historian to revise his notions and correct his views. Each age wrote its history, not to make new errors but increasingly to get rid of old ones. The historian could not consciously or conscionably accept a role of playing tricks upon the dead. Using the methods of science, playing an impartial role, exercising sound judgment, reducing one's own prepossessions to the barest minimum and reentering the earlier age to the very maximum: these were the means by which the past could be recaptured. And that the past was there to recapture Andrews did not for a moment doubt.

That Andrews largely fulfilled the image of an historian that he had made central to his system of historiography is a commentary on his personal ability, on the constancy and consistency of his effort, on the zeal with which he pursued his ambition. "To do something and to be somebody has always been uppermost in my mind." [111] Yet his success in playing a role as difficult as the one he had defined for himself was in no way an assurance of the validity of his historiography. Other criteria for validity must be consulted. Had Andrews *actually* attained that goal of objectivity which he sought? Had he come nearer the truth than the generation before him? Had he indeed removed from himself all his own prepossessions and those of his age, the personal contours and detours of his thinking? Was history speaking through Andrews, as he himself believed, or was Andrews really speaking through history?

In what touched upon the ultimate meaning of the role of the historian, Andrews himself was baffled. His letter to B. A. Konkle, written in the last months of his life and coming (as Andrews saw it) by way of "confession," carried these significant comments: "I have never tried to analyze the exact state of my mind and do not care to do so now . . . . I don't know that I have ever before made an effort to find out what kind of mind I had and I am not sure that it is worthwhile doing so now." [112] It is not sufficient for his biographer to accept, at face value, Andrews' own observation that "I have never had any axe to grind or thesis to prove. I have never believed that it was necessary to plead a cause in writing history." Not believing it to be necessary and yet doing it all the same is a distinct possibility. Moreover, there are all varieties of causes to be reckoned with, some gross and obvious, some less pronounced and more subtle. In certain aspects of his self-evaluation Andrews was quite correct. He observed that, although he was genealogically a Puritan of Puritans, nowhere in his view of the past had he accorded them any particular favor; on the contrary, his attitude toward his New England ancestors was distinctly hostile.[113] Nor did he anywhere reflect that he was the scion of ministers in general or of a Republican father in particular.

If Andrews rejected the direct influence of his heredity, however, he could not reject the indirect and more subtle influence of his environment. Eliminating the prepossessions of one's family could not be deemed tantamount to eliminating all prepossessions. There can be no serious doubt, certainly, that Andrews played the role of the scientific historian as nearly perfectly as it could be played, or that, as one of his critics wrote, he displayed throughout his magnificent achievement "a sanity of judgement, a realism, and a competence of scholarship which compel admiration." [114] Nor will any one doubt that in this distinct sense of personal striving and attainment Andrews represented the very best of his school. What remains to be ascertained is whether the larger patterns of his thought were not, in the final sense, shaped and fashioned by his own personal predilections and by the dictates of his age.

3. THE TENDENCY OF HISTORY

Nowhere in the vast array of facts that constituted his work on American colonial history did Andrews lose sight of the larger pattern of things. He was concerned with the ultimate meaning of the past, he wished to find out "what the course of events is all about." [115] The distinctive claim of his school, and it was a claim he made for his own work, was that it did not impose its ideas upon the past, that it came to the past "without any ready-made philosophy." [116] On the contrary, the philosophy would arise from the materials. But if the young Andrews felt he knew what was arising,[117] the older Andrews said he was not entirely certain. To some degree, the uncertainty stemmed from the fact that in his earlier years Andrews had taught the whole range of history "from Adam to McKinley" and had sought and formulated a larger perspective, whereas from about 1903 on he began to narrow his attention to the relatively brief span from Jamestown to Yorktown, a span which, affording as it did a closer and more detailed examination of historical tendency, put a strain upon any facile or sweeping philosophy. More than that, however, the age of the new history itself had started by seeking an answer and ended with little more than a question; certainly, its hope that a mass of facts, tested and verified, would inevitably lead to a *summa* of incontrovertible truth had hardly been realized. For that reason, the historian of sixty-one who addressed the American Historical Association in 1924 in his capacity as president declared himself to be "very much in doubt as to whether or not there is such a thing as a philosophy of history, for all interpretations couched in terms of philosophy are proving vague and unsubstantial." [118]

That did not mean that Andrews had renounced the quest for pattern in history. Whatever else they indicated or failed to indicate, the processes of historical development revealed "a constant series of adjustments on the part of man to meet continuous and recurring changes in the conditions that surround him and in the thoughts that impel him to action." [119] If there were no other laws, then at the very least there were "laws of impermanence." If any process was a constant in history, then it was certainly the "waning of the old and the waxing of the new." [120] The task of the historian was to discover the nature of this process, what forces brought it about, to what degree the individual was its agent, to what degree he was its governor. Looking through a glass darkly, inferring if not seeing directly, the historian might "predicate in a large and general way the trend of history and the tendencies that are to govern the future movements of human society." [121] Predication, however, was not to be confused with prediction; nor, for that matter, looking through a glass darkly with crystal gazing. "I refuse to commit myself to any opinion regarding the future," Andrews wrote his friend Hubert Hall. "I always feel that the historian should stick to his task and not attempt to play the part of a prophet." [122]

At the very best, then, Andrews argued a scientific history, not a science of history: the past ought to be approached rationally, not reduced to a Procrustean rationale. To his friend Burton Alva Konkle he wrote: "History is not an exact science, certainly, but it is a form of interpretation that should be devoid of prejudice, prepossessions, and bias of any kind."[123] Doubting that a single key could unlock the past, Andrews rejected the various determinisms which he encountered in his long career: whether those of the 1880's that had been inspired by Comte, Buckle, or Darwin, or those of the 1930's that had been inspired by Marx and Engels. The memorable "note" which Andrews appended to the last volume he ever wrote disclosed what he considered to be the pitfalls of a deterministic view of the past:

> It is too great a simplification of history to regard the events of the past as nothing but a struggle of classes, a clash of economic interests, for such an oversimplification of the problem leads inevitably to an oversimplified solution. . . . To emphasize the economic aspects to the exclusion of all else is to interpret human affairs in terms of material things only, to say nothing of the spiritual power necessary to use these material resources for human welfare, to ignore the influence of sentiment and morality, and to underrate the rich and varied stuff of human nature, the distractions of statesmen, and the waywardness and uncertainty of events. . . . No one should deal with the past whose ambition it is to find a single cause for all that has happened or who is unwilling to admit the existence of many causes acting simultaneously.[124]

Whether he was fighting a devil theory of history, in which the Hanoverian who had been maternally advised to be a king turned out to be the devil, or a theory of history bursting with inner contradictions and shrinking markets, Andrews decried what he termed "seemingly plausible but really superficial manipulations of fact and logic in the interest of a preconceived theory."[125]

Though hardly constrained by superficial manipulation, the facts of his own history revealed an inner logic; and if not so self-evidently preconceived, theory could be found in his account of the past. That is not to say that Andrews came anywhere near to formulating a comprehensive synthesis of historical experience. Yet if he had no composite view, neither was he an aimless wanderer. If the guideposts which led him in his travels through the past were concealed, it ought not be supposed that they were nonexistent. Andrews saw the past in the light of principles (or were they better called values?) which derived from the larger outlook of his age. He shared with his contemporaries a heterogeneous set of formulas that could be traced to Hegel, Ranke, Comte, Darwin, Spencer, to say nothing of the currents of national and international history which impinged upon the consciousness of that generation.[126]

The story of the past, to Andrews, was the story of tendencies that were in a state of evolution, of ideas and conceptions that waxed, grew ripe, and waned. A tendency defined an age: it gave an age its tone, its mood, its spirit. The processes of history, thus, had their own inner logic of events, their own irresistible sequence. Far from being apparent, however, this logic and sequence were "generally hidden even from the far-seeing men of any given age"; [127] they were deep-lying, almost invisible, elusive, difficult to comprehend.[128] What patterns of the American colonial past had Andrews comprehended? Looking backward from his own century, he discerned two major lines of development: that of the English experiment in colonization and that of the American experiment in self-government.[129] But what of history as a whole: where was it tending? To this Andrews answered as many of his age had: the past was gravitating toward improvement of social values, it was following the path of progress. A commentary on improvement and progress, the past was for Andrews the story of the growth of the liberal and democratic ideals and of the ideal of self-government. It was the story of the evolution of "progressive" and larger aggregates of states, such as the British Commonwealth and the League of Nations. It was the story of the renewed affinity between the American and British nations.

In explaining the first appearance, during the rule of Cromwell, of a program for managing the colonies, Andrews fairly well summarized his views on the pattern of history: "The times were hardly ripe for conceptions of this kind and the translating of visions into realities is always a slow process, in which hidden forces are often working toward ends that are unforeseen."[130] Indeed, the essence of Andrews' contribution to American colonial history was his account of the rise and development of this conception of colonial management. Andrews began, naturally enough, with the birth of the English experiment in colonization. Attempting to anticipate it, Gilbert and Raleigh were doomed to failure: "They represented an idea for the application of which the world was not yet ready . . . the experiment was premature."[131] But the removal of obstacles, internal and external, cleared the path for the plan to establish plantations designed for permanent residence. Nor was clearing the path and opening up the age of England's expansion overseas mere chance. The settlement of Jamestown was, to Andrews, the result of "no fortuitous series of circumstances."[132]

The seventeenth century, the century of the settlements, was divided into two periods of fairly equal length. The period of the early Stuarts, which witnessed the first successful attempt at colonization, was an age of flux, of "conflict between the old and the new," a time when that very capitalism and commerce which lay at the root of the new historical process were seeking to break through "the barriers that hedged in their medieval life."[133] The capture of Jamaica signalized the beginning of the second period. Looking out over a widening domain, with increased possibilities for trade and shipping, the English had become possessed of the colonial idea.[134] It was an idea evidenced in a "new and ambitious spirit," in "the moods of the people";[135] there was quite discernibly "something new in the air shaping England's destiny in the field of commercial and colonial expansion."[136] In contrast with the first period of colonization, the second was tolerant in religion, more wordly and opportunistic, more matter of fact in its approach to the phenomena of existence, entirely taken up with its interest in material prosperity. If the first age had taken its cue from the past, the second "was preparing the cues for the future."[137]

Gradually the program of colonial management emerged. It could not appear before 1655, certainly, because "the times were not auspicious." Afterwards, however, the notion of expanding trade and increased control over the plantations "began to filter in, almost imperceptibly, to the English mind." [138] Andrews did not cease to explain that the emergence of the English program was not an act of awareness, that England at first merely "rough shaped" a policy, that her statesmen "were feeling their way," that "men rarely envisage the trend of their own time." [139] However, it was clear to a latter-day historian, such as Andrews, that after 1655 a new rationale began to govern the course of English history. It made the adoption of a policy of centralized colonial control "inevitable." It made the "logic" of the movement against the Dutch at New Amsterdam "irresistible." [140] Processes and institutions that were not consonant with its purpose could not survive. The proprieties in America would thrive only momentarily and then expire, because the climate about them was growing increasingly more hostile, "because the times were no longer medieval but were becoming modern." [141] It was thus that Andrews explained the failure in America of the Duke of York and of the Baltimores. Their purposes were "foreign to the spirit and trend of the times." [142]

What Andrews wrote, then, was essentially an account of the development of English colonial policy. Tracing its rise and growth through the seventeenth and eighteenth centuries, he presented it, logically enough, from the viewpoint of the country out of whose historic life it had evolved. Concerned for the greater part with restoring the English ideal of empire to what he deemed its proper significance, Andrews never came to dealing adequately with the American ideal of self-government. For all that, it was clear enough that he saw the Anglo-American relationship as one that was shaped by the deeper purposes of each of its members. The movement toward American independence was a counterpart of the English movement toward control. The century from 1660 to 1765 Andrews considered to have been a century of "silent revolution," during which "the colonies and the mother country were moving in exactly opposite directions, each in obedience to historical tendencies that could not be resisted, the former toward intensive self-government, the latter toward empire." [143] The Americans proposed a new view of the relationship between the colony and the metropolis; they took a new approach to sovereignty, arguing that it was inherent in the people, that it rested on the consent of the governed.[144] Striving "half-consciously" and with no "deliberate purpose," opposing the system of central control that was being imposed on them, the growing communities in America achieved virtual independence long before they began actual revolt.[145] Integral to the process of achieving independence was the slow and imperceptible change of that which had been English into that which was becoming American.[146] That the Revolution was inevitable Andrews explained in terms which were axiomatic to his system: the inability of the English statesmen to fathom the deeper meaning of the problems confronting them; [147] the conflict between the need for change in history and the resistance to it; [148] the fact that "the time had not come" for the men in command to grasp "that higher solution of the colonial problem" toward which the tendency of history was gravitating.[149]

His commentary on the American Revolution was a commentary on all revolutions. Never sudden in origin, they were caused not by overt circumstances alone but also by conflicting mental attitudes and convictions.[150] Every revolution reflected the struggle of two great and powerful influences in history, the conservative and the radical.[151] What was more, every revolution reflected "the one indisputable law of history . . . impermanence." [152] A refusal to recognize this law or to admit the need for readjustment to new conditions "has led to the cataclysms of history—resistance, revolt, and revolution—and to the eventual disappearance of the more conservative elements of society." [153]

In this historical drama of tendencies and processes which were waxing and waning, Andrews never lost sight of the role of the individual. True, he recognized that "collective man" was, for the historian, far more significant than the individual.[154] Nor was he unaware that "the individual in every age is surrounded and dominated by the conditions about him, and that no man can be taken out of his setting and construed as an independent agent." [155] But, Andrews also knew, the setting was infinitely large, and the agency of the individual open to an infinite number of variations, improvisations, and even deviations. He well knew that, if consonance with the ideals of one's time-period was the rule, the historian had also to reckon with the exceptions of personal "whimsicalities, oddities, and prepossessions of the human soul"; what was more, he would have to reckon with the fact that many individuals were "far from always in accord with the spirit of an age." [156] One has merely to go to the index of any of Andrews' volumes to understand the significance he attached to the great individuals who dominated the colonial scene. Through his pages walk a group of men whose personalities and differences of background and temperament are closely bound to the policies they shape at Whitehall and to the fates they guide within the settlements. No major historian of the American colonial scene made as integral to his system so complete a portrayal of the role of each of the proprietors. Feeling that "they deserve a fuller recognition than has been accorded them by writers on British colonization in America," [157] Andrews devoted a volume and a half of his tetralogy to give them that "fuller recognition." Whether he was concerned with the role of the Calverts in Maryland, Penn in Pennsylvania, or of the future James II in the province of New York, Andrews was everywhere impressed with its significance. He sought to respect the individuality of the man with whom he was concerned, while yet seeing that man within the larger framework of his age. He rejected any view that exaggerated the power of any single individual to control the tendency of an age.[158] For that reason, Andrews believed that charging George III with responsibility for the American Revolution was "to accept a trivial explanation for what in reality is a mighty cosmic event." [159] In saying, however, that the activities of Raleigh were "symptomatic" of his age, Andrews never denied him his individual will or scope of action. In noting that Edward Randolph "would have accomplished little or nothing had not the spirit of the times been attuned to his efforts," [160] Andrews nowhere lost sight of the personal characteristics of his subject. What was even more crucial, it was no accident of juxtaposition that he argued the attunement of the times to Randolph rather than the reverse.

These were the principles with which Andrews construed the American colonial past. But how did he relate that past to the rest of Western history? Believing as he did in the unity and continuity of human experience, he had always seen his problem as one of understanding "the place of our thirteen colonies in the history of civilization." [161] His answer to that problem could be found in the interstices of his vast writing: here could be found that larger view of mankind's past which Andrews retained throughout his life. History, in its ultimate meaning, was a narrative of the great forward movements of man, of the development and fulfillment of great ideas and ideals, of the "general evolution of human society toward higher and broader forms of government and social relations."[162] Human experience was motivated by an "eternal law of progress." [163] It was a progress achieved not in a straight line of ascent, but only after society had passed through times of intense crisis, of strain and stress, or of moral laxity and decline. When the tumult and the shouting had died, however, mankind would emerge on a higher plane of social existence. Coercion and force might momentarily put a stop to the course of progress, but before long the ascent would be resumed and the worthier ideals would emerge.[164]

This larger theorem concerning the progress of civilization found its proof in the pages of his history. American colonial history, terminating in the Revolution, had contributed a great idea to the treasury of mankind. It was an idea which claimed a new status for the colony, one involving self-government and political liberty. The new status represented a "higher solution of the colonial problem," [165] a solution which Britain would arrive at only after a century of further experience and evolution. The American Revolution, therefore, was "a great cosmic event in the world's history." [166] Its meaning, Andrews contended, transcended the national confines of American history: it was not merely our revolution alone, said he, but more significantly "a part of the history of liberty, of humanity, and of progress." [167] It was a great progressive movement, a great cause, and one which did not need the justification of the historian, for it well justified itself.[168] The men of the revolutionary generation were governed by ideals of living that were "designed to be of service to the future of the human race." [169] As a world movement contributing to the progress of society, the American Revolution was far more significant than the Glorious Revolution of the English and could find its equal only in the French Revolution of 1789.[170] The last he deemed to have been of vast importance, for it had germinated the principles of national unity and individual liberty. "In watching the working of these forces," Andrews wrote in 1896, "we shall be studying the history of Europe" during the nineteenth century.[171]

How would he fit the decades of his own lifetime into his pattern of progress and improvement? While arguing that the present ought not be read back into the past, Andrews had always argued the validity of a contrary direction, that is, of extending the historical continuity of the past "to its logical conclusion . . . to the present day." [172] Probing for the direction of his own era, he found that the great war of 1914 marked a turning point in the course of history similar to those that he had studied in earlier periods. War burned away extravagances and subtleties in human conduct, and threw the world back on simpler ideas and finer instincts.[173] Speaking in 1917, Andrews saw the conflict between America and Germany as a conflict of ideals, the one based on individual right and governed by public opinion, and the other based on the supremacy of the state and on individual discipline.[174] Looking to the future, he saw the emergence of "a higher ideal than either, in which the best of each will be conjoined." [175] More than that, he was convinced that "the progress of civilization must be the progress of international comity . . . that some concert of the nations must come into existence." [176] Here was reason enough for him to condemn the staunch isolationists in the Senate who had undertaken to wreck the ardent vision of President Wilson. Having read much of the past, Andrews felt he could read much in the present: the action of the Senators would not stand the test of time; a League of Nations was bound to come. "The tendency of the time," he wrote in 1919, "is toward a closer cooperation among the nations and the reactionaries at Washington can no more stem this tide than could Mrs. Partington sweep out the Atlantic with her broom." [177] The emergence of the League summarized for him the whole course of history. Born in a cauldron of destruction and death, the League marked a transition to higher forms of political and social organization and to higher ideals of equity and justice. The twentieth-century crisis in human affairs had produced another onward surge of inexorable forces. Representing "perhaps the most daring innovation in human political organization that the world had ever known," the League was to Andrews the "mighty forward movement" of his own day and age.[178]

No less meaningful to him was the emergence of a British commonwealth of nations and of a new relationship between Great Britain and the United States. The transformation of the British Empire into a system of autonomous states he adjudged to be "an event in the history of the world only less significant than the founding of the League of Nations." [179] What especially touched his sense of history, all the more so because he was an historian of the First British Empire, was the fact that the great war had signalized a reunion of the English-speaking people. In that war, the two greatest democratic nations on earth, America and Great Britain, had joined in spiritual agreement; in their "battle with the German colossus," both had served as "the guardians of the same civilization." During the period of human history that was presently taking shape, Andrews felt, both nations, essentially similar in their political and social ideals, were committed perhaps more than any of the others to the sponsoring of "a progressive and liberal civilization" as well as to the cause of "progress in the sphere of international comity and enlightenment."[180] That unity of the English-speaking peoples which had been adumbrated, as he saw it, by the efforts of Sir Walter Raleigh had at last been achieved.[181]

In the final years of his life another world war burst into the realm of history. Again the question of the world's direction was thrust up, and again Andrews construed that direction in the light of his larger values and principles. The moral laxity of this latter-day generation in all parts of the civilized world he regarded as one of the elements which "precede and accompany forward movements in social organization."[182] He would not venture to predict what the world of the future would be. Yet he was convinced that democracy would triumph, and that it would be "a cleaner, more just democracy, in which the higher, juster principles will prevail and a better balance of power . . . created between the different classes of society."[183] History taught him optimism, he said, and he had no fear for the future of the democracies.[184]

He ended as he had begun. Throughout his life the view he took of mankind's past had changed but little. The doubt about the tendency of history that he had formally addressed to the American Historical Association in 1924[185] was banished by the optimism which he sounded in his correspondence and less formal addresses and which entered laterally into his histories. Almost without exception, the tendency he saw was one wherein ideas and world movements were gravitating toward ever higher planes. When he died in 1943 Andrews retained in essence the belief he had pronounced fifty years before, that "in the long course of man's development the good has survived" and that each generation saw "deeper, further and truer" than the one before.[186]

The way Andrews assessed the past had much to do with the way he and his generation assessed the present. His faith in the tendency of history was a composite of the tenets of progress and optimism which were basic to late nineteenth-century American thought. It will not be argued, certainly, that he made his history the instrument of a particular philosophy.

Nowhere in his writings can any evidence be found that he subscribed to a special orientation or that he was deeply concerned with formulating a system of principles. For all that, it is apparent that, whether intentional or no, his history was fashioned by definite principles and attitudes and that these had the stamp not merely of his sanguine personality but also of his sanguine age. His thought could hardly have escaped the impact of the transcending ideas and developments of the world about him: the implications of Darwinism, the suggestions of Comte and Buckle, the quest for a science of society, the widespread belief in progress and science, the peace and material advances that had characterized American life. One need not pursue the discrete elements: the stray gleanings from his mentor, Herbert Baxter Adams, or from John Burgess, or perhaps even from the sound orientation of his early childhood. Whatever the mainsprings of his orientation, he felt he had little cause to change it. The First World War in no substantial way afforded him a basis for despair; on the contrary, he saw it leading not merely to a parliament of man, which was wonderful enough, but to a parliament of Briton and American, which was even more wonderful. Nor did he find any cause for despair in the Second World War. He died, in 1943, in the midst of a great vision about the brave new world which would come after the dross had been purged away and the peace had been won.

His synthesis of the past had the limitations of the subject he dealt with. The progress he saw was a progress limited to the political and constitutional aspects of human experience. His world movements were concerned with the constitution of an empire, with the assertion of political freedom, with the quest for national unity, with the emergence of a federation of nations. In the same sense, his was a limited optimism. It never extended to the wider reaches of society. It rarely touched upon the economic and social questions of his day, or upon the emergence of the state as a lever in the tug-of-war among the conflicting interests and purposes in society. Moreover, the tendency he found in the past was confined to a particular historical area. It extended neither beyond the Atlantic community of nations, in width, nor beyond the seventeenth century, in depth. In its broadest sense, his history was little more than a commentary on the cleavage of a mother country and her colonies. In this respect, his optimism was merely a postscript to what his master, Herbert Baxter Adams, had predicted about the evolving unity of the Teutonic nations in the modern world.[187] Andrews corrected his master's fact about the past but subscribed to his prediction about the future. More limited even than that of Adams, his canvas portrayed little beyond the rise of the Anglo-American community, and his coloring revealed his sense that the bleakness of 1776 was being dissipated in the glow of the twentieth century. His was the sanguine hope that disunion then be replaced by a growing union now.[188]

Chapter 6

THE MASTER the APPRENTICES and the GILD

The historiography of Andrews was the mainstream of a life that had many tributaries. In his more than fifty years as a professional historian, Andrews became deeply involved in nearly every aspect of historical enterprise. If his historiography was the summary of a long career, note ought at least be made of those elements within his career which it summarized. Andrews was more than a writer of history. He was a maker of historians, an editor, a lecturer, a member of many societies, an administrator, an advisor, a friend, and the founder of a school of history: he was even constrained to serve as president of the American Historical Association. The plane surface of his historiography found a third dimension in the fullness of his varied activities. He was a jack of all historical trades and, what was more, a master of all of them too.

This did not mean, of course, that his primary goal was anywhere forgotten. The essence of the new history was that it put the writing of history into the hands of those who taught; and those, including Andrews, who had come into the legacy of the new critical standards for historiography had generally not come into the legacy which would permit a full-time practice of those standards. There were very few historians of the Beer and Rhodes variety. Beyond the responsibilities of teaching and a host of other professional activities lay, for Andrews, the greater aspiration of raising a new history upon the *hic jacet* of the old one. The difficulty was (and it has troubled not him alone) how to combine the many obligations of teaching and administration with the writing of history. His odyssey from Bryn Mawr to Baltimore and thence to New Haven was a commentary on his persistence in seeking the best conditions for writing the new history rather than administering it. One can well appreciate why he abandoned Bryn Mawr to accept, in 1907, at Johns Hopkins the post left vacant several years before by the death of his old master, Herbert Baxter Adams. It was not so much the additional money as the hope of emerging into the larger orbit of things, of doing more work on the graduate level, of reviving the glory of a department whose reputation was sagging, of embarking more fully upon his own work.[1] He found the reality of Johns Hopkins not at all conducive to satisfying his aspirations. College duties interfered, leisure time was nowhere to be found. The pioneering vision which he had always seen clear was being blurred. To Turner he lamented that he had "almost ceased to be a scholar. It does very well for a while but I cannot stand it permanently."[2] When he accepted the call to Yale in the early part of 1910, it was to get rid of administrative duties, "to throw off the character of general utility-man which I have had to assume here" at Johns Hopkins.[3] Going to Yale had, however, more than a negative meaning for Andrews. It meant working on the graduate level exclusively; it meant teaching nothing but American colonial history; it meant the opportunity of becoming editor of the Yale Historical Series.[4] Doubtless, underneath it all, was the hope of entering fully the realm of the early American past, of doing for himself what his notable friend, Herbert L. Osgood, had been doing at Columbia University since 1890—building a new school of colonial history.

Whether its mainsprings had been the Puritan ethic of his upbringing or the yet deeper recesses of his psyche, that drive "to do something and to be somebody" was impelling him onward. An appreciation of Andrews would hardly be complete, his wife has said, unless it included the phrase "my own work"; and this indeed was the refrain that could be heard throughout his years, a refrain indicating not only his sense of mission but also his impatience with having impediments thrown in the way of fulfilling that mission.[5] To Jameson he had written, even before embarking on the *Guides*, that "I am on the warpath with a magnum opus, which I mean to pursue till captured." [6] The same ideal he avowed to Turner in 1910: "I want to have a try at something that may be of value. Possibly I shall not succeed but at any rate I want to use up a little ink and paper in the process." [7] He came to Yale because the conditions seemed favorable to using ink and paper. When he found the burden of administration getting heavier as the years progressed, he thought of retiring.[8] "I am eager to get down to real work. . . . When I retire I shall hope to amount to something, or at least to die game." [9] As he grew older, the urgency of turning to the "real work" became increasingly greater: "I want to get down to writing and to finish, if I can, what I have put my hand to." [10] Retirement from teaching, in 1931, gave him his chance. The decade of his seventies was the decade of his magnum opus. It was a commentary on his ability to reconcile the goal he had always aspired to with the "chores" (as he called them) which he always had to perform that he wrote his great work only when he had retired from teaching. He felt that the years of his work on *The Colonial Period of American History* were "the happiest and most contented of my life." [11] The writing of history had always been the touchstone of his work, the objective he had most sought to achieve.

It was not so much release from teaching that Andrews sought as release from those many responsibilities with which the teacher had been encumbered. Teaching itself was integral to his historiography: it was both a testing ground for his ideas and a vehicle for his principles. No more than the writing of history could the teaching of history be taken lightly. As a matter of fact, the teacher had the additional requirement of not merely being a trained historian himself but a trainer of historians-to-be as well. To the teacher of history Andrews prescribed those very principles which he had made pivotal to his own system of historiography. The student being trained in research was to be encouraged to gather ideas as well as facts and to avoid distorting the evidence in the light of his own prejudices and partialities. The student's concern was to be directed to the larger significance of historical developments, just as his enterprise was to be directed to seeking the ultimate in historical research—interpretation of the evidence and a presentation of "an increasingly truer estimate of men and events." [12] The spirit and personality of the teacher were every bit as important as the principles of history in which he was to train his students. He had to have an ability to impart an enthusiasm for his study,[13] to inspire and stimulate his students, "to awaken in them the zest of the explorer and the investigator for further discoveries." [14] Andrews was convinced that a first-rate teacher could not be fashioned out of second-class material. A good teacher was born, not made.[15] To be a successful historian was one thing; to be a successful teacher and maker of historians was something quite different.

His own personality and spirit, to be sure, made it possible for Andrews to become both a successful teacher and an outstanding historian. The ideal he prescribed to his students he tenaciously pursued himself. It was, as his daughter once described it, something of a monastic ideal, one of intense devotion to duty, of seclusion, of equating work with prayer. It was also a Puritan ideal, that of following his calling, of pursuing "that one thing and one thing only" which he knew "to be his objective in life," [16] of "begrudging even the three distracting days" during which he was much feted for his having won the Pulitzer prize, and of "hurrying to get back to my metier." [17] That he constantly portrayed the role of the historian as a crusader, an explorer, a conqueror, was not mere chance; it was in every respect a self-portrait. He measured out his life in quantities of "things done and the hope of others to be done." [18] He was utterly devoted to "the cause to which I have given the greater part of my life." [19] His efforts commanded not merely "intellectual labor" but "physical" as well. Each volume he wrote went through two versions in longhand and frequently two in typewritten form.[20] "Nor did revision stop with the final correction of page proofs," wrote Professor Leonard W. Labaree, one of the foremost students of Andrews and his successor at Yale. The corrections, additions, and improvements in his own copies of his books bespeak the same general fact, that Andrews would not hesitate to revise his work, or even his outlook, "in the light of fresh information or further study." [21] Even after a major operation at the age of seventy-five, when it became clear to him that he could not finish his great work, he persisted in historical enterprise. Even at that "sere and yellow stage," as he called it, he managed to work some five hours a day, keeping occupied with writing and editing up to the very last months of his life.[22]

There was something more than compulsion, however, to spur him to the pursuit of his ideal. An important factor was his hearing, which had always been impaired, but which deteriorated so much after 1905 that he could not get along without a hearing aid.[23] It was only with difficulty, thereafter, that his wife could pry him away from his work to attend gatherings of the historical clan or other professional groups.[24] It was not that he did not enjoy the company of others, but it was company which he could enjoy, from now on, only in a particular, certainly more intimate way. His participation in the meetings of the American Historical Association began to fall off. To Jameson he explained:

> The Association meeting as a social centre is something of a snare and a delusion. The only way to do the friendly, social act is to have you here in my study, with a roaring fire, such as is now before me as I write, and anything else, cigar or pipe or neither, as one pleases, and then to sit up till two o'clock in the morning. . . . The Association meetings are too big and too busy.[25]

If his history was made out of ambition, it was made to no small degree out of his inability to hear, for both encouraged his growing withdrawal to the study of that world of the past which he was trying so ardently to reconstruct. No less considerable a factor in the work of Andrews was the role of his wife, who helped to insure that her husband's work "should have complete priority. Their house, their summer plans, everything which they arranged, was carefully thought out to make it easy for him to accomplish the maximum amount of work." [26] That his wife attended to all business matters was of course a boon. More than that, however, she served him always as critic, and twice as collaborator, in his many writings. He regarded his work as a joint enterprise in which Mrs. Andrews was a partner.[27] In effect, if personal striving made him pursue his ideal, external circumstances helped him attain it.

To his students, Andrews was the embodiment of the ideal he had espoused. They found in him a varied and rich basis for attraction. He was a man of outstanding reputation in his subject, having shared with Osgood the leadership in the study of American colonial history and having assumed unique command with Osgood's death in 1918. He was not merely an excellent and productive scholar, he was also a superb teacher. "We had a feeling of great reverence for Andrews," said Dumas Malone, who took courses with him at New Haven. "Lecture notes are generally not of enduring worth, but *his* were. They contained materials that you could not find in any book." [28] Here was reason enough to seek out Andrews. Yet the meaning of Andrews for his students went far beyond that. His guidance exceeded scholarship and teaching. He was not merely a master, he was also a paterfamilias. He was personally attractive, a tall, commanding figure, handsome and genial, an "entirely charming and sympathetic person." [29] There were qualities enough to prevent too open and easy a relationship between Andrews and his students: his deafness, the Acousticon there on the table in front of him, his magisterial appearance and bearing, indeed his magisterial knowledge, his sense of dignity and seriousness about everything he was doing. But once the student had grasped the sense of his master, and once he had become a devoted and serious follower in the cause which Andrews was leading, his relation with the master changed. Then the student would learn something of Andrews' real warmth, humor, devotion. Those who would meet the high standards he set were brought within the compass of his personal life, a matter which involved no serious bridging of gaps, because his personal life was his history. For those who had proven themselves to him, Andrews spared neither time nor effort. Nor did he hesitate to advise them about personal concerns which he thought might bear upon their work. He believed, for example, that productive scholarship could not proceed without a favorably circumstanced domestic life, and it was a belief he had no doubt founded on his own happy experience. He urged bachelor students to marry and married students to free themselves from encumbering responsibilities at home until they had completed their doctoral work.[30] When his wife once complained that he was devoting more time to his students than to his children, Andrews replied that "fortunately, my children have you to look after them, but my students have no one but me." [31] He was always concerned with what his students were doing—the histories they were writing, the jobs they were getting, the families they were raising. "Nothing," he declared, "can compare with my delight in the students that I have had and in their successful careers." [32] The school of Andrews grew out of something more than the teaching of American colonial history.

Yet it can hardly be doubted that his role as a teacher was the most important element in the growth of the school, the pivot upon which everything else turned. Andrews believed that an active scholar was the product of enthusiastic and inspiring teachers, and that it was principally the interest of the teacher which stimulated the student to activity.[33] His own practice, certainly, bore out what he believed. It was fortunate that he never had to offer more than one lecture course and one seminar at any given time and that the total number of students in both courses was about fifteen. This permitted Andrews to pay close attention to each of them. True enough, they were not always grateful for the attention, and particularly at such times when the master had done lecturing, set up his Acousticon, and started asking questions. Recalled Dumas Malone: "He used the Socratic method to extract information, and it was both terrifying and paralyzing, because there was so little information to be extracted." [34] For all their occasional lapses into terror and paralysis, the students of Andrews were constantly encouraged by his patience and were inspired by his great wealth of knowledge.[35] At all points, he communicated to them the vital importance of the research they were doing.[36] His seminars were alive with "a sense of the excitement of scholarship, of its comradeship, and of its permanent and abiding importance." [37] Insofar as the quality of work was concerned, he was a stern master. "One's second best was never good enough," recalled Nellie Neilson, "and sometimes neither was one's first best." [38] With careless effort he was utterly impatient. His seminar courses exacted a "rigid mental discipline." [39] Yet if he was impatient with shoddy work, he gave the interested scholar his complete attention, and it was attention not limited to his own students but extended to all those, from every part of the country, who sought out his knowledge and advice. In this way, his home at 424 St. Ronan Street, in New Haven, became during the final decades of his life something of a Mecca for students of American colonial history. Professor Labaree has described an experience that many scholars must have enjoyed:

> During his teaching years at Yale he did not maintain an office on the campus, largely because he did not want to waste time on trivial interruptions. But if a student or an out-of-town visitor took the trouble to make an appointment and go the mile or so out to his home, he assumed that the man or woman really meant business. He would receive his caller in his book-lined, third floor study, drop his own work, and draw up easy chairs before the fire. Then they would talk—for an hour, two hours, or half a day—without his ever betraying signs of impatience or of anxiety to get back to his own affairs. The conversation might begin with discussion of the questions which brought the visitor, but it was likely soon to expand to broader aspects of the central topic, and go on from there to a consideration of the fundamentals of historical interpretation, to the problems of historical writing in general, or, perhaps, to some other special topic with which Mr. Andrews was grappling at the moment in his own writing. This was teaching at its priceless best.[40]

Every seminar of Andrews was a practical application of his system of historiography. It was guided throughout by principles he considered crucial to sound history. Each member of the class would be assigned a set of problems, generally confined to a particular colony, and would then be sent to the primary sources for the solution to the problems.[41] The quest for facts was the initial point, and it was a quest which Andrews stressed endlessly.[42] Minuteness was in and of itself no fault. Had not Maitland's work revealed that? However, insisted Andrews, "the facts, no matter how minute, should be shown to be worth investigating."[43] The student had to understand the larger meaning of the facts, and had to be capable of interpreting them. The problems investigated were, in keeping with Andrews' orientation, largely of an institutional nature. Admonishing his students to "keep your horizons broad," he felt in his seminars, as he felt in his writings, that the institutional framework of history should be the primary concern of the historian.[44] It was a precept which guided his various seminar courses at Yale, whether they dealt with colonial institutions during the eighteenth century, British colonial administration and policy, plans for and experiments in colonial union, colonial currency, colonial land and labor systems.

He preferred that the subject of the dissertation be chosen by the students themselves.[45] And once the choice had been made, he undertook to guide them at every turn. He led them to the source materials, pointed out errors of fact and interpretation, asked them to define their theses more clearly, insisted that they weed out extraneous material, encouraged them for their good work, corrected their English, reminded them that history was a problem to solve and a case to prove.[46] It was a prodigious effort for both himself and his students. He insisted upon the worthiness of the dissertation, feeling that the reputation of Yale rested on the work that was turned out.[47] Until but a few years before his retirement, he kept his seminars limited and permitted the awarding of no more than one doctoral degree each year.[48] Nor did he fail to make clear that a dissertation was not at all the same as a book. "Every dissertation he directed had to be rewritten completely to turn it into a book."[49] A published volume required further exploration of the problem with which the dissertation was concerned. He cautioned against rushing into print, urging always that the manuscript could be made yet a little better, advising repeatedly that the student ought "to let [his] own mind mature and [his] method of presentation grow and mellow." [50] Out of the doctoral dissertations, then, would eventually come what Andrews deemed "a work of real importance to the historian." [51] It was thus that, under the direction of the master, and in accordance with his principles, the apprentices of Andrews ventured into the varied ground of American colonial history. It was thus, too, that out of a generation of seminars arose the school of Andrews.

In essence, the school itself was an extension of his own system of historiography. The best produce of the apprentices, appearing as volumes in the Yale Historical Series which Andrews himself edited for some twenty years, reflected at every turn those very principles which their master had underscored. The approach to the past was mainly institutional, and the scope of concern almost entirely political and administrative. Biography, which Andrews himself had questioned as a vehicle for understanding an earlier age, served as a form of administrative study more than anything else.[52] It was the story of the high command held by Loudoun rather than Loudoun himself which constituted the primary interest; Blathwayt was selected not as a fit subject for biography, but "as a prototype of administrators of his day." [53] Of history as literature, said Dumas Malone, Andrews was generally suspicious. Pretensions to style were pretensions to popular history, and both came under his ban. "In fact," recalled Professor Malone, "there was little in my own dissertation which I considered good writing, for me, that he did not consider questionable." [54] The discrete elements of Andrews' system were visible in the various writings of his students: the concern with factual detail, the setting of the physical scene,[55] the solving of historical problems,[56] the substantial impersonality of the account, and the attempt, in general, to present a monograph in accord with the most stringent dictates of historical science.

The development of English colonial policy and administration was the dominant theme of the historiography of his apprentices as it had been that of the master himself. Perhaps the most significant single contribution of the entire school, Labaree's *Royal Government in America,* was an attempt to study the system of English control "by the direct authority of the king which, sooner or later, was installed in nearly every colony." [57] Gipson's treatment of *Jared Ingersoll* was subtitled "a study of American loyalism in relation to British colonial government," and undertook to reveal something of "the very complex relationship existing between England and her American colonies during the later colonial period." [58] Integral to the writing of history done under the direction of Andrews was that it adopted England as the vantage ground for surveying the colonial scene and that it surveyed a scene wider than the thirteen mainland colonies.[59] It was axiomatic that each study would be based predominantly upon documentary materials, and that each would tap a large body of hitherto unexplored sources. Considering the theme they undertook to visit, it was not accident that the grand tours of the seventeenth and eighteenth centuries which began in a New Haven seminar almost always ended up in the Public Record Office. The driving aim of the school of Andrews was the need to present the other side of the colonial picture, the side of the mother country, revealing her purposes and trials, and the institutions with which the trials were made and the purposes effected. Inevitably, the studies were revisionist. Inevitably they reconstituted the Stuarts, looked askance at the less moderate Americans, and threw a far more favorable light upon British colonial administration and British colonial administrators.[60]

The faith of a great master is often consummated in the good works of his students. A generation and more of scholars were trained in the school of Andrews and it was through their historical productions that his system was given a constantly renewed and ever widening currency. Both in the field of American colonial history and elsewhere, many of the school of Andrews achieved high individual distinction. Of those who gained fame in areas other than American colonial history, some of the more renowned included Nellie Neilson, Edward Raymond Turner, Douglas Southall Freeman, and Dumas

Malone. Miss Neilson had studied under Andrews at Bryn Mawr, where, as she said, he turned her "from a pleasant dalliance in the paths of early English literature to the strict discipline of English legal and economic history"; that she was the only woman ever elected to the presidency of the American Historical Asociation indicated well enough that Miss Neilson had more than adequately fulfilled the demands of "the strict discipline" which she had taken up.[61] Turner, a student of Andrews at Johns Hopkins, achieved distinction by his studies of the English privy council and of the English cabinet during the seventeenth and eighteenth centuries; and though not primarily concerned with the colonial relationship, these studies, which had been inspired by Andrews,[62] helped to understand that relationship by throwing further light on the principal executive agencies of the mother country. Freeman also took courses with Andrews at Johns Hopkins; and if Freeman's contributions to biography and to military history did not seem to owe much to the historiography of Andrews, the influence of the master upon the student was, as Freeman himself avowed, substantial indeed.[63] Much the same could be said of Dumas Malone, who came under the tutelage of Andrews at Yale, and who distinguished himself by his editorship, with Allen Johnson, of the *Dictionary of American Biography* (22 volumes, 1928–44) as well as by the large-scale reappraisal which he was undertaking of *Jefferson and His Time* (2 volumes thus far, 1948–54).

In the area of American colonial history itself, notable contributions were made by many of the master's students. Among these, probably the most distinguished were Professor Labaree of Yale and Professor Gipson of Lehigh, both of whom had studied under Andrews at New Haven. In nearly all his major efforts Professor Labaree pursued the cause and sustained the precepts of his master: in his initial study, *Royal Government in America* (1930), one of the finest examples of the work done in the school of Andrews; in his edition of the *Royal Instructions to British Colonial Governors, 1670–1776* (2 volumes, 1935), a work designed, again, to lay bare, through the primary sources, the British system of administration; and in his seminar at Yale, in which the tradition of the master was nowhere lost, and which continued as one of the foremost centers in the nation for the study of American colonial history.[64] The work of Professor Gipson on *The British Empire before the American Revolution* (8 volumes, 1936–54) constituted, without doubt, the most important single effort of the whole school of Andrews in the field of early American history. In a sense, what Gipson did was to apply to a smaller segment of the colonial period those premises which his master had applied to all of it. If the history of Gipson was lacking in Andrews' philosophic patterning of the past, it was given over to the master's cause of revisionism and myth-blasting. Scaled to the breadth of an empire, skillfully cast in both institutional and narrative forms, Gipson's history carried much further that understanding of the British cause for which Andrews had so much argued. Here could be seen to some degree what was evident to an even greater degree from the works of most of the school of Andrews: the master's ideas and assumptions were the base from which his students conducted their journeys through early America.

Here, indeed, could be seen the great meaning of his school for the contribution of Andrews. It helped him prove and demonstrate his theses. It afforded him the constant opportunity of presenting and testing his ideas. In his courses and seminars he defined his subject matter and formulated his principles. Writing to one of his students, Andrews mentioned the last volume of his magnum opus, the volume on *England's Commercial and Colonial Policies* (1938), which remains probably his greatest single book. "I have no doubt," said he, "that you will find much in it recalling our Seminary discussions on British Colonial and Commercial Policy. The content of the volume is of course built up on the Seminary work." [65] As the experience of Bentham and Mill well demonstrated, a man with a doctrine needs a school. The school of Andrews had, in sum, this significance for his contribution: it was a laboratory for his ideas, a testing-ground for his principles. It was his system of historiography in motion.

One must seek farther than the immediate vicinity of his school to understand the wide realm to which Andrews' system of historiography extended. Unlike Osgood, Andrews did not close himself off from the varied contacts and channels of professional activity. It is entirely beyond the scope of this study to enter into an account of those contacts and channels: yet, inasmuch as they added a new dimension to his writings and spread his name abroad, some note ought be taken of them. Andrews offered his guidance and criticism not only to his own students but to all scholars within his field who would seek him out. Many a significant manuscript concerning colonial America passed the hands of the great master before it appeared in print.[66] That same prudence and knowledge which saved scholars throughout the country from substantial error were in evidence too in his work as editor of the Yale Historical Series, during the period from 1913 to 1933. His editorial labors were extended with particular care and concern to the field of documentary materials. Testimony to this could be found in a variety of examples: in his work with the Legal History Committee of the American Historical Association, and especially in his concern with the records of the vice-admiralty courts; [67] in his guidance and advice to the Library of Congress on its program of transcribing British archival materials for the use of American scholars; [68] and indeed, in his own famous editions of *The Journal of a Lady of Quality* (1921) and of *Jonathan Dickinson's Journal* (1945, posthumous). His interest in opening up the materials of the past to the scholastic world of the present was not limited to his own editorial efforts. He offered his aid in the editorial efforts of others; and quite often was his advice sought on the value of particular manuscript collections.

The influence of Andrews' views on the past was thus exerted by means other than his writings. He rendered capital service to his cause through his work on the Advisory Committee of

Historians associated with the project of restoring colonial Williamsburg; [69] no less effective was his service as chairman of the Committee on Historical Publications of the Connecticut Tercentenary Commission. He furthered his cause by his membership in many professional societies. These included, to name but a few, the Royal Historical Society, the Colonial Society of Massachusetts, the American Philosophical Society, the American Academy of Arts and Letters, and many historical groups, not the least significant of which was the American Historical Association. He was an active participant in the work of the Association, having been a member of the Justin Winsor prize committee, the Public Archives Commission, and the Executive Council. In 1924 he became acting president of the Association in the stead of Woodrow Wilson, who had died earlier that year; he served again in 1925, in his full capacity of president. In both instances it was a service which he accepted reluctantly, feeling perhaps that his choice had been more a decision of the few than a sentiment of the many.[70] Another factor in the spread of his views was the extensive correspondence that Andrews carried on with members of the gild both in his own country and in England. His correspondents constituted a veritable who's who of American and English historiography. Yet perhaps the most significant means for carrying his "good news" about the colonial past from New Haven and Baltimore to the historical world at large were his lectures. Whether he was addressing the American Historical Association, the International Historical Congress (which met at London in 1913), the Maryland Society of the Colonial Dames of America, the New England Teachers Association, or the students and faculty of the universities of Helsinki, Georgia, or Wisconsin, Andrews reiterated without cease and sometimes without change of text the basic elements of his orientation.

The magnitude of his contribution was recognized by his own generation. He was the recipient of many honorary degrees; he was the only American, except Alvord, to be invited to contribute to the Cambridge History volume on *The First British Empire;* [71] in 1935 he was awarded the Pulitzer prize for the first installment of his *Colonial Period of American History;* and in 1937 the National Institute of Arts and Letters bestowed upon him its distinguished gold medal for history and biography. In the last decades of his life he was universally recognized as the dean of American colonial historians.

The recognition had been hard earned. He had achieved it not merely by writing alone. He had also served as teacher, critic, editor, guide, lecturer, and correspondent. And it was by means of these varied capacities that he amplified and extended his system of historiography, giving it a broad and vital currency in the historical world of his own day.

PART IV

THE HISTORIAN AND HIS TIMES

Chapter 7

ANDREWS and the NEW COLONIAL HISTORY

1. ONE GENERATION PASSETH AWAY . . .

The contribution of Andrews was part of a larger effort. The matrix of his work was the new American society of the late nineteenth century. A changing present was dictating a changed view of the past. These were the years of the rise of the new school of American history and of the professionalization of historical study and writing. These were the years, too, of the wide dominion of the "scientific" ideal of historiography, the ideal of Ranke. Trained to be a master at his craft, the historian was to undertake to see the past as it actually was. It seemed self-evident to the young gildsman that the techniques of "historical science" had to be applied to those periods of American history that had until this late year of grace been a pile of false goods and poor craftsmanship. The colonial period in particular attracted the attention of the new school.[1] Proclaiming as they did a science of facts and impartiality, the growing gild of historians began to put out the new history of early America.

The central thesis of that new history had first been set forth by Herbert Levi Osgood. From 1887 on, he urged more and more that the pre-national period could not be properly understood unless one had a sound knowledge of English colonial policy and of the constitution of the English colonial empire.[2] "During this entire period," he argued, "our history is not only American, but English," and "the central thread of our colonial history" was the growth of a system of imperial administration and of the conflicts it engendered.[3] Either communally or severally, the new historians incorporated these views in their writings. Some of the more notable individual contributions of the early years of the new history were Beer's *Commercial Policy of England toward the American Colonies* (1893), Tyler's *Literary History of the American Revolution* (2 volumes, 1897), Greene's *Provincial Governor* (1898), Fisher's *True History of the American Revolution* (1902), and the volumes of Channing's *History of the United States* that dealt with the colonial period (3 volumes, 1905–12). Most significant, certainly, was the work of Osgood, whose articles in the *Political Science Quarterly* had long been pleading and expounding the new colonial history,[4] and who put out in 1904 the first instalment of the fullest study the colonial period was to receive.[5] That the rewriting of the story of colonial America was regarded as something of a joint-stock venture could be seen from the co-operative histories edited, respectively, by Justin Winsor and Albert Bushnell Hart. The former's *Narrative and Critical History of America* (8 volumes, 1884–89), more important for its analysis of materials than for its synthesis of them, had marked a beginning in the newer approach to the American colonial past. Including among its contributors such notable proponents of the new history as Edward Channing, Mellen Chamberlain, Charles Deane, and Justin Winsor himself, it was hailed by Andrews as "almost the first recognition in this country of history as a science." [6] The full arrival of the new colonial history was signalized, in 1904, by the appearance of the first volumes of Hart's American Nation Series. Among the more important contributions were Cheyney's *European Background of American History, 1300–1600,* Andrews' *Colonial Self-Government, 1652–1689,* Greene's *Provincial America, 1690–1740,* and Van Tyne's *American Revolution, 1775–1783.* The younger historians' canvassing of the sources and of the facts represented the most comprehensive redrawing of the early American scene by the new school of scientific history.

Nothing was so characteristic of that new school as the scorn it had for the old. Pleading the case of modern historical science, the young advocates charged their predecessors with "unwarranted conclusions" and with "haphazard guesses of no scientific validity."[7] If Osgood noted coolly that American colonial history had not hitherto been well understood,[8] Andrews ventured warmly that it had indeed been in a "state of petrifaction"[9] and that in no other field of American history could there be found "such serious limitations and defects as in those portions dealing with the period before the Revolution."[10] W. T. Root detailed what the new school had found wrong with the old: the latter was characterized by lack of balance and perspective, by insularity, by failure to appreciate either intercolonial relations or the relations of the colonies with the mother country, by Calvinistic certainty that the colonies were destined for independence and democracy, and by hindsight view of the years before 1776 as merely a prelude to the birth of the United States of America.[11]

The new school pronounced its unfavorable judgment not only upon the earlier historians of the "dark age," such as Palfrey and Hildreth, but also upon those, such as Doyle and Fiske, who were living in the very age of scientific history but who had nonetheless resisted its enlightenment.[12] Bancroft above all was singled out for attack, representing as he did to the new history the spirit incarnate of the old one.[13] Van Tyne took him to task for giving "scant justice to the British side of the controversy," and commended his facts but spurned his opinions.[14] C. K. Adams voiced a similar sentiment, noting that Bancroft's "fierce democracy" had made him blind to anything but the patriotic cause.[15] Osgood dismissed his treatment of the colonial period as "little more than a sketch."[16] S. G. Fisher found his account of the Revolution to be "the most violently partisan and timorously defensive one that had appeared."[17] Andrews hardly approved of Bancroft's strong hostility to English colonial policy:[18] it was hostility based on "ignorance and national bias." To perpetuate his outlook toward the English colonial system was "nothing less than a crime against historical truth."[19]

Young stalwarts, Andrews and his generation unfurled the banner of historical science to march against their enemies. The preface to Bancroft's last revision is a somewhat pathetic commentary on his awareness that the cloud of the new school was becoming a good deal bigger than a man's fist. Osgood, Beer, McMaster, Rhodes, Channing, and Andrews all staked themselves out vast domains for reconquest in the name of the new learning.[20] It was not so much that they were a race of giants as that they had conjured up for themselves a gigantic vision. Whether or not they were entirely justified in the heroic view they took of themselves, or in the dismal view they took of their predecessors, it is yet significant to know the ideal which inspired them and the image which they saw in their mirrors. To Andrews, the last two decades of the nineteenth century, those very decades during which he had grown to professional maturity,

> were a time of great awakening in the American historical world, as effective in its way as was the corresponding awakening already taking place in the field of the natural sciences. It was a time of exhilaration and almost religious fervor among the younger scholars, who saw new spheres of opportunity opening before them and entered on the quest with the zeal of explorers making new discoveries or of crusaders advancing to new conquests. . . . The result of all these activities was a true renaissance, in which the conception and treatment of history, under the inspiring leadership of men who saw visions and dreamed dreams, rose above the level of mere schoolmastering and became creative. This was the springtime of the historical movement in America.[21]

Out of the springtime and the renaissance, out of the zealous explorers and the conquering crusaders, had risen the new school. And colonial history, said Andrews, had "shared the general advance of scientific historical study in America." [22]

2. THE PRINCIPLES OF THE NEW COLONIAL HISTORY

What it had found wrong with the old history constituted a program of activity for the new. It was a program animated by the conviction that things historiographic were improving. Andrews, for example, knew that American colonial history was making "rapid strides in the direction of sounder scholarship . . . and more thorough appreciation of the problems involved." [23] Osgood announced that "the era of partial views and isolated efforts . . . is passing away." [24] Root hailed "the advance of sound historical scholarship in America," [25] declaring that the older provincial attitude was being replaced by "the modern and normal imperial point of view." Perhaps unimpressed by the fact that each age puts its own construction upon both modernism and normality, the new historians, for their part, equated the two with the pursuit of a scientific ideal. The very word "scientific" covered a multitude of purposes: it pointed to the progress being made in the natural sciences as a worthy example for the new history to follow; it set a lofty goal before the new historians, however partial their fulfillment of that goal might be; it served, above all, to distinguish the history of *now* from the history of *before*. Channing and Hart noted in 1896 that only within the past few years had "the seed of scientific treatment of history . . . begun to germinate throughout the system of American education." [26] Osgood specified the large areas of American colonial history that awaited "comprehensive scientific treatment." [27] In evaluating the general trend of historiography during "these forty years," Andrews believed, in 1924, that a parallel could be found between the progress of historical science and that of natural science. The historical state of mind that had come into existence was, he knew, a scientific mind. The varied works of the new historians revealed, of course, that there were many ways of being scientific. But if they lacked a common practice, they shared a common ideal.

That truth ought to be the central goal of all historical inquiry seemed clear enough. Andrews echoed the sentiments of his school when he declared "the truth of history" to be the exclusive aim of the historians, adding that here was a principle which had come into acceptance only in the past few decades.[28] The pursuit of truth could not be delayed by preoccupation with style. Osgood's prose, unadorned and severe, reflected a fairly universal feeling that time spent in seeking better expression were better spent in seeking out the truth.[29] It was a quest, moreover, which ought have no partisan or ulterior motive. Sydney George Fisher, for example, berated earlier historians for having used the American Revolution "to build up nationality, and to check sectionalism and rebellion." [30] In the gild at large there was no lack of argument that the past ought to be employed to serve the needs of the present,[31] but among the leading historians of colonial America the consensus was, as Andrews had summarized it, to study history for its own sake.[32]

Implicit in the whole concept of truth as a goal in historical study was of course the feeling that, whatever may have been sought in earlier decades, that which had been found came nowhere near the goal. Hart saw the volumes of his American Nation Series as concerned with discovering the "real motives" in the colonial situation; they would "show what the issue really was." [33] Sydney Fisher undertook to write the *true* history of the American Revolution. Inevitably, the role of the historian became that of an iconoclast. He had to pierce beneath the myths and distortions of the earlier history. Beer, subscribing in essence to views which Fisher had been arguing, submitted that the place of the American Revolution in the history of democracy had been "unduly exalted." It was not really the revolution itself that had been influential in the growth of democratic ideas but rather "the legend that has developed around the movement." [34] The new historian would seek to separate myth from reality. He would, like Channing, blast the fables agreed upon by the filiopietists and hero-worshippers.[35] The new age was, as Andrews had indicated, the age of doubt, of skepticism, of "believing rightly." [36] And who would deny to the men of his generation, with their intensity of purpose and zeal of spirit, that theirs indeed was the right belief?

To free the past from legend, the scientific historian began by canvassing the sources. Indeed, the phrase "from original materials" was part of the title of Hart's American Nation Series and reflected its editor's conviction that "no accurate history can be written which does not spring from the sources." [37] The campaigns mapped out by the generals of the new colonial history, Osgood and Andrews, were concerned with the matériel of the battle as much as with the conduct of it. Characteristic of each major contribution to the new history was a prefatory explanation of what new bodies of documentary sources had been incorporated.[38] It was axiomatic that a new view of the past would proceed from the hitherto unused materials. Throughout his life, Andrews reiterated this belief that advancing knowledge of the British archives would yield "a new version of our colonial history." [39] Osgood would certainly have agreed with his observation that "the older insularity of treatment was due quite as much to want of documents as to American patriotic bias." [40] In its stress of source materials, the school in which Andrews belonged was doing the same thing as every national school in the Western world: indeed the very thing that the Nestor of them all, Ranke, had made the stamp-mark of the new historiography. Andrews' monumental *Guides* were part of the grandiose scheme carried on by the Carnegie Institution of Washington to survey all documentary materials for the history of the United States that were deposited in the various archives throughout America and Europe. His volumes were more than a guide to an individual's historiography: they were a commentary on the ideal of that generation of historians.

The attainment of that ideal required more than sources. Historical science depended ultimately upon the historical scientist. The document itself was not the only thing with which to catch the conscience of an age: the historian's conscience was just as important in catching the real meaning of a document. In order to maintain their partisan view, said Sydney Fisher, the Whig historians had had to "conceal or ignore more than half the evidence and testimony of eye witnesses and contemporary documents of the Revolution." Bancroft in particular had elected to use but very little of the vast amount of documentary materials that he had at his disposal.[41] The older historians, said Andrews, had made history "an object lesson for the encouragement of patriotic virtues." [42] Their writings could be of no permanent value "because they do not rest on the bed rock of adequate knowledge; they are far too often built upon the shifting sands of ignorance and prejudice." [43]

What was new about the new history was its insistence on the impartiality of the historian. To Root, for example, "the advance of sound historical scholarship in America" could be computed in terms of the growth of "a catholic attitude, the spirit of the judge." [44] But the spirit of judgment, Channing and his contemporaries well knew, was affected by "the time and place of one's birth and breeding." [45] For which reason historians such as Beer warned against the distortion of historical data "by the investigator's personal theory of social philosophy." [46] Osgood's summation of Ranke was a summation of the role of the historian in the pursuit of historical science:

> He had also the loftiest conception of the duty of the historian to discover the truth and to state it with absolute impartiality. Again and again in his letters and elsewhere does he rebuke partisanship and insist upon thoroughness in research and objectivity in statement. This is the priceless lesson which his life and work have taught the scientific world.[47]

If Andrews had learned the lesson from the English master, Maitland, and from Maitland's co-workers in the field of English medieval history, it was nonetheless something which he too made central to his historiography. With the rest of his school, he believed that an ultimate truth about the past could be found, and that the role of the finder was the key to the problem.

It was universally agreed among the new writers of American colonial history that recapturing the past as it had actually happened was not only a matter of impartiality but one of seeing the past in its own light. Beer's study of *The Commercial Policy of England toward the American Colonies* (1893), one of the first contributions to the new history of early America, argued against a condemnation of that commercial policy "in the light of the modern ideas of *laissez-faire* and free trade." [48] He was no more than echoing the sentiments of his master, Osgood, who asked that "the principles of historic relativity" be applied to the colonial situation and that English policy be judged in terms of "how it worked at that time" rather than on the basis of "latter-day ideals." [49] Channing and Van Tyne made similar asseverations.[50] With these Andrews was in full agreement. Historical-mindedness was the prime substance out of which his system of historiography was being fashioned.

Nor was there any lack of correspondence between Andrews and his contemporaries with respect to the scope and contents of history. The matter of historical science could no longer consist of annals, dramatic narrative, personal biography, or political administrations; it had, instead, to become a sober and earnest study of the development of institutions and ideas. No less significant was the understanding that the domain of the historian was, as Andrews put it, "the entire life of the times . . . man's every activity." [51] Certainly the prefaces of the major works of the new colonial history proclaimed the historian's hope to encompass the breadth of man's historical experience. In embarking upon his magnum opus in 1905, Channing expressed his desire to treat the growth of the American nation "as one continuous development from the political, military, institutional, industrial, and social points of view." [52] Hart's introduction to the American Nation Series indicated that his own purposes were no less considerable than those of his Harvard friend and colleague. The series was "not intended to be simply a political or constitutional history: it must include the social life of the people . . . their economic life . . . their wars and their diplomacy." [53]

The truth of it, however, was that the text of the new history but little fulfilled the claims of the preface. Indeed, a few chapters could be found at the end of each of the volumes in the American Nation Series which touched upon some elements of social and economic life, almost in the manner of an afterthought, and which left these elements largely unrelated to the account that had preceded. For the larger part, the volumes by Andrews, E. B. Greene, G. E. Howard, and Van Tyne were devoted almost entirely to issues of a political, constitutional, or military nature. No less true was this of the contribution of Channing, which was given over largely to political and constitutional developments [54] and which, as Van Tyne put it, displayed "astonishing blindness to social forces." [55] Two of the most significant monographs on the early American period, those of O. M. Dickerson and W. T. Root, undertook to explore the theme of imperial policy and control, and gravitated inevitably toward subjects that were political, military, and constitutional.

In the case of the foremost contributor to the new school of American colonial history, Herbert Levi Osgood, there was no difference between what he proposed to deal with and what he actually dealt with. His purpose at the very outset was "to trace the growth of the British-American colonies as institutions of government and as parts of a great colonial system." [56] Social and economic factors would concern him not directly but merely insofar as they explained political growth; and while he nowhere denied the importance of these factors, he insisted that the historian ought "never lose sight of the fact that they operate within a framework of law." [57] Accordingly, his own work he described as an effort "to interpret early American history in the terms of public law." [58] That he achieved a relatively greater success than others of his school was due in measure to the smaller historical area which his philosophy sought to encompass. Certainly the primary materials for the canvassing of an area much larger than the political were not yet at hand. Perhaps, too, the new history of any given age always starts with the hope of widening the scope of historical inquiry and always concludes with explaining the course of political development by a slightly different mechanism—whether institutional, economic, intellectual, or psychoanalytical. Howsoever that may be, the school in which Andrews belonged laid its stress on institutional development in general and on the development of political institutions in particular.

There was no lack of awareness on the part of Andrews and his contemporaries of the need for finding the larger pattern and rationale of the past. It was a need recognized at the initial meeting of the American Historical Association, in 1884, when Andrew D. White, the Association's first president, called for "a philosophical synthesis of human affairs." [59] By virtue of that "philosophical synthesis" the light of the past might be thrown upon some of the darkness of the present. Osgood, though he might not have agreed that the tendency of history had to be put to practical application, would certainly have underscored the need to find it. His famous address of 1898 called for seeing "the colonial period as a whole," for "keeping in mind what the essential nature of this period is," for ascertaining its position "in the general history of the world." [60] The task of the historian, according to Hart, was to look for sequence and integration, for history meant nothing unless it was "consecutive history, in which events shall be shown not only in their succession but in their relation to one another." [61] In regarding the historian as ultimately concerned with those undercurrents, influences, and tendencies that lay deeply hidden in the past,[62] Andrews reflected his concurrence with the avowed interest of his school.

It was an interest, as he himself explained it, that derived from the larger intellectual currents of that age: "the teachings of Darwin, Buckle, Draper, and Lecky began to simmer in the American historical mind." [63] The belief in progress and evolution that had become the orthodoxy of the late nineteenth century had inevitably worked its way into the creed of the cult of scientific history. The gild of historians pursued the analogy of biological science: institutions were viewed organically and surveyed in stages of origin, evolution, and maturation.[64] Channing's purpose, declared solemnly at the outset of his great *History of the United States,* was to treat "the growth of the nation . . . as one continuous development," and "to view the subject as the record of an evolution." [65] Andrews reiterated the formulas of his age and the premises of his school in noting that history was concerned with "the problems of development, of growth, of progress." [66]

Man's institutions were a commentary not only on evolution but also on the unity and continuity of human experience. Applying this understanding to the American colonial past, Channing rejected the older "isolated" and "antiquarian" approach which had seen "the colonists as living a life somewhat apart from the rest of mankind." [67] The proper approach, submitted Cheyney, was that "the history of America is a branch of that of Europe" and that "the beginnings of American history are therefore to be found in European conditions at the time of the foundations of the colonies." [68] If the beginnings of the colonial period were to be seen as a continuity from European conditions, then the period itself was to be seen as a unity with conditions prevailing in all of Europe and particularly in England. It was Osgood who first suggested that the tangled problem of diversity in the colonial period could be resolved only by making England one's point of observation. In the growth of imperial administration and "the conflicts which arose in consequence of the application of its restraining influence to the colonies," Osgood found "the central thread of our colonial history." [69] The work of Andrews was largely a cloth woven out of that thread.

Their observations on the American Revolution revealed not only how the new historians were making their synthesis of the past but also how that synthesis contained some of the values and premises of their present. The ultimate meaning of the Revolution was, for them, a triumph of the American ideal: that of "self-government by the main body of the people, the principle of American democracy." [70] The triumph was one particular in a general record of advancing American society. G. E. Howard, for example, saw the break with Great Britain as a milestone in "social progress," a step toward "the full development of the American people." [71] Channing, though he did not explicitly appraise the wider historical significance of the Revolution, construed the basic trend of American history as "the victory of the forces of union over those of particularism," an observation which he doubtless would have applied not only to the Civil War but to the Revolutionary War as well. Viewing his subject "as the record of an evolution," Channing saw in the past a "story of living forces, always struggling onward and upward toward that which is better and higher in human conception." [72] This optimistic summation of history was very similar to that of Andrews. No less close a similarity could be found between the larger observations of Andrews and Beer. To the latter's way of thinking, the political evolution of the Western world had been characterized by two movements: the one tending toward the creation of increasingly larger political entities, the other tending in the direction of democracy.[73] The American Revolution, as Beer saw it, had simultaneously encouraged and hindered both of these underlying movements; for which reason, he could not join others of his school in proclaiming it a distinct contribution to progress.[74] Andrews, however, who owed more to Beer perhaps than to any other historian of the new school, had no such misgivings. The Revolution, for him, marked the beginning of "a great experiment in self-government"; only the French Revolution of 1789 could equal it "as a factor in the world's progress"; it signalized anew that "law of general evolution of human society toward higher and broader forms of government and social relations." [75]

Yet if the new school of colonial historians had found patternings in the past, the crucial point was that it had found nothing of a single pattern. Its philosophic insights did not amount to the insight of a philosophy. The truth of it was that, for the larger part, the generalizations it made came by the way of being *obiter dicta*. Its synthesis was nothing frontal, but crept into the interstices. Indeed, this was consonant with the Rankean ideal, at least as the gild of American historians construed it, an ideal which to them prescribed a regimen of scientific procedures for recapturing the actuality of the past. Historic truth was to be dug out of the documents, smelted with skillful criticism. Truth would emerge slowly, item by item, *fact by fact*. Authentic philosophy would be the product only of authenticated fact. The ideal of the manuscript and the monograph was an ideal of the specific rather than the universal. Eventually, after all the parts of the cosmic jigsaw puzzle had been carefully recovered, they might be put together; it would be more nearly expressing the opinion of the school to say that the parts would put themselves together, would simply fall into place.[76] Little favor could be found in the new historical gild for the idea of a science of history, for bringing the past under the governance of laws and for making it possible to predict the future.[77] More favor could be found for seeking the patterns of the past and showing their significance for the present.[78] But the exhortations of several of the presidents of the American Historical Association to their fellow gildsmen to look for tendency in history was something of its own commentary that it was not being sought. The purview of the new colonial historiography was hedged in by the limited subject matter of its works, to say nothing of the limited number of these works—a single monograph, in the instance of the greater majority of the new historians, the doctoral dissertation itself. Of those who ventured beyond the statutory requirement, not many, at least in the field of American colonial history, undertook the formulation of that fuller synthesis to which the presidents of their gild had encouraged them.

George Burton Adams, himself a medievalist, expressed a sentiment that aptly summarized the preponderant sentiment among the colonial historians. In 1908, in his presidential message to the American Historical Association, he urged that generalizations could wait. Not that he denied the possibility of a philosophy of history. But such a philosophy could grow only out of scientifically established fact, not out of half-baked and unsupported generalization. The historian who helped in the sound establishment and classification of fact, he felt,

> will make a more useful and a more permanent contribution to the final science, or philosophy of history, than will he who yields to the allurements of speculation and endeavors to discover in the present stage of our knowledge the forces that control society, or to formulate the laws of their action. None of the new battle-cries should sound for us above the call of our first leader, proclaiming the chief duty of the historian to establish *wie es eigentlich gewesen*.[79]

The cause which Adams was pleading had already, though more unconsciously than otherwise, enlisted the support of those contributors to the American Nation Series who were concerned with the colonial era. With them, the footnoted fact took precedence over the philosophy. Indeed, among the principal historians of the new school of American colonial history there was not one who presented, in his historical works, a full *summa* of man's experience, or, for that matter, anything more than stray insights of a summary nature. Osgood and Beer offered their readers the order and logic of a historical system, viewed from different sides of the Atlantic and with a somewhat different stress of subject matter. Their history was more a legal brief than an abbreviation of historical law: it was a history of description without too much explanation, of analysis without too much synthesis, of institutions without too much humanity, of fact without too much reason. In Channing, the outlines and movements of history were completely submerged beneath the tidal waves of fact. His *History of the United States,* the greatest such venture of its age, summarized the inclination of the new history to speak its mind in syllables rather than in sentences.

The historiography of Andrews, it is true, showed a greater concern with the underlying currents of history than could be found in the efforts of most of his distinguished colleagues. At thirty, he had postulated the need for combining "the grasp of the philosophical historian and the scholar's keenness for exact and precise statement," urging the importance of treating "the particular with a full understanding of its relation to the universal." [80] This was a precept which guided all his work. For all that, it ought to be stressed that Andrews rejected any single or simple key to the complexity of man's experience, and that he agreed entirely with Beer that preconceived ideas could not be inflicted upon the past.[81] What pattern he did find in history, moreover, stood out in very low relief: its surface had been worn down by his abrasive wariness of generalizing and by his grinding concern for the fact of the thing. His work revealed the thread of a philosophy: but he never called it that, nor did he proceed to weave it into a whole cloth. *The Colonial Period of American History* was, as Carl Bridenbaugh correctly saw it, yet another installment in the scientific historian's "perennial search for completeness and accuracy in his facts." [82] It was part of his age's quest for the ultimate truth of the past, *wie es eigentlich gewesen.* It offered scientific history, not a science of history. What historical tendency it offered was much more apparent in the preface than in the text. Created out of countless documents, fashioned by a surpassing attempt at objectivity, the history of Andrews was a tribute to the everlasting dominion of the fact.

3. THE CONTENTS OF THE NEW COLONIAL HISTORY

The principles of the new historiography were inevitably reflected in the actual contents of the new American colonial history. Again, though the rising school spoke with many voices, a tone of relative uniformity prevailed; and again, the contribution of Andrews was in essential correspondence with the newer views, not only arising out of the changing context of American colonial historiography but helping in no small measure to produce the change. Basic to all further considerations was the fact that the period before 1776 had to be freed from the provincialism which had made it merely a prelude to independence and which had cut off colonial America from the larger currents of Western history. That famous address of Osgood's in 1898 had submitted that "the greatest need to-day" in the study of the colonial era was "the ascertainment of its position in the general history of the world." [83] Bancroft's lofty preface had proclaimed, in 1834, the maturity of the American state, its equality with the states of Europe, and its independence from them. The opening statement of the new history, on the other hand, was but a minor variation on the theme that "America is a child of Europe," [84] and that the institutional and political origins of the New World were to be sought in the Old.

If America was a child of Europe in general, it was the child of England in particular. Decrying the older approach, Channing noted that his own work undertook to consider "the colonies as parts of the English empire, as having sprung from that political fabric." [85] The logic of the newer approach had been well argued by Osgood. The colonial period belonged not merely to American history but to English history as well. American growth was nothing more, after all, than a phase of English expansion. Necessarily, it was only in the light of their English roots that American institutions could be understood. "They were," Osgood contended, "English institutions, worked by Englishmen, but under new and strange conditions. They therefore underwent modification." [86] The founder of the new colonial history wondered that the English side of the story should hitherto have been either omitted or "referred to as something foreign and inimical to the colonies." [87] But the English side, asserted Osgood, was "the very essence of the colonial relationship, and without it the meaning of the period is to a large extent lost." [88] Beer relentlessly underlined the argument of his master. The colonies, he said, had to be restored to their "real historical setting," and in that setting they "were part of a larger system which influenced their development in various ways." [89] The work of Andrews was dedicated to these self-same propositions. The "colonial" had to be put back into "the colonial period of American history": the fundamental reality of that period was the dependence and interdependence of mother country and colonies.[90] Writing in 1908, Andrews hailed the general advance of the scientific study of the years before the Revolution; he noted with satisfaction that "points of view, once parochial, are becoming imperial." [91] Indeed, the imperial viewpoint characterized the new school. In 1898, it had been enjoined upon the rising generation by Osgood, who asked the new historian, in his imagination, to take up his stand at London, "that he may thus view colonial affairs in their proper perspective." [92] It matters little perhaps that the plea of Osgood was more fully satisfied by the work of Beer and Andrews than by his own. What matters is that the imperial perspective which he had pleaded for became the touchstone of the new history.

To get that perspective the new school undertook a comprehensive analysis of the workings and agencies of the British system of colonial management.[93] Integral to the analysis was a desire to understand the contemporary meaning of the principles by which the British system had been governed. The historian could not in justice condemn the idea of a self-sufficient empire, argued Beer, for "to the man of those days it was as true as is the theory of evolution or of diminishing returns to us." [94] Far from agreeing with Bancroft that the acts of trade were a "badge of servitude," Osgood tried to understand them as "a natural and necessary phase in the development of colonization." [95] Channing rejected the view that the men who passed them "were actuated by a spirit of despotism or disregard of colonial interests." [96] Asserting that English policy was in no wise more severe than that of the other European states, Van Tyne felt that it did not seem to have worked to the disadvantage of the colonists.[97] Here was a view which was carried to its farthest extent in Beer's favorable appraisal of the old colonial system.[98] It was a view with which, moreover, Andrews was in basic agreement. If Beer and Andrews represented at most the extreme point to which the historiographic pendulum had swung, they represented at least the general direction in which it was swinging.

The vantage ground of the empire afforded, to the new school's way of thinking, a deeper insight into the main lines of development during the colonial period. No longer would Bancroft's simple polarization of British tyranny on the one hand and American love of liberty on the other suffice.[99] Nor could the story of the American Revolution be made a matter of historical romance or the product of personal influences. History was cast, rather, in the form of long-range developments and remote causes; moreover, the role of the individual in the larger play of things was substantially reduced. In this light, and in the light of the wider view which they took of the empire, it will be understood why Osgood and his contemporaries found the central theme of the colonial period to be the tendency toward imperial control on the part of the British and the tendency toward an independence from that control on the part of the colonies.[100] The story of growing conflict between the centralizing purposes of the British and the decentralizing purposes of the Americans became, in fact, the dominant story of the new colonial history. It was variously recounted in the pages of E. B. Greene, Root, Channing, Van Tyne, and Andrews.[101] Even though the conflict was seen as one of a political and constitutional nature, and one expressed most dramatically in the struggle between the provincial assemblies and the royal governors, its reaches were extended beyond the realm of politics and the resistance to governmental authority. That "silent and peaceful revolution" which Andrews saw taking place in America during the century after 1660 was one which involved the gradual change of transplanted English institutions into institutions essentially American. By 1763, said the new historians, a very clear divergence had come about between the ways of the metropolis and those of the colonies. It was a divergence which found tangible expression in their respective social structures, in their religious institutions, in their patterns of thought, no less than in their economic systems and forms of government. This expanded view of the pre-national period, however limited the treatment it received in the pages of the new history, was fairly universally accepted; but probably no better presentation of the new synthesis could be found than in Van Tyne's *Causes of the War of Independence* (1922). In explaining the Revolution, which was after all the summary of the whole colonial era, the generation of Andrews saw deeper than the decade before 1776 and wider than the sphere of politics.

That larger view of the empire which the new history had made central to its presentation of the colonial period became even more meaningful in its appraisal of the nature of the Revolution. Root was stating the prevalent sentiment of his school when he observed that the French and Indian War had revealed the weaknesses of the imperial structure and that Britain's primary concern, with the advent of peace, was to reorganize her colonial system.[102] It was a view of course which Beer's *British Colonial Policy 1754–1765* (1907) had first argued, cogently and at some length. It was Beer, too, who had contended that whatever differences may have existed prior to

1763 were greatly intensified by Britain's tightening up of her system of control.[103] This construction of the imperial situation made intelligible the subsequent course of events. "Fundamentally," said A. M. Schlesinger, "the great problem of the decade following the peace of 1763 was the problem of the reconciliation of centralized imperial control with colonial home rule." [104] Again, Van Tyne's *Causes of the War of Independence* served as the summary of his school's orientation. Its dominant theme was the problem of imperial organization which faced that earlier generation of Britons and Americans. The road to revolution, ran the theme of the new history, was paved with good intentions of solving the imperial problem and a calamitous failure to do so. And 1776 was the point upon which, as the historiography of Andrews together with that of his generation undertook to demonstrate and prove, all paths of the imperial relationship ultimately converged.

4. ANDREWS AND HIS CONTEMPORARIES

Thus, in the actual contents of his contribution no less than in the historiographic principles by which that contribution was fashioned, Andrews was at one with the new school. If he was not first to formulate either the principles or the contents, he served just as significantly by sustaining the one and popularizing the other. His *Colonial Background of the American Revolution* (1924) was, in this respect, an admirable summation of the precepts of the new history concerning the century and a half before 1776.

Not that there was an inflexible adherence on the part of Andrews to every aspect of the newer orientation. It would be as invalid to suppose *that* as it would be to suppose that the newer orientation was an entirely uniform one, or indeed, that it represented anything more than a prevalent direction of thinking about the colonial period. G. E. Howard, for example, could never quite accept the implications of the new historically-minded approach to the old colonial system; to him that system remained "the fruit of ignorance and inexperience," "selfish in motive . . . and false in principle." [105] And

Beer, to cite another instance, would hardly have subscribed to Channing's retrospective view of imperial conditions in 1760, a view which found the colonists to have been "patient and long-suffering" and which asserted that "only prolonged misgovernment on the part of the rulers of Britain compelled them to declare themselves independent of that empire from which they had sprung." [106] That a general similarity of approach by no means meant a uniformity of approach was equally evident in the case of Andrews. There can be no doubt that he pushed the imperial viewpoint farther than most of his contemporaries. Few of his school took up their vantage ground solely in Whitehall and Westminster; few extended their survey to include the island colonies of Britain as well as the continental ones; few felt that looking at the American colonies from without would, by itself, suffice. Indeed, Root warned that "it would be a serious mistake . . . to try to explain colonial history largely from the standpoint of the mother country." [107] Yet, if Root reflected the sentiment of his school in warning against an extreme, it was nonetheless true that the extreme indicated the larger pattern of thinking. The pattern was essentially imperial, if not exclusively so.

No small measure of the degree of correspondence between the contribution of Andrews and that of his school could be found in the judgment which his contemporaries passed upon his efforts. If a later age would mix its praise of Andrews with damns which were not so faint, his own age greeted the work he was doing with fairly universal acclamation. The *Guides* (1908, 1912, 1914), which represented the greatest of his labors during the decades of the rise of the new colonial history, were uniformly hailed by his peers. Whether sounded by Channing, Jameson, Root, or Osgood, the theme was a recurrent one: that Andrews was "opening the door to students of our colonial history," [108] that he had provided his generation with "a chart of an hitherto imperfectly discovered country," [109] that he had brought "a new vision" to the study of the past,[110] that his work marked "an era in American colonial history, by putting it at once on a new and higher basis." [111] No less glowing was the tribute paid the works of revisionism and of the newer synthesis which were coming from his pen. Willis Mason West found his *Colonial Self-Government* to be "the best volume in the [American Nation] Series so far [1904]." He lauded Andrews' use of the sources as well as his freedom from a provincial attitude toward England; the discussion of English colonial administration, something of an innovation in 1904, West considered to be "the best . . . outside of special treatises, if not the best anywhere." [112] The praise was virtually unbounded for the distillation of the new American colonial history which Andrews presented in the two hundred and fifty pages of his *Colonial Period* (1912). Herman V. Ames, who was spreading the revisionist view at the University of Pennsylvania, hailed the excellence of the volume.[113] Essentially the same sentiment could be found in Samuel Eliot Morison's evaluation of *The Colonial Background of the American Revolution* (1924). "No such balanced and masterly review of colonial conditions and British colonial policy has ever been given to the public," wrote Morison.[114] It was indeed, as he aptly called it, *une oeuvre de haute vulgarisation,* for it spread abroad the new orientation, it spoke the collective mind of the gild to the ear of a wide and interested audience. If some of his peers greeted Andrews with reservation, the reservation was posited within a larger context of approval.[115] And the approval was, self-evidently, that of an age for its spokesman. By 1924, however, Andrews had been pronouncing the tenets of the new creed for nearly three decades. Even then the novelty he was claiming in his preface was hardly being substantiated in his text.[116] Before very long the new view would itself become history, and the continuing voice of Andrews, nothing more than the voice of the past.

His own appraisal of the work of his contemporaries was no less a clue to the relation between Andrews' historiography and that of his age. Here too it could be seen that if the new field of American colonial history was being plowed severally, it was being held in commonalty. In what Andrews said of his colleagues, it was evident that, whatever difference of stress could be found in their works, it was subordinate to a larger unity of principle. He rejoiced that the study of the period before 1783 had shared "the general advance of scientific historical study in America." [117] He hailed the advent of the historical state of mind and of the scientific historian.[118] The efforts of the younger historians of the American colonial past, men such as E. B. Greene, A. M. Schlesinger, and W. T. Root, to cite but a few, were enthusiastically greeted by Andrews for having satisfactorily fulfilled the requirements of the new history. He was impressed with their sanity and good sense, their fairness, balance, and accuracy, their freedom from patriotic bias, their refusal to plead the patriotic cause, their thoroughness and impartiality: in effect, with their essentially scientific approach.[119] The historiography of his most notable colleague, Herbert Osgood, he found no less impressive. It had been characterized, said Andrews, "by fullness of knowledge, fairness of treatment, insight into the deeper springs and processes of historical development, and profound understanding of the influences at work guiding the actions of men." [120]

Commendable though he found the work of Osgood, however, it was for the work of Beer that he reserved his greatest praise. Here was, for Andrews, the scientific historian incarnate. His appreciation of Beer, the only extensive one he ever wrote of the contribution of another historian, represented something more than a biography of the famous student of Osgood: in a deeper sense, it was the biography of the new school, perhaps for Andrews an autobiography. With no one did he identify himself as much as with Beer. To his critical and exhaustive study of the sources, Beer had brought an attitude of strict impartiality. He had come to the past with no preconceived idea, with no prefabricated philosophy. He approached the past in the light of the past, pursued it for no other reason than discovering the truth. Certainly, though a loyal American, Beer "would not demean history by compelling it to serve as an object lesson for the cultivation of patriotic virtues." [121] His contribution, Andrews summarized, everywhere revealed "the same principle of thoroughness, candor, and truth, of scientific accuracy and historical impartiality that were inwrought in the very fibre of his being." [122]

Not that Andrews had words of praise for all the principles espoused and practiced by his contemporaries. Where the men of his age did not measure up to his view of the role and responsibilities of the scientific historian, he did not withhold his censure. It was his sentiment, for example, that Mellen Chamberlain, James A. Woodburn, and George E. Howard had not fathomed the depths of the American Revolution, that none of them even pretended to have made a thorough examination of the evidence, and that, in sum, none had satisfactorily solved that great historical problem.[123] He was dismayed by Fiske's failure to use manuscript materials [124] and not a little chagrined by Goldwin Smith's "historical moralizing" and present-mindedness.[125] The work of Channing he regarded with no little misgiving. It was "lacking in depth," it exaggerated the influence of individuals, it hardly satisfied its pretensions to encompassing the institutional and economic aspects of the past.[126] The Harvard professor, Andrews felt, wrote history which was prejudiced and insular and remarkably unwilling to generalize or penetrate the farther reaches of its subject.[127] Nor for that matter, did the contribution of his most illustrious compeers, Osgood and Beer, escape the criticism of Andrews. The first he found too narrow in scope, too severely concerned only with problems of government and public law.[128] He felt, too, that Osgood had "eliminated very largely the human elements" of his story and that he had failed, at times, to present "the deeper reason for things." [129] As for Beer, his work was lacking in continuity; it was more a series of discrete essays than an organic whole. Moreover, noted Andrews, the historian of the old colonial system did not adequately convey a sense of evolution: the idea of the self-sufficient empire did not unfold, it sprang forth almost full-grown. Because of these inadequacies, the feeling of movement toward some definite end was missing in the pages of Beer.[130] The reservations Andrews entertained about the work of his contemporaries, however, were little more than reservations from a general acceptance.

For the larger part, he hailed the "honest desire . . . of younger American writers to deal with American history as a subject for exact and careful scholarship in the broadest sense of the term." [131] For the larger part, his own principles of historiography were also theirs.

No less true was this of the central theme of his contribution. It was a theme which he shared with his contemporaries and one, moreover, by which he gauged the rise of the new history. In evaluating the works of his age, he measured out how far they had seen the colonies in their imperial context, the degree to which they had understood English purposes and policies, and their success in relating colonial development to the wider currents of Western history. The fourth and fifth volumes of J. A. Doyle's *English Colonies in America,* for example, he considered to have fallen lamentably short of the modern ideal, all the more so because they were the contribution of an Englishman, who should have availed himself of the vast materials offered by his nation's archives.[132] Provincial in outlook and perfunctory in their treatment of British colonial management, Doyle's volumes were behind the times; and that they appeared in 1907 made this fact painfully clear, for it was this very year that Osgood's work on English imperial control [133] marked, as Andrews saw it, "the highest point reached thus far in the scientific interpretation of our colonial history." [134] Channing's viewpoint seemed, to Andrews, to be far more acceptable than that of Doyle. Channing had adopted the imperial outlook, he had "viewed the colonies, not as isolated political and social units, but as parts of a great empire." [135] This, however, did not preclude certain grievous errors, either of omission or commission. His work revealed "an inherited dislike of the British government," a self-evident lack of sympathy with the old colonial system and "a proneness to find fault." His survey, in effect, was yet insular in its approach and far from being unprejudiced.[136]

Where Channing succeeded partially at best, the younger historians had a substantial triumph. Put to the scales of the imperial viewpoint, at least as it was construed by Andrews, the efforts of Dickerson, Root, Greene, and Schlesinger were nowhere wanting.[137] They had drawn their canvas wide, set the colonies into the world of English expansion, explored English commercial and colonial policies, and divested themselves of an American orientation and of patriotic bias. It was also gratifying to Andrews that the imperial point of view was being adopted more and more in studies concerning the American West during the pre-Revolutionary period. Here in fact was the reason for which he hailed Alvord's monumental volumes on *The Mississippi Valley in British Politics* (1917). Alvord was opening up a new and important phase of British policy, a policy which Andrews held to be the essence of the colonial story. And the crux of it, as Andrews emphasized, was that Alvord was "taking his stand with those who would study American colonial history as a phase of European history, realizing that the day is past when colonial history can be viewed solely as an American interest." [138]

It was natural enough that Andrews would warmly commend the orientation of both Osgood and Beer toward the American colonial past. They were, after all, together with himself, the foremost "exponents of a version of colonial history that is destined in the long run to supplant all older versions." [139] Andrews agreed that Osgood could easily claim the distinction of priority in sounding "the modern note regarding the relations between England and her colonies." [140] It was he who had drawn attention to the fact that the colonies were part of an expanding English empire and that understanding English commercial policy was necessary for an understanding of American colonial development.[141] It was he, "more than anyone else," who had "revolutionized the writing of our early history." [142] The praise which Andrews had for his colleague was not, however, unmixed. He recognized that it had never been Osgood's purpose to take his stand in England or to survey any more than the thirteen colonies which finally revolted. Even so, felt Andrews, Osgood was hardly justified in omitting all mention of British policy and control after 1730.[143] More significant than that, however, was the fact that his exclusively

American point of observation tended "to create in him a dis-relish—I would not call it a prejudice—for the British system and all who upheld it, and to make it difficult for him to understand just what was the British outlook before 1763." [144] Certainly, said Andrews, it was not quite fair for Osgood to call British mercantile policy "a system of benevolent despotism." It could be viewed as despotic only by someone who had taken his view at a distance.[145] Osgood had seen the British mind from America, "and distance had lent disenchantment to the view." [146] Indeed, said Andrews, the sum of it could be found in Osgood's feeling that his major disciple, George Louis Beer, "had gone too far in his reaction from the old, specifically American way of interpreting colonial history." [147]

Here, of course, Andrews revealed his sentiment not only about the master but also about the student. His enthusiastic approval of the work of Beer was in essence the approval of his choice of observation point. Beer knew, with compelling clarity, that to do justice to British policy one had to study it through the eyes of contemporary British officials. He knew "that colonial settlement and development were more a British than an American matter, requiring for their elucidation a knowledge of contemporary British thought and opinion, motives and needs, social conditions and tendencies." [148] He knew he could find the answer to his problem only in the British documents and only in Whitehall and Westminster. He knew, Andrews might have concluded, what Andrews knew, and he was no less justified in his conclusions.

In effect, the degree to which they had adopted the imperial outlook served as the basis for evaluation which Andrews made of the members of the new school. Having himself completely and unequivocally taken up the vantage ground of Whitehall and Westminster, it was perhaps inevitable that his criteria for evaluating the works of his colleagues were too much inclined to the imperial viewpoint. For all that, whether underscored in his case or simply stated in theirs, it was a viewpoint which lay at the root of the new history in general and of the contribution of Andrews in particular.

The relationship of Andrews to his age was, in an ultimate sense, the relationship of his own contribution to that of Osgood and Beer. The individual quality of his work derived from the fact that, moving between the essentially American world of Osgood and the essentially English world of Beer, he undertook to reveal the American scene as one of English action. This explained something of the difference of attitude between Osgood and Andrews on elements of English colonial policy, with Andrews taking a view which was uniformly more sympathetic than that of his colleague; it explained, at least to a degree, why the work of Andrews, having its own outlook, made such a painfully small acknowledgment of its debt to the work of Osgood. For the larger part, however, the difference among the great trio was a difference of formula, and the remarkable fact of it was that each was, so far as he went, essentially successful in the satisfaction of the demands of his particular formula. In that respect, the work of Osgood, Andrews, and Beer complemented each other, forming a substantially integrated picture of the Anglo-American world during the century and a half before 1776. To some extent, perhaps, the historiography of Andrews, though dedicated to the same propositions, was withal built of more durable materials than that of his great colleagues. His history was less severely a legal brief than theirs, less than theirs the proof of a historical theorem. He demonstrated, better than they, that history was a richly human affair; his pages were alive with human complexity and confusion. His portrait of the American scene was wider than Osgood's, in a way, not merely because he saw thirty colonies where Osgood saw only thirteen, but also because he more consciously tied up the colonial scene with the wider currents of Western history. More than Osgood, he sought to probe the mainsprings of historical action. It is not merely the regard in which he is held by his biographer which suggests that, while the imposing structure of Osgood's contribution is essentially the external one of a theorem and seven volumes of proof, that of Andrews cannot be superficially gleaned. It must, instead, be sought in the depths of his account, in his skillful weaving of a rich cloth of history: in the unfolding of historical ideas, in the subtle and complex interplay of historical forces, in the changing currents of economic and political philosophy, and in the drama of personalities and the problems with which they were confronted.

The individuality of his contribution, however, could not obscure the larger truth of his belonging to a definite age and to a certain school. His historiography grew from the same matrix as that of Osgood and Beer. Indeed, it might almost be said that no major principle of Andrews was uniquely his own, that every one of his basic tenets had earlier been formulated either by Osgood or Beer. It was Osgood who had underlined the need for seeing American colonial development as a phase of English expansion. If Osgood furnished Andrews with the premises of the new approach, Beer furnished him with the details. In his comprehensive studies of the origin and development of the old colonial system Beer first presented the particulars which constituted the heart of Andrews' own contribution: the growth of the colonial idea, its rapport with the deeper currents of Western history, its evolution in the course of the seventeenth century, the changing currents of English purposes and plans at the time of the Restoration, the significance of the last French war in producing reorientation of British policy, and the American Revolution as a product of Britain's entirely understandable needs for reconstituting her new territorial empire. If it was true that he put the borrowed materials together in a way that was entirely his own, it was no less true that the materials had indeed been borrowed. Yet the significant point is not so much that they had belonged either to Osgood or to Beer, but that they were the products of a particular historiographic age.

The imprint of that age could be found upon the works of all three of the great triumvirate. Theirs was an historiography which pursued what they deemed to be a certain truth in the soundest scientific manner. It was an historiography of archival materials, of objectivity and historical-mindedness, of institutional origins and development. All three historians, moreover, were predominantly concerned with problems of government in their larger institutional framework. They were worshippers at the shrine of Ranke, revisionists, explorers of *terra incognita,* dominated by a zealous singleness of purpose in taking over and claiming for the new science the lands of the American colonial past.

Perhaps the ground was no longer as fresh in 1934, when Andrews embarked upon his magnum opus, as it had been in 1904, when Osgood embarked upon his. Perhaps too Andrews should have been more aware than he seemed to be, impressed as he still was with the novelty of his orientation, that the grounds were no longer new, indeed that the soil was becoming exhausted. Did this mean that his contribution was one of ill gleaning after Osgood and Beer? Hardly. It was, despite its delay, a contribution of the greatest magnitude. Possibly it was that very lapse of three decades which explained the enhanced richness and depth of his account, its wider scope, its humanity, its philosophic structuring. If that was so, it did not come too late; coming earlier it would not have been the same. Andrews served by waiting. It did not matter that his viewpoint was not as new in the 1930's as he felt it to be. For he had written not another installment of the new history but rather a *summa* for his age. Indeed, THE *summa.*

Chapter 8

NEW TIMES NEW HISTORIES

1. . . . ANOTHER GENERATION COMETH

But the *summa* was its own commentary on the fact that things historiographic were in a state of change. The lines of the great tetralogy stood forth in clear contrast against a background of new historical thinking. Appearing in the 1930's, *The Colonial Period of American History* had been fashioned largely out of the materials of an earlier age. The decades since 1898 had gone quickly by. A new generation was opening up "wider" vistas, proclaiming "deeper" understandings, discovering "sounder" truths, and declaring the inadequacies of the generation which it was ushering out. The wheel had, in fact, come full circle. During the 1930's, in the last decade of his life, Andrews had to undertake a defense of his system against the critique of the still newer history. It was reminiscent of the defense which George Bancroft had had to undertake a generation earlier, when the age of "scientific" history was beginning to bring to the past its own vistas, understandings, and truths, to say nothing of a declaration of the inadequacies of its predecessors. Neither history nor the history of history would have a stop; the writing finger, having writ, was moving on.

In what direction was it moving? For one thing, the axioms and attitudes of the older school were being revised. Lawrence Harper, for example, challenged Beer's view of the old colonial system, indicating that the colonies were far from being as unexploited as the notable student of Osgood had contended.[1] Samuel Morison removed the seventeenth-century Puritan from the pillory of disdain to which he had been consigned by the generation of Andrews, and saw the New Englander's intellectual achievement as a pronaos to the American mind of the nineteenth and twentieth centuries.[2] Carl Bridenbaugh threw up a counterpoise to that imperial viewpoint which had caught the fancy of the earlier school by suggesting that primary stress had to be laid on the continental American scene.[3] Indeed, the work of Bridenbaugh and of the younger generation was very much taken up with exploring anew that continental American scene.

It was more than reexploration that was under way during the 1920's and 1930's: it was also a discovery of new areas of interest. The publication of Jameson's brief volume on *The American Revolution Considered as a Social Movement* (1926) revealed a growing attention to the Revolution as an internal conflict, as one which had produced great changes in the structure of American society. This heightened interest in social history was further evidenced by the appearance, beginning in the late 'twenties, of the History of American Life Series, to which T. J. Wertenbaker, J. T. Adams, and E. B. Greene made notable contributions. The first works of Perry Miller signalized an increasing emphasis on intellectual currents in early America. That the historian as sociologist could add a new dimension to the colonial period was excellently displayed in Bridenbaugh's *Cities in the Wilderness* (1938). In this year appeared Curtis P. Nettels' *Roots of American Civilization,* a work which further proclaimed the advent of a newer history: Nettels not only saw the early American past in its many aspects but urged that the unifying element for the whole view would be found in class conflicts and in the determinism of economic forces. Nor was it insignificant, as a commentary on the rising school, that Nettels regarded history as "man's guide to action in the present and future."[4] The real question was whether he and his colleagues had not made man's action in the present his guide to the past. The lights of postwar and depression America were strongly reflected in their portraits of the early American scene.

Not only was the subject matter of history changing, however. As a matter of fact, the very principles which had constituted the historiographic ideal of the generation of Andrews were themselves being undermined. A growing doubt was being voiced about the ideal which Ranke had come to represent in America: a growing doubt that ultimate truth was attainable, that the essence of sound history was objectivity and nonpartisanship, that the historian could ever really present the past as it had actually occurred. Perhaps the Rankean ideal might do for a generation which had been schooled in the teachings of Comte, Darwin, and Spencer. But the generation which followed the First World War had come into an entirely different legacy. Theirs was a shaken optimism, a growing disbelief in absolutes, a certainty that the certainty of their predecessors had nowhere been justified. And if they agreed with some of the older historians that the lessons taught by the past might serve the needs of the present, the new historians differed radically as to the lessons which the past was teaching. Historical relativism was not exactly a new way of looking at man's experience; what *was* new, however, was the larger frame of circumstances which gave it validity and currency.

The relativists, led by Charles A. Beard and Carl Becker, opened an attack upon the "scientific" ideal, an attack fraught with significance for all fields of American historiography. They questioned, in essence, whether the historian could attain a real objectivity; they asserted that every historian was limited by the framework and controlling assumptions of his age. As they saw it, historical thinking was social thinking, the philosophy of one age concerning the ages which had preceded it. Itself part of a larger intellectual pattern, historiography was mutable and unenduring, constantly refashioned by the changing patterns of an ever changing present. Not that the relativists despaired in the face of these impediments to historical truth. On the contrary, they believed that their very awareness of the impediments would make them less likely to stumble. And they felt that their understanding of the variable nature of historical truth would make the study of the past a richer study and an instrument of greater social usefulness.[5] The issue between the Rankeans and the relativists did not, of course, lend itself to ready solution. Indeed, at the midpoint of the century, the presidential addresses of Conyers Read and Samuel Morison to the American Historical Association revealed that the issue was very much alive and substantially unresolved. To the argument of Read that the pattern of the past was imposed upon it by the climate and problems of the present,[6] Morison rejoined that he doubted the validity of a "frame of reference" approach to history, and that, for himself, he preferred to "stand firm on the oft-quoted sentence of Leopold von Ranke." [7]

It seemed to the reviewers of Andrews that he was not only standing firm on Ranke but standing still on other vital aspects of historiography. The disparity between his own system and that of the younger historians was all the more pronounced because it was not until the 'thirties, when the newer trends had become more clearly defined, that Andrews published his magnum opus. He found, as others had found before him, that two generations could not be spanned with the ideas of one. His reviewers put his four volumes to the scales and found them wanting. For all its virtues, many of them felt, *The Colonial Period of American History* seemed to belong to an earlier age. What Andrews had done, noted one reviewer, would have been new in 1904, not 1934; as it was, his work constituted "the last and perhaps the best of a series . . . rather than the first of a new historical deal." [8] If they mitigated the severity of their censure by indicating that Andrews had himself played no small role in making traditional the views which lay at the center of his major contribution,[9] his reviewers took him to task, and perhaps rightly so, for failing to acknowledge his indebtedness to the prior work of his contemporaries, Osgood, Beer, Cheyney, and Root.[10]

That Andrews had driven the thesis of the imperial vantage ground with such persistence tended, of course, to heighten the intensity of the criticism. Bridenbaugh, for example, urged that the imperial viewpoint afforded only one side of the picture, that it was just as significant to study "the colonial outlook on its own problems and towards England." [11] But even apart from this consideration, the consensus was that Andrews had presented an essentially incomplete portrait of the colonial scene. His history, said the men of the new school, was a history of institutions, of political and legal development, of governmental agencies, of patents and charters and land titles.[12] It touched lightly upon, or left completely untouched, the vast areas of economic, social, and cultural development within the American scene. Curtis Nettels, sensing what he thought might be an "aversion for economic factors," noted that Andrews had failed to consider "wages, prices, profits, creditor-debtor relationships, and the distribution of income and wealth." [13] What was more, observed Nettels, even within his delimited area Andrews had not surveyed all the relevant problems. Thus, in analyzing English colonial policy, Andrews had failed to consider such questions as the disposal of land in America, immigration into the colonies, currency regulations, the protection of Britain's overseas investments, and a host of others.[14] Samuel Morison declared that "on the social history of these colonies, Professor Andrews is not so happy . . . it would have been better to have left out social history altogether, rather than bring it in as an afterthought to the institutional." [15] It was Bridenbaugh, however, who best summarized it for his generation:

> There are questions which Professor Andrews does not answer. We must know more of social composition, of racial intermixtures, of the actual processes of gaining a living, of folkways, of religious and cultural tendencies. And we need to know more of individuals limned against their backgrounds. Most of all an examination of the relative effect of the tug of the frontier and the restraining force of an ever-increasing overseas influence on the colonists is called for. Like the empire, like colonial political institutions, colonial economic and social life was dynamic. Nor was the colonial mind static.[16]

But an age of depression might extend even further its list of grievances against an older historiography. It might venture, in the light of its own limited social thinking, a disapproval of what it presumed to be the limited social thinking of the earlier age. In the new light, the history of Andrews would be found to be "animated by a conservative spirit." [17] It would be deemed no less true that his "sympathies are plainly with the ruling class, whatever it happens to be."[18] To some members of the new school, and they constituted no more than a minority, it was regrettable that Andrews had not entered into the class conflicts of the colonial period, that he had not adequately described the workings of the English capitalist economy, and that he had not clearly seen the American Revolution as the inevitable outcome of inner tensions and contradictions within an oppressive mercantilist system.[19]

The state of Ranke was withering away. It mattered little that a few of the new historians were far more critical of their predecessors than the rest; what really mattered was that all of the new historians were, at the very least, critical. They were looking at the contribution of Andrews in a retrospective light; they were putting a time-stamp and date-seal upon it; they were beginning to tie it up in a bundle for placement in the archives of historiography. They respected his "perennial search for completeness and accuracy in his facts and for objectivity in his interpretation."[20] But they knew that the ideal under which he had labored so long, so patiently, and so arduously was itself becoming history. The ideal of Ranke they had come to recognize as unattainable. "Never can we recover all of the facts, nor can we divest ourselves as historians of the preconceptions that are part and parcel of us as people. No account can tell us of the past *wie es eigentlich gewesen.*"[21] Andrews was universally praised, true enough, but it was praise for having put the finishing touches to the colonial portrait which his great contemporaries, Osgood and Beer, had begun some thirty years before. He was hailed for having brought his age to a close, rather than for having opened up a new one.

Privately and publicly, Andrews undertook to respond to the charges that had been leveled against him. If what he said was the answer of an individual to his critics, it was not any less the answer of one age of historiography to its successor. The most recurrent of the adverse comments had been that Andrews had written narrow history, that he had largely omitted the social and economic aspects of colonial development, and that he had written a history of politics and of institutions. To this he replied that institutional history was a necessary prerequisite to all aspects of history: it afforded the structural outline within which other forms could be correctly understood. "The economic, social, and cultural aspects of a people's life," contended Andrews, "cannot be given their proper place until the essential features of their political institutions—the framework of constituted authority—are made unmistakably clear." [22] The question of social history troubled him sorely. Had he been able to continue his *Colonial Period of American History,* Andrews would have had to treat of the changing pattern of American colonial life during the eighteenth century. To some degree, he confused the problem. Seeking a formula with which he could proceed to the next volume of his history, and undertaking too an answer to those who had found the preceding volumes limited in scope, Andrews tended to link social history to "social science"; and by proving the case against the scientific possibilities of social studies, he seems to have concluded that the case against social history had also been proven.[23] As for that history of the "common man" which he had failed to write, he felt it would tend to be a very barren history, if for no other reason than the fact that the materials for such a history were slight and fragmentary.[24] What was more, he was not exactly sure what the term "common man" was designed to mean.[25] For the larger part, however, he argued that social currents could not be understood without first understanding institutional and political currents.[26] "History," said Andrews, "ought to be woven of many factors and the moment you separate one of the factors and deal with it by itself you destroy the unity of the whole." [27]

This answer was of course equally applicable to the charge that he had been deficient on the side of economic history. Here Andrews undertook to defend himself by questioning the view, one increasingly popular during the 1930's, that history was the product of materialistic determinants and of class conflicts. Such a view he categorically rejected. It impressed him as a "superficial manipulation of fact and logic in the interest of a preconceived theory." [28] Human affairs could not be interpreted in terms of material things alone. To interpret them that way was to reduce them to absurdity. Nor could history be reduced to a single cause or understood in the light of anything less than a whole complex of causes acting together.[29] For that reason, the efforts of Louis Hacker impressed him as highly unacceptable; for that reason too, he questioned the value of the contribution of Charles Beard.[30]

There was, as Andrews himself recognized, an element of negativism,[31] indeed of tu quoquery, in the way he met the challenge of the 'thirties. Casting doubt upon the validity of a self-contained social history was no more than a counterblast to the doubt that had been cast upon fairly self-contained institutional and political history. Nor was the question of his failure to give fuller consideration to economic factors answered any more satisfactorily by Andrews. He tended, as John Krout justly observed, to link economic history with economic determinism and then to proceed blithely to obliterate the determinists.[32] Perhaps indeed there was no really satisfactory answer that the historian of one age could make to the charges of another; and perhaps Andrews did as well, by way of answering, as he might have. The sum of the critique advanced against Andrews by the new school was, as Bridenbaugh and Nettels both observed, that he had written something less than a Colonial Period of American History.[33] To this he answered in private correspondence what he doubtless should have said in a public preface. "I never promised to write a complete history of the colonies and I do not want to be understood as ever having had that in mind. All that I have ever pretended to do was to make a contribution to the elucidation of what our colonial history is all about and to set some people straight in regard to the point of view that ought to be taken." [34] In a way, this represented something of a retreat from what he had aspired to; and the very tangible difference between his reach and his grasp was the result of spending in a later age the intellectual legacy of the earlier one.

Andrews never squarely faced either the problem of historical relativism or its meaning for the scientific ideal which he had always pursued. He made no extensive attempt to explore the view that the historian, whether or not he could free himself from personal bias and predilection, was at best an imperfect instrument in attaining truth, blunted as he was by the social and economic pressures of his age. It was, perhaps, too late for the contemporary of Osgood and Beer and the colleague of George Burton Adams to be a relativist. He never spoke of Croce, and when Beard and Becker were translating the ideas of the Italian philosopher into a pragmatic American philosophy during the 'thirties, Andrews was very definitely disturbed about it.[35] The problem touched him personally when some of his reviewers suggested that his magnum opus was the product of a conservative frame of mind and that his "sympathies are plainly with the ruling class." To these charges he issued a sharp rebuttal, one in which, it ought be understood, was involved the very essence of his ideal, the very touchstone of his calling. His reply to the animadversions of Louis Hacker was something of a minor classic:

> I think that his characterization of my personal attitude should have been deleted. I am, I believe, entirely devoid of class-consciousness, and Mr. Hacker's opinion to the contrary is a curious commentary from one who is class-conscious to the core. As a historian I am neither conservative, liberal nor radical, but possessed of sufficient flexibility of mind to go wherever the evidence leads and to accept the truth where I find it. Can Mr. Hacker say the same of himself?[36]

The criticism that a conservative spirit dominated his work brought forth a similar reply: that he had "reached the conclusions that had to be reached" in the light of the evidence he had used.[37] To his friend Konkle he reiterated, in the final months of his life, the precepts which constituted the core of the scientific ideal. His own contribution, Andrews felt, had been governed "by a strongly grounded desire to know the truth of a matter without leaning one way or another." He had undertaken to plead no cause, to uphold no thesis. That history was a form of interpretation he agreed readily enough, but he insisted even more that it "should be devoid of prejudice, prepossessions, and bias of any kind." [38] Here, in effect, was the reaffirmation of a creed to which he had held for more than half a century, for the entire length, indeed, of his professional career. Nor did he, in this vital issue, stand alone. Many of the gild took up a defense of the Rankean ideal. And if Andrews did not openly join the controversy, it was eminently clear where he stood on the pronouncements that were being made by the historical relativists. Against their belief that the historian was merely performing an act of faith, he pitted his own belief that a historian was at every turn bound to act faithfully.

2. THE HISTORIAN AS SOCIAL THINKER

But was not the history of Andrews, whatever else he may have deemed it, itself an act of faith? Did it not reflect the predilections of its author and the outlook of his times? Something of an answer to these questions could be found in those very explanations which Andrews had offered about his own historiography. He claimed to be "possessed of sufficient flexibility of mind to go wherever the evidence leads." [39] But the doubt was not merely about his flexibility of mind, it was also about his evidence. Where, indeed, would evidence found in the British archives tend to lead? Might it not at once define his sympathies as well as the scope and subject matter of his history? If his work was conservative in outlook, he wrote, it was "an entirely unconscious attitude and one that was taken as the result of the evidence which I used in connection with my subject." [40] That the attitude was unconscious did not make it any the less an attitude. There was, moreover, in this sentiment of Andrews' a bit of Fustel de Coulanges, a bit of that rather questionable belief that the past, in all its documentary regalia, spoke through the voice of the historian. Could it have been that the opposite was more nearly true? To Konkle, Andrews wrote that "I have never believed it was necessary to plead a cause in writing history. All I have wanted was to find out what history is all about and to interpret it in my own way." [41] But could not the act of interpreting it *in his own way* be tantamount to pleading a cause? Particularly revealing was his statement, in the last year of his life, that "I have never tried to analyze the exact state of my own mind and do not care to do so now." [42] An analysis might have disclosed that, despite his ideal, elements of personal inclination had entered his writing. It might further have disclosed that the personal inclination had, to no small degree, been governed by the problems and currents of his times. It might have disclosed, finally, that in a very distinct way, Andrews, no less than the Bancroft who preceded him and the Beard who followed, was pleading a cause in history and was bound, not so much to truth eternal, but to truth for his epoch.

That is not to say that the contribution of a major historian can be neatly fitted into the social age in which he belonged. Nor is it to suggest that the historian is little more than a puppet whose strings are pulled by the conventions of his times. At most, an age sets up the larger potential for the writer of history. His own achievement, self-willed and highly personal, is one of reducing to actuality what the age has offered as a potential.

The major principles of Andrews' system of historiography flowed from the intellectual and historical currents of late nineteenth-century America. The generation of historians that followed Appomattox came into a various legacy. It was a legacy wherein the precepts of Ranke had been confirmed and amplified by the implications of Positivism and Darwinism, and the whole translated into a system consonant with the needs and problems of an expanding American society. That the potpourri of philosophic and historical elements constituted a uniform or stable compound can hardly be suggested. For all that, within the milieu of late nineteenth-century American society, some ideas tended to dominate. The universal creed was science. It was an age which worshipped the machine and the laboratory. The findings of Darwin linked to the postulates of Comte offered the historian much to think about. Society could be studied in the same way as the natural sciences. The primary need was to collect facts and statistics, in a scientific manner, and let the facts speak for themselves. The facts should be concerned with man in the mass rather than individual man. By an exact and impartial reporting of the facts, one could discover the inner lines of historical development. There could be no doubt, and Herbert Spencer underlined this, that social statics would speak what the dynamics of nature had spoken: that human society was an evolving organism, and that the "laws" and "trends" governing that society pointed in a direction that went upward and onward. Indeed, progress no longer had to be proven; it was a law of nature and of science; it was inevitable. What more comforting answer could there be for a nation seeking comfort? Caught in the throes of an expanding industrial economy and facing the problems of an increasingly urban culture, America listened eagerly to the social Darwinists and to the Comteans, the prophets of optimism, the postulators of a science of man—to John Fiske, Lewis Henry Morgan, John Wesley Powell, and their numerous adherents.[43]

The principles with which Andrews recreated an earlier age were those that had been fashioned by his own. It was not at all fortuitous that his structure of history was built to a pattern of progress and that, whatever his occasional misgivings, he retained his belief in the "forward movement" of Western society to the very end of his days.[44] Such a belief derived, though hardly exclusively, from the translation of the precepts of Darwin into a language that had a wide social currency.[45] The implications for the gild of American historians of what the great English naturalist had postulated went beyond the notion of progress, however. The new history, wrote one of its most outstanding leaders, A. B. Hart, in 1907,

> has consciously or unconsciously learned from Charles Darwin, who is the great historical master of our age in that he has taught us how, in the world of mind as in the material universe, there is steady progression from one condition to another; for human institutions also follow a law of natural selection, by the survival of those which are best adapted to their surroundings.[46]

If Andrews never arrived at a law of natural selection, he went a goodly distance down that much-traveled Darwinian road: with his generation, he saw human experience in lines of waxing and waning institutions, of organic evolution and growth, of the genesis and maturation of historical tendencies and processes.[47] There was nothing fortuitous, again, about the foremost principle of the system of Andrews: that the historian was a scientist, a highly trained collector of facts, an impartial interpreter of the past, a seeker after ultimate truth.[48] Yet if his principles were part not merely of the history he wrote but also of the history he lived, there were important questions to be asked. What would become of these principles when it grew clear that the "scientific ideal" had major imperfections, that the facts had not really spoken for themselves, that they had been selected and ordered, and that they had been interpreted in a way that was, in many respects, meaningful for one age alone? What would become of them when history, characterized less by international expositions of peaceful arts and more by international exhibitions of nuclear warfare, could no longer be seen as a progressive evolution toward an ever higher plane?

If the principles governing his view of the past were largely the products of an evolving phase of the present, no less so were the actual contents of his history. Again, the dominant themes of his work were nowhere unique to him. Andrews shared with his contemporaries that imperial viewpoint toward the American colonial period which constituted the outstanding feature of his contribution. With them he believed that the time had come for looking at the British side of things as well as the American. Where the American past had hitherto been treated arbitrarily, it seemed to Andrews and his compeers, it now had to be submitted to arbitration. Where American historians had hitherto stood on the colonial shores proclaiming the justice of independence, they now had to revisit the shores of the mother country to understand the justice of interdependence.

The change of outlook derived from the change in Anglo-American relations after the Civil War. The colonial status of

America had been terminated neither by the war for independence nor the war of 1812; and the treatment accorded Charles Francis Adams, the American ambassador at the Court of St. James', during the Civil War, revealed that the mother country expected the collapse of the century-old effort at forging an American union. With the American conflict clearly resolved, the tensions between Old and New England could come to an end, and the Treaty of Washington (1871) indicated nothing so much as a recognition by Britain of the success of the American experiment and a willingness to deal with the federal republic as an equal.[49] What was at best a state of receding animosity between the two powers up to 1898 became during that year a state of distinct friendship. Forced by new conditions in world politics to reconsider her policy of isolation, Britain was casting about for allies and connections. America seemed to be a likely associate. And America took more than passing interest in suggestions for association when, as a result of the Spanish war and her new career in imperialism, she found herself facing a European hostility broken only by British sympathy for both her war and her imperialism. It was a reciprocal sympathy that America extended to Britain when the latter became involved, in 1899, in a war with the Boers.[50] Mutual understanding grew into cooperation in all major areas of international tension. If understanding did not produce the formal alliance that London had hoped for, the great number of diplomatic agreements between the United States and Great Britain during the years after 1898 produced a condition of affinity such as both states had never before enjoyed. By 1914, on the eve of the Great War, Anglo-American friendship was a factor to reckon with in the world of diplomacy.[51]

It was also a factor that was being reflected in the Anglo-American world of opinion and letters. After the Civil War, there began to emerge on both sides of the Atlantic a Pan-Anglian state of mind, one which embraced a various and nebulous set of beliefs. Because of the strains and stresses of British circumstances, the Pan-Anglian outlook was adopted with particular warmth by British educators, lawyers, writers of novels, and writers of history. Its basic tenets were that the British or Anglo-Saxon "race" was a unified one, that British institutions had been spread throughout the world by means of colonization, and that, whatever differences might temporarily arise between two branches of the "race," it was ultimately true that "blood is thicker than water." [52] Little Englanders and Greater Britons alike envisoned the development of an Anglo-Saxon federation, one that would contain all independent British colonies, including the United States. In his notion of a *Greater Britain* (1868), Charles Dilke saw "the American Republic as an amplifier for England's voice to the world, offering to the English race 'the moral dictatorship of the globe, by ruling mankind through Saxon institutions and the English tongue.' " [53] Edward Freeman, whose ideas were being so widely disseminated at the Johns Hopkins University,[54] lectured to Americans during the 1880's about their "everlasting ties of blood and speech" with the British.[55] Frequently related to the concept of an Anglo-Saxon race which had spread its kin and its institutions all over the world was the concept that the welfare of the world depended on a union of the English-speaking peoples. Conan Doyle dedicated his *White Company* (1890) "To the Hope of the Future, the Reunion of the English-speaking Races." [56] Mandell Creighton, historian and Bishop of London, felt certain that the future of the world rested on "the existence of the Anglo-Saxon civilization on a religious basis." [57] The idea of Anglo-American unity was nowhere more ardently espoused than among British statesmen. To them it was apparent that America was their mighty fortress, that the New World had to be called into friendship to help the British redress the balance of the Old. Joseph Chamberlain, the Earl of Rosebery, Sir Cecil Spring-Rice, and Lord Cromer, to cite but a few, sounded many variations on the theme that the British nation would not hesitate joining with America "in defence of the ideals of the Anglo-Saxon race—of humanity, justice, freedom, and equality of opportunity." [58]

American opinion and letters after the Civil War also began to mirror the growing diplomatic cordiality between Washington and London. That sentiments of fraternity were hardly as intense or widespread among the Americans as they were among the British was due not only to the long-standing tradition of isolation in the United States but also to the far less pressing needs of American foreign policy. Views were nonetheless changing, a fact which was evident from the writings of the younger American historians: if pro-British feeling was hardly universal among them, it was certainly discernible and growing. John Fiske cast his philosophic eye over the past and linked it prophetically to the future: with its settlements in America, the English race had begun a work which would continue until it had spread English language, political habits, and traditions over most of the world. That race would retain the commercial and naval supremacy which it had started to win with its colonization of Virginia and Massachusetts.[59] As for the destiny of America and Britain, it appeared certain to Fiske that these "two great branches of the English race have the common mission of establishing throughout the larger part of the earth a higher civilization and more permanent political order than any that has gone before." [60]

If Alfred Thayer Mahan used the history of sea power rather than the history of Anglo-Saxon evolution to teach lessons to the present, his lessons were not very different from Fiske's. He believed that a "cordial understanding" with Great Britain was "one of the first of our external interests." He argued for a policy of "close sympathy" between America and Britain, feeling that "the best hope of the world is in the union of the branches of that race to which she and we belong." [61] Moses Coit Tyler's *Literary History of the American Revolution* (1897) further revealed that if the story of the past was being rewritten, the events of the present were playing a considerable part in the rewriting. Tyler lamented "the tragedy and the pathos of the period between 1763 and 1783, as the birth time of a most bitter race feud . . . between the two great branches of a race which, at this moment, holds an historic position in the world and an historic opportunity, not only the most extensive and the most splendid, but the most benignant, that was ever attained by any similar group of human beings upon this planet." [62] The feud, Tyler urged, ought to be ended. Together, Britain and America could lead "the whole human race upward to all the higher planes of culture and happiness." [63] The spirit of his history, in this light, he deemed to be peaceful rather than polemical, and he hoped that his work would yield "one practical consequence . . . namely, the promotion of a better understanding, of a deeper respect, of a kindlier mood, on both sides of the ocean, among the descendants of those determined men who so bitterly differed in opinion, so fiercely fought, and, in their anger, so widely parted company a century and a quarter ago." [64] From what Tyler was saying it could be surmised that history might involve something more than past politics. It might, conceivably, involve present politics as well.

And the course of present politics, at the end of the nineteenth century and at the beginning of the twentieth, saw America's emergence as a world power and a growth of friendship with Britain. Would the gild of historians really be an impartial supreme court on the past or would it, to no small degree, actually follow the election returns? Had it been merely fortuitous that the new age of American colonial history was formally opened by Osgood and Andrews the very year (1898) which saw America's entrance upon the stage of world affairs and Britain's warm applause for that entrance? Historians who had adopted the imperial viewpoint were not at all unaware that conditions which were altering the outlook of American diplomacy were also altering the outlook of American historiography. W. T. Root found that America's new imperialistic career, her growing concern with colonies, commerce, sea power, and international relations, had been reflected in changing attitudes toward Britain's position in the old colonial system.[65] "The American adventure in imperialism," observed A. M. Schlesinger, "should enable Americans of the present generation to view with sympathy the British experiment of the eighteenth century." [66]

Sympathy, growing out of the rapprochement of the present,

would clear up the separation of the past. In his volume on *The American Revolution* (1905), Van Tyne revealed how much the Pan-Anglian ideas of Charles Dilke had become part of the intellectual apparatus of the new colonial history. After the war for American independence, wrote Van Tyne, Great Britain

> was still to be the mother of nations, and the English race was not weakened though the empire was broken. In political, social, and intellectual spirit England and America continued to be much the same. English notions of private and public law still persisted in independent America. The large influence which the Anglo-Saxon race had long had upon the world's destiny was not left with either America or England alone, but with them both. America only continued England's "manifest destiny" in America, pushing her language, modes of political and intellectual activity, and her social customs, westward and southward—driving back Latin civilization in the same resistless way as before the Revolution.[67]

In *The British Empire and the United States* (1914), William Archibald Dunning, a colleague of Osgood's at Columbia University, surveyed the century of peace in Anglo-American relations that had just ended. America and Britain, said Dunning, shared "an intimate like-mindedness," one that had been fashioned out of similar conceptions of democracy, liberty, and law.[68] His review of a century of their history had shown, he concluded, that the English-speaking peoples sensed "that some special fiat of God and nature enjoins enduring peace among those whose blood or language or institutions or traditions, or all together, go back historically to the snug little island of Britain." [69]

In trying to understand how the structure of politics might shape the structure of American colonial historiography there is perhaps no contribution more relevant to that of Andrews, and indeed to the imperial viewpoint as a whole, than that of George Louis Beer. It was Beer who was associated with Andrews in pleading the cause of a sympathetic understanding of British colonial policy; it was Beer, moreover, whom Andrews hailed as the scientific historian incarnate. If differences with Britain over freedom of the seas were, during the first years of the Great War, temporarily disaffecting some segments of

American public opinion, the opinion of the historian of the old colonial system suffered no such disaffection. Summarizing views he had been formulating for some time, Beer suggested, in *The English-Speaking Peoples* (1917), that it was time to consider seriously the question of a reunion of Britain and America.[70] If he doubted the wisdom of forcing the pace of such a reunion, he did not in the least doubt that it would be, whenever it came, a most inspiring and laudable "consummation." Surveying the course of "historical evolution," Beer felt certain that the only way in which the "progress" of law and justice was achieved was "by the integration of ever larger and larger political aggregates." [71] There was, in this regard, much that linked America to Britain: their cultural solidarity, their economic interdependence, the common ideals of their foreign policies. Of all the great powers, said Beer, they were the ones least spurred by military visions or the hope of gaining territory. [72] Scanning the past, he found the evolution of the British Empire, of the United States, and of English civilization throughout the world to have been "the most momentous political development of the last three centuries." [73] Scanning the future, he saw with equal clarity that an alliance of the United States and the British Commonwealth would "secure the general peace" of the world to come and would "well-nigh guarantee the development of the world along progressively democratic lines." [74] From what Beer was saying it was apparent that, no matter how much a "scientific" ideal might be invoked, history as it actually *was* had much to do with history as it actually *is*. From what he was saying it was also apparent that a plea for seeing the past in its own light might really be a plea for turning on in the twentieth century a light of affinity that had been extinguished in the eighteenth. Certainly, his own castigation of American policy against Britain in the early 1800's as "provincial" and due to "myopic absorption . . . in its own development " [75] could hardly be called in the best tradition of historical-mindedness or of the "scientific" ideal. It could hardly be called anything, in fact, but reducing the past to the Procrustean bed of a current Pan-Anglian outlook.

The historiography of Andrews was governed to no lesser

degree by the immediate problems of America's role in world affairs. With Beer, indeed, he went farther than most of his colleagues in sympathy toward British causes, whether the causes involved eighteenth-century colonial Americans seeking to break an empire apart or twentieth-century colonizing Germans seeking to build one up. The increasingly favorable disposition of his age toward Britain's role in history was enhanced, in the case of Andrews, by factors of a personal nature. If there was any country other than his own to which he felt bound by ties of affection, it was England. Andrews' father had been a minister in the Catholic Apostolic Church and had, in this connection, made several trips to England, where the church had originated and where it possessed its greatest membership.[76] Many of the friendships which his father had made were taken up by the young historian during his very first visit to England, in 1892.[77] Beginning this very year, indeed, Andrews came to know personally an evergrowing number of English historians, among whom were included Maitland, Seebohm, T. F. Tout, H. A. L. Fisher, A. P. Newton, and Hubert Hall. His own work, devoted as it was to canvassing the British archives, made recurrent visits to England an integral part of his scholastic regimen. The eight or ten trips which he made in the course of his life, the first in 1892 and the last in 1926, brought Andrews many close friendships and made England a second homeland for him.

For such an historian of Anglo-American relations, the renewed friendship between America and Britain carried a message. It was a message most dramatically conveyed by the physical reunion of the kindred nations on the battlefields of France in 1917 and 1918. At once, it seemed to Andrews, the outlines of the past and the tendency of the future had been clarified. The present was joining together the two English-speaking peoples who had for a moment in history been torn asunder:

> Whatever may have been the controversies in the past between the two great branches of the Anglo-Saxon race, both before and since the shock of revolution broke the ties of colonial relationship, the

events of the World War have banished without likelihood of return the bitterness engendered thereby and have aroused to an extent never before known a feeling of respect, charity, and good will. The two nations have awakened to a consciousness of common kinship and common ideals and to a realization of the fact that despite differences of opinion, habit and temperament—the inevitable consequences of environment and historical circumstances—they are fundamentally alike in their views of political liberty and their standards of social justice, for which each has in its own way struggled in the past. Great Britain and the United States stand as sponsors for a progressive and liberal civilization, not as unwilling allies but as two great powers actuated by principles and traditions derived from a common source and united to defend common ideals in life and government.[78]

Here was another voice in the Pan-Anglian chorus that included Dilke, Freeman, Fiske, Tyler, Van Tyne, and Beer. Talking as a protagonist of Anglo-American friendship in the present, Andrews was also talking as an interpreter of the failure of that friendship in the past. Inevitably his plea for moderation and judiciousness in Anglo-American relations became linked to his views of the earlier period when, as he saw it, the conduct of those relations had been in the hands of the immoderate and the injudicious. Inevitably too the past which Andrews was writing up began to reflect his own sense of the larger tendency of the present.

This could be seen from the fact that, starting with the years of the Great War, Andrews began to argue the spirit and implications of the imperial viewpoint to a greater extent than most of his colleagues. For one thing, he came to see the colonial world of the seventeenth century as one which was almost entirely English and essentially undemocratic; the world of little democracy and less Americanism which emerged from the pages of his magnum opus was a very different one indeed from that which had been portrayed in his earlier writings. In an extensive correspondence with Andrews during the 1930's, Marcus Jernegan was to delight in setting the later Andrews against the earlier one and in asking an explanation for the contradictory views.[79] What had been, moreover, at most an understanding attitude toward British policy in his *Colonial Self-Government* (1904), grew more sympathetic in his *Colonial Period* (1912), and reached the point of espousal rather than appraisal in his *Fathers of New England* (1919). He was settling more and more upon the conviction that the old colonial system had not worked to the disadvantage of the colonists, that its purposes were equitable, and that, indeed, agencies such as the vice-admiralty courts were more instruments of benevolence than of oppression. Toward the Puritans, and particularly insofar as their objections to English commercial policies were concerned, Andrews was expressing constantly stronger feelings, feelings which bordered on outright hostility.[80] Significantly too, his understanding of the Revolution began to change. If he had been fully decided before that the break between the mother country and the colonies was the product of long accumulating and irrepressible forces, he now began to ruminate that "a little more yielding, a little more of the spirit of friendship and compromise on both sides, would have calmed the troubled waters and stilled the storm that was brewing." [81] What is more, in the views that he was formulating during and after the First World War, Andrews was coming to see the Revolution as a clash between extremists on both sides: it was a view which caused him to pronounce not a little antipathy toward the "muscular radicals" in America, those whom he saw as men of violence, breakers of law, destroyers of property, subverters of government.[82] His sentiments were running close to those of a growing and vocal group of historians and political leaders on both sides of the Anglo-American world, a group which included Jan Smuts, George Louis Beer, and H. E. Egerton, and which had come to see the Revolution as an altogether regrettable occurrence.[83]

But no matter what the deviations of the past, it was clear what ought be the directions of the present. That present, as Andrews saw it taking shape, was one in which the progress of the world depended to no small degree upon the friendship of the United States and Great Britain. Here indeed was a basis for understanding the past. In an address on "Raleigh's

Place in American Colonization," delivered during the war, Andrews considered the ultimate significance of the adventurous Elizabethan to be this, that he stood "as the representative of a great union, the union of the English-speaking peoples." [84] Raleigh's effort foreshadowed, to Andrews' way of thinking, what had at last come into existence: "an Anglo-American fraternity, committed to the maintenance of political liberty, high standards of social justice, and a permanent peace." [85] This construction of the role of the United States and Great Britain in world history he reiterated in 1919, when he asserted that "these two peoples working in harmony [are] trustees for the civilization not only of the Old World but also of the New." [86] It was imperative, in order to effect "a harmonious rapprochement between the two countries," to remove the obstacle of misunderstanding about that earlier conflict which had separated the American branch of the English-speaking peoples from the European. To this task Andrews addressed himself in his most important single volume, *The Colonial Background of the American Revolution* (1924), where he explored both the current meaning of the past and the past meaning of the current. He undertook to rebuke the patriots and the filiopietists, those whom he accused of using history "to keep alive the ancient grudge against Great Britain." [87] But if his volume had any larger significance it was that Andrews was using history to kill off "the ancient grudge against Great Britain" once and for all.

Was he not himself pleading a cause? Indeed he was. He was arguing that an erroneous view of the past must not be permitted "to destroy the spiritual agreement of the two greatest democratic nations on earth," and that hereafter "both must work together, not in a spirit of mistrust or jealousy, but as brothers and comrades joined in a common service, the political and social good of all the world." [88] If the historiography of Andrews carried any message for the times, the message was that it was too late in history to be merely a patriot, too late to be merely a Whig. That imperial view of the American colonial period which had grown out of America's new diplomatic standing at the end of the nineteenth century had been confirmed and enhanced by the First World War. For this reason, Andrews attacked those who opposed America's entrance into the League of Nations, declaring that "the tendency of the time is toward a closer cooperation among the nations." [89] For this reason, too, he reprimanded those who kept up the ancient American animus against Great Britain, with whom, he felt, history had clearly prescribed "a closer cooperation." Little wonder that the Hearst press read clearly the thinly disguised message of Andrews' *Colonial Background* and denounced the historian for his "poisonous propaganda" and for working "to the end that our great republic may become seduced into an Anglo-American coalition for English-speaking domination of the world under British imperialistic leadership." [90] It matters little whether the propaganda of the Hearst columnist was any the less "poisonous" or whether his own uses of the past were not the more questionable. What is noteworthy, however, is that in attacking the "scientific" validity of the history which Andrews was writing, he was unwittingly touching upon a larger truth: that the techniques of historical science might be used to achieve a variety of current purposes, even indeed a variety of utterly conflicting purposes. It will hardly be ventured, of course, that Andrews was consciously molding the past to serve more immediate needs. Yet it can hardly be denied that the present and the past had become so strongly interconnected in his mind that the world about him began to impinge upon the earlier world of which he was writing. If Andrews was finding a message in history for present politics, it was because he also was finding a message for past politics in the present. In this sense, his *Colonial Background* as well as the many addresses he delivered during these wartime and postwar years were indeed political tracts for the times, history given tone and shape by the circumstances of the present, history written as an act of faith, history with a lesson.

The lesson Andrews was teaching could not but lose its vitality and meaning with the passage of time. And time was passing. A newer history had arisen, with different lessons to teach and different acts of faith to perform. By the 1930's the American nation was preoccupied with staggering domestic problems of an economic and social nature. It had turned its back on international involvements, convinced that this was the way to avoid giddy minds and foreign quarrels. Americans were not very much interested in befriending Britain in the present and even less so in understanding why they had unfortunately become enemies in the past. For all that, Andrews continued to inveigh against the "writers of the older generation," against those whose antagonism and criticism prevented their understanding the nature of England's influence on colonial affairs or their fathoming the depths of her colonial policy.[91] It had been a fitting purpose for his contribution a decade or two earlier. But as it was, the purpose had lost its timeliness. More than that, he was continuing to wave the flag of heterodoxy into an age when what he was saying had already become orthodox. By the 1930's one could not help feeling that Andrews was something of a Don Quixote fighting windmills, challenging enemies long since vanquished, fighting battles long since won.

He continued the fight until the end of his professional career, even though the course of history had reduced the battles to skirmishes. By the early 'thirties, the issue that Andrews had to face was no longer the cosmic one of defining America's role in international affairs, and particularly her relations with England, but rather the local one of celebrating the tercentenaries of the New England colonies. The first issue had gushed from the mainstream of the present; the second trickled from the backwaters of the past. For all that, Andrews went on teaching the lessons of history. If the time had passed for him to help usher in the Anglo-American friendship of the future, it was not too late to continue ushering out the Anglo-American enmity of the past. It is not at all difficult to understand why he would have little to do with either the patriotism or the provincialism attending the tercentenary celebrations, particularly that of his native Connecticut. His state's foremost historian, Andrews served as chairman of the Committee on

Historical Publications of the Connecticut Tercentenary Commission and continued to help in an advisory capacity even after resigning from the chairmanship. He contributed several pamphlets on the early history of the Connecticut colony. It was inevitable that the sanctifying spirit of the Commission and the iconoclastic spirit of Andrews should come into conflict. The Commission was frankly distressed by the introduction that he had written for the Fundamental Orders, an introduction which, according to Albert C. Bates, secretary of the Committee on Historical Publications, was "a little too critical of things considered in Connecticut necessary in order to give a little halo to the Fundamental Orders." [92] The introduction was withdrawn, and the historiography which hailed the Puritans and that which hailed Britannia went their separate ways. "More sheer nonsense," declared Andrews, "has been and is to be talked during the spread of this epidemic of 'celebrationitis' than is good for the historian's digestion. I cannot get up and talk that way." [93] The way he *could* talk was evident in his magnum opus, which represented something of Andrews' answer to the tercentenarians. In the chapters on New England he undertook to put in their historical place, at least so far as he saw it, both the Puritans and the documents of which their descendants were making so much. The last decade of his life was thus linked to the first, for at the very outset of his professional career he had enlisted in the ranks of an anti-patriotic and anti-provincial historiography. Indeed, the fight against the Whig interpretation of the colonial period constituted the central message of his contribution.

If he had not pleaded his cause as volubly as the Bancroft who preceded him or the Beard who followed, it did not mean that he had had no cause or had done no pleading. The historical significance of the scientific ideal which he pursued was after all precisely this, that the partiality it cast out in the preface had long since come back by the time of the index. The scientific ideal opened no broader avenue to the truth of the past than the ideal which had dominated a prior age or that which was to dominate a subsequent one. Primary sources were nothing more than inanimate commodities: they needed selecting, ordering, interpreting. And impartial interpretation could at best be a goal, not a certitude. History was not merely a two-way relation between the historian and the past. The third and inescapable component was the historian's own world. It impinged upon the past at every turn, subtly, almost unconsciously. It was an omnipresent voice, speaking a message of self-assertive American patriotism in one age, contending for a materialistic view of American development in another, and urging the need for Anglo-American friendship in still a third.

CONCLUSION

The course of historiography is no less vital and changing than the course of history itself. Every age wishes to know the truth about itself and its forebears. And every age seeks not merely to solve its problems but also to find in the past something of a key to their solution. But truth is a various commodity, and what is found in the past is largely dependent on who does the finding. To that degree, the history of history is a mirror both to the historian and to the age in which he belongs. In the larger sense, writing about the past is merely one facet of the intellectual currents of an age; and, in that sense, it is no less shaped and patterned by the age than any other element of contemporary social thinking. Inevitably, the story of the past will carry the message of the present. Inevitably, it will illuminate the past with its own light. In that respect, it will, for all its good intent, play tricks upon the dead. In that respect, too, despite its protestations, it will carry the imprint of Mr. Everyman upon its pages.

But this is merely to suggest a potential for historiographic development and not actually to define it. The definition itself becomes a matter of modifying the governance of the potential. For one thing, the lines that flow from one age into the next are frequently blurred and unclear; an age of historiography is no more distinct and separate than an age of history. Moreover, within any age the lines of historiographic development may vary or conflict, no less than the broader lines of historical development which they reflect. Above all, the role of the individual historian must be reckoned with. The ultimate repository of any corporate ideal is after all within the individual.

And intellectual history is, in the final analysis, the composite of the history of intellects.

It is only in the light of these understandings that the contribution of Charles McLean Andrews can be assayed. The system of historiography which he fashioned was the product not only of a man but of a man working within the framework of his times. If he shared the attainments of the school in which he belonged, he also shared its limitations. That ideal of science which he and his colleagues pursued carried the date-stamp of the late nineteenth century. It conjured up a man of impartiality and objectivity, a seeker after ultimate and unalterable truth. Andrews never seriously questioned the validity of the ideal, nor did he ever doubt his own ability to fulfill it. He rehabilitated the Stuarts and reprimanded the Puritans with an almost scientific certainty that the facts called for a rehabilitation of the one and a reprimand of the other. He never ventured, as did some of his contemporaries, to inquire whether "scientific" facts really spoke for themselves, whether historic "truth" could not be heard in various and sometimes contradictory voices, whether the trappings of Rankean "objectivity" might not conceivably adorn a past as it actually was *not*.

He had seen the past not only through the values and prepossessions of an earlier age but also through the values and prepossessions of his own. His *summa* bore upon it the imprint of a sanguine age no less than that of a sanguine personality. The enterprising Connecticut Yankee spoke well for an age of enterprise. Dipping into the future, he saw a vision of the world which centered more on a Parliament of man than on argosies of magic sails. It was a vision which might readily have filled the eyes of the historians of that generation, heartened as they were by the teachings of Comte, Darwin, and Spencer and by the statistics of a united and burgeoning America. A later generation, however, one coming after Versailles rather than before Sarajevo, would tend to speak of the decline of the West rather than of its continuing rise. It would see the course of history less as progress than as poverty. It would accept neither the philosophic conventions nor the factual selection of its predecessors. The *summa* of Andrews could not outlive its age. Neither, for that matter, could that scientific ideal which was integral to his historiography.

No less did the contents and scope of his contribution reflect the limitations of his age and those of his own individuality. Perhaps the essence of it was that Andrews pushed to an extreme a formula which the times had thrown up as a means of recapturing the past. Out of the new and friendly relations between America and Britain in his own day had come a new and friendly approach to their relations in the past. Restored to the larger English system of which they had been part, the American colonies were revisited with an awareness of the spirit and purpose of that larger system. But what was to have been merely one avenue in approaching the past tended, in the historiography of Andrews, to become *the* avenue. In driving the imperial viewpoint too hard, he became its captive rather than its master. His colonial world was bounded by the Public Record Office on one side and by the details of imperial acts, agencies, and administration on the other. Taking up the vantage ground of Whitehall and Westminster had its virtue; but doing so to the exclusion of the more native ground of America was in some measure to repeat that earlier vice of provincialism which Andrews had so much decried. If his life's work consisted, as he saw it, of putting the "colonial" back into American colonial history, he did so at the expense of removing not a little of the "American."

That he had not builded better than he knew, nor perhaps even as well, revealed not so much the limited attainments of Andrews himself as the limitations that had been imposed by his age. And if he spoke for a particular age, it nowhere meant that he had not spoken well. His was no small achievement. The system that he had fashioned was one of the finest expressions of the scientific ideal of American historiography. Within the restrictions of his age, he had sought and he had found. To his work he brought the highest qualities of the master craftsman. Long training, sound judgment, fabulous knowledge, and an indefatigable will had brought him as close as any of his age to the achievement of the scientific ideal. Indeed, he exceeded the requirements of his craft. To the demands of science he added the skills of art. His contribution was more profound than Channing's, broader in scope than Osgood's, more vital and less constrained than Beer's. He made his history a richly human document and kept his vision wide. Offering no simple answer nor a single key to the problem of causation, his historiography was wrought out of the varieties and contradictions of man's experience. The precepts of Ranke, Maitland, and George Burton Adams inspired him to determination rather than to determinism.

Better than any of his compeers he demonstrated the significance and validity of the imperial viewpoint for American colonial history. If the viewpoint had been the common legacy of his age, it was a legacy which his own tremendous effort converted into a substantially personal possession. He was not merely a Hakluyt, he did his own principal voyaging; he not only drafted plans but did his own construction. The house of colonial history which Andrews built was in every wise an imposing one. If the *Guides* were the broad foundation, the *Colonial Period of American History* was nothing less than a monument. More than a monument to the contribution of a great historian, it was one to the scientific ideal and to an epoch of American historiography.

NOTES

INTRODUCTION

1. No reference is being made here to that "New History" which James Harvey Robinson later espoused. The "new history" (without capitals) of the late nineteenth century had its own particular characteristics, some of which may be understood from this paragraph and the next. Each age, for all its particular characteristics, makes the same general discovery and proclamation of a "new history."

CHAPTER 1: THE LEGACY OF HERBERT BAXTER ADAMS

1. Elizabeth Parkhill Andrews, "A Memoir of Charles M. Andrews," p. 28. Five years younger than her brother Charles, Miss Andrews wrote this charming "Memoir" after his death; in its thirty-odd pages, she has given some delightful pictures of Wethersfield in the 1860's, the friends of the Andrews family, and the early schooling of her famous brother. A carbon copy of this unpublished manuscript is to be found among the Andrews papers.

2. *Ibid.*, p. 30.

3. *Ibid.*, p. 31.

4. *Ibid.*, p. 32.

5. "Necrology," *Trinity Coll. Bull.*, XLI (1944), 14.

6. Andrews to his mother, Mrs. William Watson Andrews, January 6, 1886; January 10, 1886; March 18, 1889. Unless otherwise indicated, all letters referred to in the footnotes are part of the Andrews papers, a collection which is presently to be found at the home of Mrs. Charles M. Andrews, New Haven, Conn.

7. Statement of Mrs. Charles M. Andrews to author, November 11, 1952.

8. Elizabeth P. Andrews, "Memoir," p. 33.

9. See P. E. Shaw, *The Catholic Apostolic Church* (New York, 1946), chaps. 14, 15. Further details concerning Andrews' father

may be found in Samuel J. Andrews, *William Watson Andrews, a Religious Biography* (New York, 1900).

10. Andrews to Burton Alva Konkle [Spring, 1943].

11. Elbert V. Wills, *The Growth of American Higher Education* (Philadelphia, 1936), p. 190.

12. W. Stull Holt, ed., *Historical Scholarship in the United States, 1876–1901: As Revealed in the Correspondence of Herbert B. Adams* (Baltimore, 1938), p. 127, n. 2.

13. *Essays in Colonial History Presented to Charles McLean Andrews by His Students* (New Haven, 1931), pp. x-xi.

14. "These Forty Years," *American Historical Review* (hereafter cited as *AHR*), XXX (1925), 233, 236.

15. *Herbert B. Adams: Tributes of Friends* (Baltimore, 1902), p. 46.

16. A survey of his life and services, by Richard T. Ely, may be found in *ibid.*, pp. 27–49.

17. See the excellent introductory sketch in Holt, *Historical Scholarship.*

18. Adams corresponded with Henry Adams, Hermann Eduard von Holst, Edward Channing, George E. Howard, James Bryce, Andrew Dickson White, Charles Kendall Adams, William F. Allen, Justin Winsor, Edward P. Cheyney—men who, whether younger or older, stood at the forefront of historical science in late nineteenth-century America. The correspondence was generally concerned with matters of an administrative nature, involving always one of the implements or problems of the new history: courses that were being given, lectures and addresses to students or to full members of the profession, questions of appointment to different posts throughout the United States, or observations about the progress of historical science. Nothing is more fascinating than this correspondence, which reveals, detail by detail, how the structure of the new history was being built during the last quarter of the nineteenth century. See Holt, *Historical Scholarship, passim.*

19. Cited in Holt, *Historical Scholarship,* p. 15.

20. Herbert B. Adams, *The Study of History in American Colleges and Universities* (Washington, 1887), p. 175. See too Charles Kendall Adams, "Recent Historical Work in the Colleges and Universities of Europe and America," Amer. Hist. Assn., *Papers* (New York, 1890), IV, 39.

21. Herbert B. Adams, "Special Methods of Historical Study," in G. Stanley Hall, ed., *Methods of Teaching and Studying History* (2d ed., Boston, 1885), p. 122.

22. Adams, *Study of History,* p. 172.

23. Cited in Holt, *Historical Scholarship,* p. 15.

24. Quoted in letter, K. R. Greenfield to Andrews, March 20, 1939.
25. Andrews to his mother, December 12, 1886.
26. Andrews to his mother, May 7, 1888.
27. Andrews to his mother, February 26, 1888.
28. Johns Hopkins Univ., *Circulars,* January, 1888, p. 25.
29. *Ibid.,* February, 1889, p. 27.
30. Andrews to his mother, November 13, 1887.
31. *Herbert B. Adams: Tributes of Friends,* p. 45.
32. Andrews to his mother, October 24, 1886.
32. Andrews to his mother, October 7, 1888.
34. Daniel Coit Gilman, the first president of Johns Hopkins, and a friend of Andrews' father.
35. Andrews to his mother, May 19, 1889.
36. Andrews to his mother, April 22, 1889.
37. Adams, "Special Methods," in Hall, *Methods,* p. 143.
38. "Is History Past Politics?" Johns Hopkins Univ. Studies in Hist. and Pol. Science, XIII (1895), 199.
39. "Special Methods," in Hall, *Methods,* p. 124.
40. See *Herbert B. Adams: Tributes of Friends,* p. 39.
41. *Ibid.,* p. 39. 42. *Ibid.,* p. 40.
43. See "Is History Past Politics?" pp. 189–203.
44. Edward A. Freeman, *Comparative Politics* (London, 1873), p. 303; Herbert B. Adams, *The Study and Teaching of History* (Phi Beta Kappa Address, William and Mary Coll., February 18, 1898), pp. 9–10.
45. "Special Methods," in Hall, *Methods,* p. 132.
46. Adams, *Study of History,* p. 173.
47. "The Germanic Origin of New England Towns," Johns Hopkins Univ. Studies in Hist. and Pol. Science, I (1883), 8–9.
48. "Special Methods," in Hall, *Methods,* p. 124.
49. *Ibid.,* p. 163. 50. *Ibid.,* p. 131.
51. Adams, *Study of History,* p. 178.
52. Quoted by Mellen Chamberlain, "Remarks on the New Historical School," in his *John Adams and Other Essays* (Boston, 1898), p. 179.
53. Johnston's views were presented in two studies: "The Genesis of a New England State," Johns Hopkins Univ. Studies in Hist. and Pol. Science, I (1883), No. 11; and *Connecticut: A Study of Commonwealth-Democracy* (Boston, 1887).
54. *The River Towns of Connecticut* (Baltimore, 1889), p. 29. The volume appeared as part of the Johns Hopkins Univ. Studies in Hist. and Pol. Science, Vol. VII (1889).
55. *River Towns,* pp. 118–19. See, too, Andrews, "The Begin-

nings of the Connecticut Towns," Amer. Acad. of Pol. and Soc. Science, *Annals,* I (1890), 172–73.

56. "Beginnings," p. 180–81; *River Towns,* p. 120.

57. *River Towns,* p. 123; "Beginnings," pp. 184–85.

58. "Beginnings," p. 190.

59. *River Towns,* p. 41.

60. *Ibid.,* pp. 50–51.

61. *Ibid.,* pp. 68–69.

62. *Ibid.,* p. 98.

63. *Ibid.,* p. 30, n.

64. "The Theory of the Village Community," Amer. Hist. Assn., *Papers* (New York, 1891), V, 47.

65. *Ibid.,* p. 50.

66. *Ibid.,* p. 53.

67. *Ibid.,* p. 48.

68. *Ibid.,* pp. 56–58.

69. *Ibid.,* p. 60.

70. *Modern Language Notes,* June, 1889, p. 378.

71. *The Old English Manor* (Baltimore, 1892), p. 137. The study appeared as Extra Vol. XII in the Johns Hopkins Univ. Studies in Hist. and Pol. Science.

72. *Ibid.,* p. 156.

73. *Ibid.,* p. 59.

74. *Ibid.,* pp. 146–47.

75. Nor was Andrews unaware of this. To his mother he wrote: "It is my most ambitious work and . . . it will show how audacious a youngster can be in taking up a much disputed problem & attempting to solve it. But my solution is put forth with due humility I trust & certainly no one will accuse me of dogmatism. One becomes less & less inclined to domgatic assertion as the years roll on." January 24, 1892.

76. *Old English Manor,* p. 5.

77. *Ibid.,* pp. 27–29.

78. *Ibid.,* p. 51.

79. *Ibid.,* p. 58; italics mine.

80. *Law Quarterly Review,* XXXII (1892), 339.

81. Seebohm to Andrews, July 8, 1892.

82. Vinogradoff to Andrews, July 13, 1892.

83. Maitland to Andrews, October 15, 1892.

84. Unidentified review, Andrews papers.

85. *English Hist. Rev.,* VIII (1893), 540.

86. "Some Recent Aspects of Institutional Study," *Yale Review,* I (1893), 382.

87. *Christian Union,* July 2, 1892.

88. "Some Recent Aspects of Institutional Study," pp. 392, 394.

89. *Ibid.,* p. 386.

90. *Christian Union,* August 1, 1891.

91. "Some of the Vagaries and Amenities of History," Assn. of Hist. Teachers of the Middle States and Md., 4th Annual Convention (March, 1906), *Minutes,* pp. 48–49.

92. Amer. Acad. of Pol. and Soc. Science, *Annals,* XIII (1899), 402.

93. *Pol. Science Quarterly,* X (1895), 693.
94. *AHR,* III (1897), 133.
95. *Christian Union,* August 1, 1891.
96. This glittering generalization on the dominant views of the new school of American historians is that of William A. Dunning, "A Generation of American Historiography," Amer. Hist. Assn., *Annual Report for 1917,* p. 350.

CHAPTER 2: A PORTRAIT OF THE HISTORIAN AS A YOUNG MAN

1. For a further discussion of the meaning of the scientific ideal for the new history that was arising in late nineteenth-century America, see below, chap. 8, pp. 203–5. The bibliography cited in n. 43, chap. 8, affords a view of the framework of ideas at that time. Excellent discussions of this problem will also be found in Herman Ausubel, *Historians and Their Craft* (New York, 1950), chap. 6, and W. Stull Holt, "The Idea of Scientific History in America," *Journal of the History of Ideas,* I (1940), 352 ff.
2. Andrews to his mother, May 20, 1888.
3. Andrews to his mother, September 3, 1893.
4. Andrews to his mother, January 5, 1890.
5. Statement of Mrs. Charles M. Andrews to author, December 5, 1952.
6. Andrews to his mother, November 13, 1892.
7. *Christian Union,* June 4, 1892; "Some Recent Aspects of Institutional Study," *Yale Review,* I (1893), 381–410.
8. Andrews to Burton Alva Konkle [Spring, 1943].
9. *Ibid.*
10. Andrews to his mother, November 13, 1887.
11. Andrews to his mother, March 22, 1891; undated letter [late 1891].
12. Andrews to his mother, undated letter [late 1891].
13. Andrews to his mother, January 12, 1890.
14. Andrews to his mother, August 18, 1893.
15. An example of this may be found in his letter to J. F. Jameson, June 14, 1906, Jameson papers, where Andrews noted his earlier fear that deafness might bar his appointment to Johns Hopkins; also, letter to Jameson, May 18, 1908, Jameson papers.
16. Andrews to his mother, October 25, 1891.
17. Andrews to his mother, June 20, 1904; January 16, 1899.
18. His letter to his mother, January 24, 1897, describes exactly such a conversation with William Lyon Phelps, who had come to Bryn Mawr to address its Graduate Club.

19. Andrews to his mother, November, 1891.
20. Andrews to his mother, February 12, 1896.
21. Letter to his mother, September 2, 1900, mentions a typical instance of this.
22. Andrews to his mother, January 21, 1894.
23. Andrews to his mother, April 30, 1900.
24. The type of success that his wife was to have is indicated in a letter of Andrews to his mother, December 4, 1901: "I add a postscript this morning for we are all very much excited over the offer made by Rockefeller of $250,000 to the college on condition that the college raise $250,000 more. We are especially interested because the obtaining of this gift is Evangeline's work. She wrote Mr. Rockefeller last Spring and had an interview with his son and educational agent in May . . . . It is really a great gift, the largest that Rockefeller has given to any of the women's colleges and will do an enormous deal for Bryn Mawr."
25. Statement of Mrs. Charles M. Andrews to author, February 20, 1953.
26. Andrews to his mother, December 19, 1897.
27. Andrews to his mother, March 25, 1901.
28. *Ibid.*
29. Andrews to his mother, November, 1898.
30. "Some Recent Aspects of Institutional Study," p. 393. Andrews often referred to the study of history as "historical science."
31. *Ibid.,* p. 395.
32. "Some of the Vagaries and Amenities of History," Assn. of Hist. Teachers of the Middle States and Md., 4th Annual Convention (March, 1906), *Minutes,* p. 42.
33. *Ibid.,* p. 43; "History as an Aid to Moral Culture," National Education Assn., *Journal of Proceedings and Addresses, 1894,* p. 406.
34. *Christian Union,* February 11, 1893.
35. "Moral Culture," p. 400. 36. *Ibid.,* p. 404.
37. "Should Recent European History Have a Place in the College Curriculum?" Amer. Hist. Assn., *Annual Report for 1899* (Washington, 1900), I, 542–43.
38. *Ibid.,* p. 540.
39. Andrews to his mother, May 2, 1898.
40. Andrews to his mother, May 2, 1898; March 5, 1899.
41. Andrews to his mother, May 2, 1898.
42. Andrews to his mother, August 14, 1898.
43. "Recent European History," p. 547.
44. Andrews to his mother, February 28, 1897.
45. See pp. 212–19.
46. "Recent European History," p. 548.

47. *Ibid.*, pp. 541–42; Ausubel, *Historians and Their Craft,* pp. 43–49.
48. *AHR,* VII (1902), 784; *Pol. Science Quarterly,* X (1895), 523.
49. *The Nation,* October 8, 1908.
50. "Moral Culture," p. 398.
51. *Christian Union,* June 30, 1894.
52. "Recent European History," p. 541.
53. "Moral Culture," p. 399.
54. "Some Recent Aspects of Institutional Study," p. 393.
55. "Moral Culture," p. 406; "Recent European History," p. 542; *Christian Union,* February 25, 1893.
56. His perennial concern with this problem is evident from his book reviews, viz., *Pol. Science Quarterly,* VI (1894), 734; *AHR,* I (1895), 120.
57. "Recent European History," pp. 540–41.
58. Cited in G. P. Gooch, *History and Historians in the Nineteenth Century* (London, 1913), pp. 344–45.
59. Amer. Hist. Assn., *Annual Report for 1896,* p. 257.
60. "Some of the Vagaries and Amenities of History," p. 49.
61. "Moral Culture," p. 408.
62. *The Nation,* December 20, 1906.
63. *Yale Review,* New Ser., VII (1918), 867.
64. *Independent,* July 3, 1902.
65. *AHR,* V (1900), 387.
66. *Christian Union,* February 25, 1893.
67. Andrews to Herbert B. Adams, November 22, 1893.
68. Clarence P. Gould to author, October 11, 1952.
69. "Some Recent Aspects of Institutional Study," p. 395.
70. *Ibid.,* p. 396.
71. *Christian Union,* April 1, 1893.
72. "Some Recent Aspects of Institutional Study," p. 386.
73. *Christian Union,* February 27, 1892.
74. "Moral Culture," p. 408.
75. *Christian Union,* June 4, 1892, November 5, 1892; *AHR,* XI (1906), 673.
76. *AHR,* III (1898), 355–60; *Christian Union,* March 27, 1890; Amer. Hist. Assn., *Annual Report for 1896,* p. 257.
77. *AHR,* V (1900), 741; "Some Recent Aspects of Institutional Study," p. 393.
78. *Pol. Science Quarterly,* XVII (1902), 162.
79. Draft of letter, Andrews to L. H. Gipson [June, 1935].
80. S. M. Pargellis to author, September 22, 1952.
81. Maitland to Andrews, September 12, 1893; Andrews to his mother, June 20, 1904.

82. *The Nation,* October 8, 1908.
83. *AHR,* III (1897), 130–31.
84. *Pol. Science Quarterly,* XVII (1902), 163; *Christian Union,* February 27, 1892.
85. Ausubel, *Historians and Their Craft,* p. 190.
86. There is no evidence to indicate that Andrews, in his use of these words, intended to convey anything beyond their general popular meaning.
87. "Moral Culture," pp. 393, 406.
88. *Yale Review,* II (1893), 316.
89. "Recent European History," p. 542.
90. *Pol. Science Quarterly,* IX (1894), 163.
91. *Ibid.*
92. "Moral Culture," p. 400.
93. *Ibid.,* p. 404.
94. Andrews to his mother, November 13, 1892.
95. "Moral Culture," p. 407.
96. "Some Recent Aspects of Institutional Study," p. 403.
97. "Some of the Vagaries and Amenities of History," p. 53.
98. *AHR,* V (1900), 332.
99. *Ibid.*
100. Andrews to his mother, April 8, 1895.
101. *Ibid.;* also, statement of Mrs. Charles M. Andrews to author, November 28, 1952.
102. *The Historical Development of Modern Europe, 1815–1897* (2 vols., New York, 1896–98), I, iv.
103. *Ibid.,* II, iv–v.
104. *Ibid.,* I, 87.
105. *The Guardian,* June 2, 1897; *British Review,* January 23, 1897.
106. *The Speaker,* May 22, 1897.
107. *Saturday Review,* December 3, 1898.
108. *Historical Development,* II, iv.
109. *Ibid.,* I, 36.
110. *Ibid.,* I, 115–16.
111. *Ibid.,* II, 230.
112. *The Academy,* February 20, 1897.
113. *Historical Development,* I, iv.
114. *Ibid.,* I, iv.
115. *Ibid.,* I, 81, 102; II, 87, 187.
116. *Ibid.,* II, 41.
117. *Yale Review,* VI (1897), 94.
118. *Historical Development,* II, v.
119. *Yale Review,* XIII (1904), 227; *AHR,* IX (1904), 544.
120. *A History of England* (Boston, 1903), p. iii.
121. Assn. of Hist. Teachers of the Middle States and Md., 6th Annual Convention (March, 1908), *Record* (Baltimore, 1908), p. 30.
122. *Yale Review,* III (1894), 261–94.
123. *New England Magazine,* New Ser., VII (1893), 702–9.
124. *Ibid.,* p. 709.
125. *Ibid.,* p. 702.

126. Introduction to *Ideal Empires and Republics* (Washington, 1901), p. xvii.

127. Leonard W. Labaree, "Charles McLean Andrews: Historian, 1863–1943," *William and Mary Quarterly,* 3d Ser., I (1944), 10.

128. Andrews to L. H. Gipson, June 24, 1935.

129. Andrews to his mother, December 9, 1895.

130. "In Memoriam: Charles McLean Andrews," *Bryn Mawr Alumnae Bulletin,* December, 1943, p. 7.

131. Andrews to his mother, October 29, 1899; February 5, 1900.

132. Quoted by Mrs. Charles M. Andrews to author, February 20, 1953.

133. "Some of the Vagaries and Amenities of History," pp. 60–61.

134. *Bryn Mawr Alumnae Quarterly,* I (1907), 37.

135. Amer. Hist. Assn., *Annual Report for 1896,* p. 257.

136. Assn. of Hist. Teachers of the Middle States and Md., 6th Annual Convention (March, 1908), *Record,* p. 32.

137. "Some of the Vagaries and Amenities of History," pp. 47–48.

138. *Ibid.,* p. 49.

139. New York *Evening Post,* May 10, 1905; "Some Recent Aspects of Institutional Study," p. 383; "These Forty Years," *AHR,* XXX (1925), 228–29.

140. *Christian Union,* March 26, 1891.

141. *Ibid.*

142. *Ibid.,* June 26, 1890.

143. *Ibid.,* November 5, 1892.

144. Draft of letter, Andrews to L. H. Gipson [June, 1935].

145. *AHR,* XIII (1908), 570.

146. *Christian Union,* November 5, 1892; Amer. Acad. of Pol. and Soc. Science, *Annals,* II (1891), 387.

147. Draft of letter, Andrews to L. H. Gipson [June, 1935].

CHAPTER 3: COLONIES, ARCHIVES, AND GUIDES

1. See below, chap. 7, sec. 1 *passim.*

2. Andrews to L. H. Gipson, June 24, 1935.

3. Andrews to his mother, July 23, 1893.

4. Amer. Acad. of Pol. and Soc. Science, *Annals,* I (1891), 697.

5. Chamberlain to Andrews, November 29, 1894.

6. The article on the land system appeared in R. H. Inglis Palgrave, ed., *Dictionary of Political Economy* (London, 1896), II, 556–60.

7. "American Colonial History, 1690–1750," Amer. Hist. Assn., *Annual Report for 1898,* p. 49.

8. *Ibid.,* pp. 51–54.

9. Chamberlain to Andrews, November 11, 1893.

10. *Pol. Science Quarterly,* IX (1894), 753.

11. "Some Neglected Aspects of Colonial History," N. J. Hist. Soc., *Proceedings,* 3d Ser., IV, No. 1 (1901), 7.

12. *AHR,* XIV (1909), 364. 13. *AHR,* XXII (1917), 392.

14. "Some Neglected Aspects," pp. 18, 6.

15. *Pol. Science Quarterly,* XXXVIII (1923), 141.

16. *The Nation,* November 14, 1907.

17. "Some Neglected Aspects," p. 7.

18. Andrews to D. C. Gilman, October 27, 1902, Jameson papers; Andrews to A. C. McLaughlin, April 27, 1903, Jameson papers.

19. *Encyclopedia of Social Sciences,* VII, 377.

20. Justin Winsor's editorship of the *Narrative and Critical History of America* (8 vols., 1884–89) was pioneering work in tapping the sources; Winsor's presidential address, in 1887, to the Amer. Hist. Assn., was devoted to the question of "Manuscript Sources of American History." Jameson constantly appealed for help from the federal government, as in his talk on "Expenditures of Foreign Governments in Behalf of History," Amer. Hist. Assn., *Annual Report for 1891,* pp. 33–61.

21. See note of this in *AHR,* IV (1898), 156.

22. Andrews to his mother, January 5, 1902.

23. *Christian Union,* March 26, 1891.

24. Letter of Andrews to *The Nation,* February 22, 1912.

25. *The Nation,* December 30, 1915.

26. Andrews to his mother, January, 1891; *AHR,* XIX (1913), 157.

27. *Sat. Rev. of Lit.,* January 19, 1935. The letters of Andrews to E. B. Greene, chairman of the Legal History Committee, and to R. B. Morris, secretary, during the first half of the 1930's, reveal a constant interest on the part of Andrews in all problems involved in publishing the legal records of early American history. The Andrews-Morris correspondence in reference to this subject was very generously lent to the author by Prof. R. B. Morris, of Columbia University. Other aspects of Andrews' concern with the same problem are dealt with in the Andrews papers, presently to be found at the home of his widow, Mrs. Charles M. Andrews, 424 St. Ronan Street, New Haven, and in the Andrews MSS., Yale Univ. Lib.

28. "Some of the Vagaries and Amenities of History," Assn. of Hist. Teachers of the Middle States and Md., 4th Annual Convention (March, 1906), *Minutes,* p. 42.

29. *Hist. Teacher's Mag.,* I (1910), 149.

30. "Archives," Amer. Hist. Assn., *Annual Report for 1913* (Washington, 1915), I, 264.

31. *Ibid.*
32. *AHR,* XVII (1912), 825.
33. *Ibid.*
34. *AHR,* XIV (1909), 591.
35. *The Nation,* September 15, 1910.
36. *Ibid.,* July 27, 1911.
37. The account of Andrews' work on the *Guides* is given by Jameson in his preface to the *Guide to the Manuscript Materials for the History of the United States to 1783, in the British Museum, in Minor London Archives, and in the Libraries of Oxford and Cambridge* (Washington, 1908), and in the introductory note to the *Guide to the Materials for American History to 1783, in the Public Record Office of Great Britain,* Vol. I (Washington, 1912). A more extensive account of the work of Andrews in this field may be found in John Riggs, "Charles McLean Andrews and the British Archives" (unpubl. thesis, Yale, 1949). Mr. Riggs' manuscript, which runs some sixty pages, and which is concerned with the story of how the *Guides* were conceived and composed, has made admirable use of the Andrews-Jameson correspondence, presently to be found at the Carnegie Institution of Washington.
38. Andrews to L. H. Gipson, June 24, 1935.
39. Andrews to Hubert Hall, November 29, 1938.
40. *Guide to the Materials for American History, to 1783, in the Public Record Office of Great Britain* (Washington, 1912), I, vii.
41. Andrews to Hastings Eells, March 5, 1926.
42. Leonard W. Labaree, "Charles McLean Andrews: Historian, 1863–1943," *William and Mary Quarterly,* 3d Ser., I (1944), 7.
43. "American Colonial History, 1690–1750," p. 54.
44. *AHR,* VIII (1913), 592.
45. Draft of letter, Andrews to L. H. Gipson [June, 1935].
46. "Materials in British Archives for American Colonial History," *AHR,* X (1905), 333.
47. "The Value of London Topography for American Colonial History," *Hist. Teacher's Mag.,* II (1911), 102.
48. Yale Univ. Lib. has taken over the greater part of his private collection of books and it is presently housed in the Andrews Study Room.
49. "List of Commissions, Instructions, and Additional Instructions issued to the Royal Governors and others in America," Amer. Hist. Assn., *Annual Report for 1911* (Washington, 1913), I, 395.
50. *Ibid.,* p. 397.
57. "List of Reports and Representations of the Plantation Councils, 1660–1674, the Lords of Trade, 1675–1696, and the Board of Trade, 1696–1782, in the Public Record Office," Amer. Hist. Assn., *Annual Report for 1913* (Washington, 1915), I, 326.

52. Andrews, "The Story of the Transcripts," in *Essays Offered to Herbert Putnam by His Colleagues and Friends on His Thirtieth Anniversary as Librarian of Congress* (New Haven, 1929), p. 52.

53. See comment on location and amount of these materials in the Bibliography.

54. Numerous instances from the personal correspondence of Andrews could be cited relative to this point. The letters from Randolph Greenfield Adams, Custodian of the William L. Clements Library at Ann Arbor, Mich., are typical.

55. Jameson to Andrews, July 30, 1908, Jameson papers.

56. Jameson to Andrews, May 13, 1914.

57. *AHR,* XX (1915), 419; "American Colonies and the British Empire," *Hist. Teacher's Mag.,* VI (1915), 283.

58. "American Colonies and the British Empire," p. 283.

59. *AHR,* XIV (1909), 830.

60. O. M. Dickerson, *American Colonial Government, 1696–1765* (Cleveland, 1912); W. T. Root, *The Relations of Pennsylvania with the British Government, 1696–1765* (New York, 1912); M. P. Clarke, "The Board of Trade at Work," *AHR,* XVII (1911), 17–43.

61. Andrews to Jameson, November 24, 1911, Jameson papers.

62. *Ibid.*

63. Andrews to Jameson, April 20, 1902, Jameson papers.

64. Jameson to Andrews, May 13, 1914.

65. Andrews to Jameson, May 15, 1914. Jameson papers.

CHAPTER 4: MAJOR THEMES

1. *The Colonial Period of American History* (4 vols., New Haven, 1934–38), IV, xi. Hereafter cited as *C.P.A.H.* Quotations used by permission of Yale University Press.

2. Andrews to Frederick Jackson Turner, November 17, 1912.

3. "Remarks on the Writing of American Colonial History," Colonial Soc. of Mass., XX, *Transactions, 1917–1919* (Boston, 1920), p. 159.

4. *C.P.A.H.,* IV, ix; "On the Writing of Colonial History," *William and Mary Quarterly,* 3d Ser., I (1944), 29.

5. Andrews to Hastings Eells, March 5, 1926.

6. *The Colonial Period* (New York, 1912), p. v. Hereafter cited as *C.P.* Quotations used by permission of Oxford University Press.

7. *C.P.A.H.,* I, xi.

8. "Remarks on the Writing of American Colonial History," p. 161; *The Nation,* November 14, 1907.

9. *C.P.,* p. vi.

10. *C.P.A.H.,* I, xi.

11. *The Nation,* December 20, 1919.
12. *C.P.A.H.,* I, xi.
13. *C.P.,* p. 107.
14. "Remarks on the Writing of American Colonial History," p. 160.
15. *C.P.,* p. 11.
16. *AHR,* XIV (1909), 809; *C.P.A.H.,* Vol. I, chap. 1 *passim.*
17. *C.P.A.H.,* IV, ix.
18. "On the Writing of Colonial History," p. 29.
19. "The Proprietary Element in Maryland during Colonial Times" (Privately printed [1929]), p. 1.
20. *C.P.A.H.,* I, xi.
21. *The Colonial Background of the American Revolution* (rev. ed., New Haven, 1931), p. ix. Hereafter cited as *Background.* Quotations used by permission of Yale University Press.
22. *C.P.A.H.,* Vol. I, chap. 1 *passim.*
23. *Ibid.,* I, 46.
24. *Ibid.,* I, 67.
25. *Our Earliest Colonial Settlements* (New York, 1933), p. 141. Hereafter cited as *Earliest.*
26. *C.P.A.H.,* I, 77.
27. *Ibid.,* I, 44.
28. *Ibid.,* I, 76.
29. *Ibid.,* IV, 3–4.
30. *Earliest,* p. 2.
31. *C.P.A.H.,* III, 1.
32. *Ibid.,* III, 2.
33. "Virginia's Place in Colonial History," *Va. Mag. of Hist. and Biog.,* XL (1932), 214.
34. *Earliest,* p. 27.
35. "Virginia's Place in Colonial History," p. 214.
36. "The Massachusetts Bay Colony in the Seventeenth Century," New Eng. Teachers Assn., *The Leaflet* (1931), p. 4.
37. *Earliest,* p. 80.
38. *Ibid.,* p. 90.
39. *Ibid.,* p. 111.
40. *C.P.A.H.,* II, 82.
41. *Earliest,* p. 123.
42. *Ibid.,* p. 164.
43. *C.P.A.H.,* II, 270–72.
44. *C.P.,* pp. 42–43; *C.P.A.H.,* III, xiii.
45. *C.P.A.H.,* III, ix–xiii.
46. *Ibid.,* III, 6–7.
47. *Ibid.,* III, 55.
48. *C.P.,* p. 44.
49. *C.P.A.H.,* Vol. II, chap. 6.
50. *Ibid.,* III, 138, 179–80.
51. *Ibid.,* III, 99.
52. *Ibid.,* III, 182.
53. *Ibid.,* III, 251, 304.
54. *Ibid.,* II, 366; III, 209–12, 225–26, 235, 240, 279, 312.
55. *Earliest,* p. v.
56. *C.P.A.H.,* III, 327.
57. *Earliest,* p. v.
58. *C.P.A.H.,* III, 1–2.
59. "On the Writing of Colonial History," p. 29.
60. *Earliest,* p. 25.
61. *C.P.A.H.,* II, 197.
62. "Virginia's Place in Colonial History," pp. 228–29.

63. *C.P.A.H.*, III, 305.
64. *Ibid.*, III, xiii.
65. *Ibid.*, IV, ix.
66. Andrews to Frederick Jackson Turner, November 17, 1912, copy.
67. Andrews to Frank J. Klingberg, November 16, 1940.
68. *Background,* p. 121.
69. *C.P.A.H.*, III, 55.
70. "The Acts of Trade," in *The Old Empire from the Beginnings to 1783* (Cambridge, 1929), p. 268, Vol. I of *Cambridge History of the British Empire,* ed. J. H. Rose, A. P. Newton, E. A. Benians; *C.P.A.H.*, III, 37–39.
71. "The Acts of Trade," p. 276; *C.P.A.H.*, IV, 61.
72. *C.P.A.H.*, IV, 177.
73. *Background,* p. 71.
74. "Anglo-French Commercial Rivalry," *AHR,* XX (1915), 546.
75. *Background,* pp. 88–89.
76. *Ibid.*, p. 80.
77. *Ibid.*, p. 81.
78. *Ibid.*, p. 86.
79. *Ibid.*, p. 100
80. *C.P.A.H.*, IV, 354.
81. *Ibid.*, IV, 2.
82. *Ibid.*, IV, 326 ff.
83. *C.P.*, p. 120.
84. "The Government of the Empire, 1660–1763," in *The Old Empire from the Beginnings to 1783* (Cambridge, 1929), p. 411, Vol. I of *Cambridge History of the British Empire,* ed. J. H. Rose, A. P. Newton, E. A. Benians.
85. *C.P.A.H.*, IV, 336; *Background,* pp. 114, 115.
86. *C.P.A.H.*, IV, 333; *ibid.*, II, 272; *Background,* p. 95.
87. *C.P.A.H.*, IV, 228; *C.P.*, pp. 188, 192.
88. *C.P.A.H.*, IV, 349, n. 4.
89. *Ibid.*, IV, 179.
90. "The Acts of Trade," p. 270.
91. "The Government of the Empire, 1660–1763," p. 417.
92. *C.P.*, p. 147.
93. *C.P.A.H.*, IV, 205.
94. *Background,* p. 22.
95. *C.P.A.H.*, IV, 407–8.
96. *Background,* p. ix.
97. "The American Revolution: An Interpretation," *AHR,* XXXI (1926), 221.
98. *C.P.*, p. 155.
99. *C.P.A.H.*, II, 198; *Background,* pp. 180–83.
100. "Virginia's Place in Colonial History," p. 232; "Commencement Address–Trinity College, 1929," *Trinity College Bulletin,* New Ser., XXVI, No. 3 (1929), 14.
101. "The Proprietary Element in Maryland," pp. 4–5.
102. "The Government of the Empire, 1660–1763," p. 424.
103. *C.P.A.H.*, IV, 375.
104. *Background,* pp. 65–66.
105. *Ibid.*, p. 41.
106. "On the Writing of Colonial History," p. 39.
107. *Background,* pp. 187 ff.; "Present-Day Thoughts on the

American Revolution," *Bull. of the Univ. of Ga.,* XIX, No. 11 (1919), 9.

108. *Background,* p. 195.
109. *C.P.,* pp. 163–85.
110. *Ibid.,* pp. 203–4.
111. *Background,* p. 123.
112. *C.P.,* pp. 238–39.
113. *Background,* p. 129.
114. "On the Writing of Colonial History," p. 46.
115. *Background,* p. 186.
116. *Ibid.,* p. 152.
117. *Ibid.,* p. 168.
118. *Ibid.,* p. 218.
119. *Ibid.,* p. 181.
120. "Present-Day Thoughts on the American Revolution," p. 12.
121. *Ibid.,* p. 15.
122. *Background,* p. 161.
123. *Ibid.,* p. 183.
124. *Ibid.,* p. 182.
125. "The American Revolution: An Interpretation," p. 230.
126. *Background,* pp. 218–19.
127. New York *Herald Tribune,* May 12, 1935.
128. A detailed account of the critical reception of the works of Andrews by his own generation may be found below, chap. 7, pp. 183–84. The principal reviews of his *Colonial Period of American History* (4 vols., 1934–38) included those by Henry Steele Commager in the New York *Herald Tribune,* Carl Bridenbaugh in the *Pa. Mag. of Hist. and Biog.,* Wesley Frank Craven in the *William and Mary Quarterly,* Marcus Jernegan in the *Yale Review,* Samuel Eliot Morison in the *New Eng. Quarterly,* and Curtis P. Nettels in the *Annals of the Amer. Acad.* For something of the contents of these later reviews see pp. 196–98.
129. New York *Evening Sun,* January 17, 1925.
130. Harper to Andrews, April 10, 1938.
131. *Background,* pp. 189, 195.
132. Jernegan to Andrews, December 14, 1934.
133. Jernegan to Andrews, December 25, 1937.
134. *Ibid.*
135. *Pa. Mag. of Hist. and Biog.,* LXIII (1939), 464.
136. *Ibid.*

CHAPTER 5: SUMMA HISTORICA, 1903-1943

1. "Some Recent Aspects of Institutional Study," *Yale Review,* I (1893), 395; cf. review of E. B. Greene's *Foundations of American Nationality,* in which Andrews speaks of "the ultimate truth of our colonial history," *AHR,* XXVIII (1923), 761.
2. "These Forty Years," *AHR,* XXX (1925), 244.
3. *AHR,* XXXI (1926), 219.
4. *Ibid.*
5. *Amer. Eco. Review,* II (1912), 615; *AHR,* XXX (1924), 150.

6. *Background,* p. 219.
7. *Ibid.,* p. x.
8. "The Historian," in *George Louis Beer: A Tribute to His Life and Work in the Making of History and the Moulding of Public Opinion* (New York, 1924), p. 9.
9. "Virginia's Place in Colonial History," *Va. Mag. of Hist. and Biog.,* XL (1932), 220; Middle States Assn. of Hist. and Soc. Science Teachers, *Proceedings,* XXXI (1933), 15; unidentified MS., Andrews MSS., Yale Univ. Lib.
10. "The Historian," p. 9.
11. *The Nation,* December 20, 1917; *Yale Review,* XXX (1941), 426.
12. "These Forty Years," p. 249; "On the Writing of Colonial History," *William and Mary Quarterly,* 3d Ser., I (1944), 27.
13. "These Forty Years," p. 241.
14. *Background,* p. 180.
15. *Earliest,* p. 1.
16. "These Forty Years," p. 239.
17. *Ibid.*
18. "On the Preservation of Historical Manuscripts," *William and Mary Quarterly,* 3d Ser., I (1944), 124; "These Forty Years," p. 239; *Colonial Self-Government, 1652–1689* (New York, 1904), pp. 338, 344.
19. *The Nation,* November 21, 1917.
20. "On the Writing of Colonial History," pp. 31–38.
21. *Ibid.,* p. 33.
22. Statement of Prof. Dumas Malone to author, February 15, 1955.
23. See pages 196ff. for a discussion of the criticism made, on this subject, by the historians of the 1930's and for the response of Andrews to their charges.
24. "These Forty Years," p. 246.
25. *Ibid.,* p. 237.
26. *British Committees, Commissions, and Councils of Trade and Plantations, 1622–1675* (Baltimore, 1908); "The Boston Merchants and the Non-Importation Movement," Colonial Soc. of Mass., XIX, *Transactions, 1916–1917* (Boston, 1918); "Vice-Admiralty Courts in the Colonies," an introduction to Dorothy S. Towle, ed., *Records of the Vice-Admiralty Court of Rhode Island, 1716–1752* (Washington, 1936).
27. "These Forty Years," p. 246.
28. His analysis of the fall of the Virginia Company is an excellent example: *C.P.A.H.,* Vol. I, chap. 8.
29. *C.P.,* p. 206.
30. *C.P.A.H.,* III, 70.
31. *Earliest,* p. 80.
32. *Ibid.,* p. 90.
33. *AHR,* XXIX (1924), 150.
34. "These Forty Years," p. 239.
35. "The Historian," p. 20.
36. "These Forty Years," p. 229.
37. *Ibid.,* p. 244.
38. *Ibid.,* p. 228.

39. *Ibid.*
40. *Ibid.*, p. 242.
41. *Ibid.*
42. *Ibid.*, p. 244.

43. Assn. of Hist. Teachers of the Middle States and Md., 6th Annual Convention (March, 1908), *Record*, p. 30; *Yale Daily News*, April 26, 1922; "On the Preservation of Historical Manuscripts," p. 123.

44. *Background*, p. 219.
45. *Ibid.*, p. 220.

46. "Virginia's Place in Colonial History," p. 225.

47. "These Forty Years," p. 245; "The Value of London Topography for American Colonial History," *Hist. Teacher's Mag.*, III (1912), 102.

48. "These Forty Years," p. 246.

49. *Ibid.*; "Virginia's Place in Colonial History," p. 225.

50. "These Forty Years," p. 243.

51. *Ibid.*
53. *Ibid.*, p. 245.

53. "The Historian," p. 10; "On the Writing of Colonial History," p. 39.

54. Andrews to B. A. Konkle [Spring, 1943].

55. *AHR*, III (1897), 131.

56. "The Historian," pp. 26–27.

57. *C.P.A.H.*, I, xii.

58. *Yale Review*, VIII (1919), 881.

59. New York *Evening Post*, May 10, 1905.

60. *Earliest*, pp. v–vi.
61. *Background*, pp. 176–77.

62. *The Fathers of New England: A Chronicle of the Puritan Commonwealths* (New Haven, 1919), p. 185.

63. *Ibid.*

64. See for example: Samuel Eliot Morison in New York *Herald Tribune*, February 15, 1925; Henry Steele Commager in New York *Herald Tribune*, November 20, 1938; Verner W. Crane in *AHR*, XL (1935), 350.

65. T. P. Abernethy in *Va. Quarterly Review*, XIII (1937), 313.

66. Henry Steele Commager in New York *Herald Tribune*, May 12, 1935.

67. See Randall and Haines, "Controlling Assumptions," in *Theory and Practice in Historical Study: A Report of the Committee on Historiography* (New York, 1945), p. 43.

68. For a fuller discussion of this very important subject, see pp. 211–16.

69. *C.P.A.H.*, IV, 205, 221, 403–4; *Background*, pp. 79, 118, 125, 186, 193.

70. "The American Revolution: An Interpretation," *AHR*, XXXI (1926), 232.

71. "These Forty Years," p. 234.

72. "Historic Doubts Regarding Early Massachusetts History," Colonial Soc. of Mass., XXVII, *Transactions, 1930–1933* (Boston, 1935), p. 285.
73. *Background,* p. 178.
74. Quoted in *Background,* p. 178.
75. "Historic Doubts," p. 285.
76. *Atlantic Monthly,* December, 1923, p. 14.
77. *C.P.A.H.,* I, xii, xi.
78. *Ibid.,* III, 118, n. 1.
79. *Ibid.,* III, 113.
80. *Ibid.,* I, 173.
81. *Earliest,* p. 50.
82. *Ibid.,* p. 52.
83. *C.P.,* pp. 188, 192.
84. *C.P.A.H.,* IV, 349, n. 4.
85. *Ibid.,* IV, 251–52.
86. *Fathers of New England,* p. 64. Quotations used by permission of Yale University Press.
87. See, for example, *Fathers of New England,* p. 62; *Earliest,* p. 131.
88. "The Massachusetts Bay Colony in the Seventeenth Century," New Eng. Teachers Assn., *The Leaflet* (1931), p. 8.
89. *Ibid.,* p. 14.
90. *Earliest,* p. 82.
91. "The Proprietary Element in Maryland during Colonial Times" (Baltimore [1929]), p. 1.
92. "Virginia's Place in Colonial History," p. 226.
93. "These Forty Years," pp. 241–42.
94. "The Value of London Topography," p. 102. The Andrews MSS. at Yale Univ. Lib. contain a notebook full of charts and plans of the administrative offices at eighteenth-century Whitehall.
95. "Some Neglected Aspects of Colonial History," p. 18.
96. "Conservative Factors in Early Colonial History," in *Authority and the Individual* (Harvard Tercentenary Publications, Cambridge, 1937), p. 157.
97. *C.P.A.H.,* IV, 318.
98. *Background,* p. 87.
99. *Ibid.,* p. 47.
100. Andrews to Frederick Jackson Turner, November 17, 1912.
101. "These Forty Years," pp. 227 ff.
102. *Fathers of New England,* p. 160.
103. *Earliest,* p. 81.
104. *Ibid.,* p. 78.
105. *Social Education,* II (1939), 71.
106. Most pertinent are Adams to Andrews, March 20, 1922; May 29, 1922.
107. "Conservative Factors in Early Colonial History," p. 165.
108. Jernegan to Andrews, December 25, 1937; April 25, 1932. Cf. pp. 102–3.
109. See *C.P.,* pp. 28–9, 60, 65, 82–83.
110. New York *Herald Tribune,* December 27, 1936.
111. Andrews to B. A. Konkle [Spring, 1943].

112. *Ibid.*
113. "Historic Doubts," pp. 282, 286–94; see pp. 123–24.
114. G. W. Brown in *Canadian Hist. Review,* XVII (1936), 70.
115. Andrews to B. A. Konkle, March, 1942.
116. "These Forty Years," p. 245; "The Historian," pp. 10–11.
117. See pp. 46–47.
118. "These Forty Years," p. 246.
119. *Ibid.,* p. 248.
120. *Ibid.,* p. 249.
121. *Ibid.*
122. Andrews to Hubert Hall, March 27, 1939.
123. Andrews to B. A. Konkle, March, 1942.
124. *C.P.A.H.,* IV, 427–28.
125. *Ibid.,* IV, 425.
126. See pp. 203–11.
127. *Background,* pp. 197–98.
128. "The American Revolution: An Interpretation," p. 220.
129. *Background,* p. 169.
130. *C.P.A.H.,* III, 5–6.
131. *Earliest,* pp. 20, 21, 26.
132. *C.P.A.H.,* I, 52.
133. *Ibid.,* I, 75.
134. *Ibid.,* III, 39.
135. *Ibid.,* III, ix.
136. *Ibid.,* III, 32.
137. *Ibid.,* II, xiii.
138. *Ibid.,* IV, 369.
139. *Background,* pp. 7, 9, 12.
140. *C.P.A.H.,* III, 55.
141. *Ibid.,* III, 183, n. 1; II, 197.
142. *Ibid.,* III, 101.
143. *Background,* p. 183.
144. "The American Revolution: An Interpretation," pp. 228–29.
145. *C.P.,* p. 204.
146. "The American Revolution: An Interpretation," p. 226.
147. *Background,* p. 197.
148. "The American Revolution: An Interpretation," p. 231.
149. *Background,* pp. 161, 185.
150. "The American Revolution: An Interpretation," pp. 220–21.
151. *Background,* p. 182.
152. "On the Writing of Colonial History," p. 31.
153. "These Forty Years," p. 249.
154. *Ibid.,* p. 248.
155. *Ibid.,* p. 241.
156. *Earliest,* p. 1.
157. *C.P.,* p. 31.
158. New York *Evening Post,* July 6, 1905.
159. *Background,* p. 181.
160. *C.P.A.H.,* IV, 158.
161. "The Historian," p. 42.
162. *Background,* p. 208.
163. "Commencement Address, Trinity College, 1929," *Trinity Coll. Bull.,* New Ser., XXVI, No. 3 (1929), 16.
164. "The American Revolution: An Interpretation," p. 232.
165. *Background,* p. 185.
166. "Present-Day Thoughts on the American Revolution," *Bull. of the Univ. of Ga.,* XIX, No. 11 (1919), 14.
167. *Ibid.*

168. "The American Revolution: An Interpretation," p. 232.

169. *Ibid.*

170. *Background,* p. 181.

171. *The Historical Development of Modern Europe, from the Congress of Vienna to the Present Time* (2 vols., New York, 1896–98), I, 87.

172. "Should Recent European History Have a Place in the College Curriculum?" Amer. Hist. Assn., *Annual Report for 1899* (Washington, 1900), I, 544.

173. "Some Constructive Aspects of the War," *Meredith Coll. Quarterly Bull.,* Ser. 10, No. 4 (1917), p. 42.

174. *Ibid.,* p. 56.

175. *Ibid.,* p. 57.

176. *Ibid.,* pp. 58, 61.

177. *Yale Alumni Weekly,* December 5, 1919.

178. "Present-Day Thoughts," pp. 1–2.

179. *Ibid.,* p. 16.

180. *Ibid.,* p. 3; "Commencement Address, Trinity College, 1929," p. 8.

181. "Raleigh's Place in American Colonization," State Literary and Hist. Assn. of N. C., *Proceedings,* 1918, in Publications of the N. C. Hist. Commission (Bull. No. 25, Raleigh, 1919), p. 75.

182. Andrews to Dr. Kwan-Ichi Asakawa, February 19, 1941.

183. *Ibid.*

184. Andrews to Hubert Hall, March 27, 1939.

185. "These Forty Years," p. 246.

186. "History as an Aid to Moral Culture," National Education Assn., *Journal of Proceedings and Addresses* (1894), pp. 403, 401.

187. See pp. 11–12.

188. See pp. 212–15.

CHAPTER 6: THE MASTER, THE APPRENTICES, AND THE GILD

1. Andrews to his mother, May 7, 1906; statement of Mrs. Charles M. Andrews to author, November 22, 1952.

2. Andrews to Turner, March 27, 1909.

3. Andrews to Turner, March 10, 1910.

4. Turner to Andrews, March 10, 1910, copy; G. B. Adams to Andrews, January 29, 1910; L. W. Labaree, "Charles McLean Andrews: Historian, 1863–1943," *William and Mary Quarterly,* 3d Ser., I (1944), 8.

5. Statement of Mrs. Charles M. Andrews to author, January 9, 1953.

6. Andrews to Jameson, April 20, 1902, Jameson papers.

7. Andrews to Turner, March 10, 1910.

8. Andrews to Hubert Hall, December 2, 1925.

9. Andrews to Jameson, March 14, 1926, Jameson papers.

10. Andrews to Charles Seymour, March 31, 1927.
11. Andrews to Hubert Hall, November 29, 1938.
12. *Yale Daily News,* March 11, 1924.
13. *Ibid.*
14. "Message as Senior Member of the Executive Council," Middle States Assn. of Hist. Teachers, 30th Anniversary (1904–33), *Proceedings,* pp. 13–14.
15. *Ibid.*
16. Andrews to B. A. Konkle [Spring, 1943].
17. Andrews to Charles Seymour, May 9, 1935.
18. Andrews to Hubert Hall, January 8, 1932.
19. Andrews to Hubert Hall, June 14, 1937.
20. Mrs. Charles M. Andrews to the Hubert Halls, September 7, 1942.
21. "The Charles McLean Andrews Memorial," *Yale Univ. Lib. Gazette,* XVIII (1944), 65.
22. Andrews to Hubert Hall, March 22, 1943.
23. Statement of Mrs. Charles M. Andrews to author, February 20, 1953. Andrews' letters to his mother during the latter part of 1905 and early part of 1906 refer constantly to his growing deafness.
24. Statement of Mrs. Charles M. Andrews to author, January 27, 1953.
25. Andrews to Jameson, December 12, 1921, Jameson papers.
26. Helen Taft Manning to author, June 20, 1953.
27. *Ibid.*
28. Statement of Prof. Malone to author, October 11, 1954.
29. Helen Taft Manning to author, June 20, 1953.
30. Statement of Mrs. Charles M. Andrews to author, January 20, 1953.
31. Statement of Mrs. Charles M. Andrews to author, February 3, 1953.
32. Andrews to Charles Seymour, November 23, 1938.
33. Andrews to G. W. Pierson of Yale University, conversation, July 10, 1942. A copy of Mr. Pierson's notes are in the possession of Mrs. Charles M. Andrews.
34. Statement of Prof. Malone to author, October 11, 1954.
35. C. P. Gould to author, October 11, 1952.
36. S. M. Pargellis review, *AHR,* XLIX (1944), 492.
37. *Ibid.*
38. "In Memoriam: Charles McLean Andrews," *Bryn Mawr Alumnae Bull.,* December, 1943, p. 7.
39. L. H. Gipson, "Charles McLean Andrews and the Re-orientation of the Study of American Colonial History," *Pa. Mag. of Hist. and Biog.,* LIX (1935), 215.
40. "Charles McLean Andrews: Historian, 1863–1943," p. 11.

41. S. M. Pargellis review, *AHR*, XLIX (1944), 492.

42. C. P. Gould to author, October 11, 1952.

43. *Yale Alumni Weekly*, March 28, 1919.

44. S. M. Pargellis to author, September 22, 1952.

45. Andrews to G. W. Pierson of Yale University, conversation, July 10, 1942.

46. A large part of the Andrews papers (those mss. which are still at the home of Mrs. Charles M. Andrews, 424 St. Ronan Street, New Haven) consists of letters from his students dealing with their dissertations and indicating the great care and attention which Andrews had devoted to them.

47. Andrews to Charles Seymour, March 31, 1927.

48. Statement of Prof. L. W. Labaree to author, December 7, 1951.

49. S. M. Pargellis to author, September 22, 1952.

50. Andrews to C. P. Nettels, May 19, 1931; the same suggestion is evident from V. F. Barnes to Andrews, November 3, 1929.

51. Andrews to H. A. Moe, November 21, 1931.

52. Prof. L. H. Gipson has written the author that when he began his seminar work under Andrews, in 1917, the latter tried to dissuade him from working on Jared Ingersoll. Andrews expressed "with great firmness" his conviction "that biography was not a proper medium for a thesis at the doctoral level. He said that he had never permitted a student working under him to select a biographical subject. . . . After the completion of Jared Ingersoll to his satisfaction, he never, so far as I know, raised an objection to a biographical subject, provided that it served to illuminate institutional history, his great specialty."

53. S. M. Pargellis, *Lord Loudoun in North America* (New Haven, 1933), p. v. G. A. Jacobsen, *William Blathwayt, a Late Seventeenth Century Administrator* (New Haven, 1932), pp. v–vi.

54. Statement of Prof. Malone to author, October 11, 1954. Prof. Malone had done his work under Allen Johnson but consulted Prof. Andrews about it before publishing it in the Yale Historical Series.

55. See Jacobsen, *Blathwayt,* chap. 1, "Whitehall in William Blathwayt's Day," pp. 1–30.

56. See Pargellis, *Lord Loudoun,* chap. 1.

57. L. W. Labaree, *Royal Government in America* (New Haven, 1930), p. ix.

58. L. H. Gipson, *Jared Ingersoll* (New Haven, 1920), p. 7.

59. See Labaree, *Royal Government,* p. 37; also B. W. Bond, *The Quit-Rent System in the American Colonies* (New Haven, 1919), chap. 13.

60. Cf. V. F. Barnes, *The Dominion of New England: A Study in British Colonial Policy* (New Haven, 1923), p. 3; Jacobsen, *Blathwayt,* chap. 14.

61. Andrews, "Bryn Mawr and the Past," *Bryn Mawr Alumnae Bull.,* July, 1943, p. 11.

62. Edward Raymond Turner, *The Privy Council of England in the Seventeenth and Eighteenth Centuries, 1603–1784* (2 vols., Baltimore, 1927–28), I, xi.

63. After the death of Andrews, Freeman undertook to appraise his own debt to his master: "He exercised more influence over my mind and my style than all the other History Professors at Johns Hopkins combined. In fact, after Professor Herbert Adams' death and prior to his coming, the history department was in the hands of mediocre, uninspiring or scatter-brained men. Your husband came down one day in the Spring of 1907, spoke to us students, and thrilled us. He had just completed his great work in Britain and had a mind full of it. I remember now how delighted we were to learn, a little later, that he was to come back to the Hopkins as Professor of History . . . . For my part, I had the benefit of his guidance the first year of his professorship when he was full of enthusiasm to bring back the department to the eminence it had enjoyed in Adams' day. As my dissertation was in American history, I did not have the privilege of doing my research under him, but I count it one of the blessings of my life that when my dissertation was being shaped to final form, I had to submit it to him. Never shall I forget the evening when, at his summons, I went to your home to get his criticisms. They concerned chiefly my literary "style," rather than my investigation and conclusions, and they were, to say the least, sharply pointed . . . . It was to Professor Andrews' help that I owed my start in historical editing and writing. I do not think I ever could have succeeded had he not prevailed upon me to do the first book in a sound manner." Freeman to Mrs. Charles M. Andrews, September 25, 1943.

64. The newer directions of Prof. Labaree's work may be seen not only from his highly suggestive appraisal of *Conservatism in Early America* (1948) but also from the vast enterprise which he has just begun as editor of *The Papers of Benjamin Franklin,* a definitive edition to be published over a decade and a half in 25 to 30 vols.

65. Andrews to Mrs. Ernest Fast, November 8, 1938.

66. Andrews read, among other similar mss., the first volume of Gipson's multi-volume work (L. H. Gipson to Andrews, September 16, 1930); Bining's *British Regulation of the Colonial Iron Industry* (A. C. Bining to Andrews, November 9, 1932); and a first draft of Nettels' *The Money Supply of the American Colonies before 1720*

(C. P. Nettels to Andrews, August 2, 1931). All letters cited are among the Andrews papers.

67. Andrews joined the Committee at its very inception in 1930 and wrote an introduction entitled "Vice-Admiralty Courts in the Colonies" to Vol. III of the Committee's publications: Dorothy S. Towle, ed., *Records of the Vice-Admiralty Court of Rhode Island, 1716–1752* (Washington, 1936).

68. Andrews withdrew in 1915 from his advisory capacity on the transcripts but offered his services for further consultation, if necessary, an offer of which the Library of Congress availed itself. Herbert Putnam to Andrews, February 23, 1915; J. F. Jameson to Andrews, December 22, 1928.

69. Prof. Labaree relates how Andrews' *Guides* contributed to the accuracy of the Williamsburg restoration: "A brief description, in the section on the Bodleian Library, Oxford, of a copper plate with views of 'buildings, probably in some town in Virginia or Carolina,' came to the notice of the Williamsburg researchers. Investigation proved that the plate depicted elevations of the principal buildings of the Virginia capital. By means of this plate the authenticity of the reconstruction of these buildings became assured." ("Charles McLean Andrews, 1863–1943," *William and Mary Quarterly,* 3d Ser., I [1944], 6, footnote).

70. J. S. Bassett to Andrews, December 14, 1921; November 3, 1922. H. E. Bourne to Andrews, October 29, 1922.

71. Alvord's death prevented his participating in the volume.

CHAPTER 7: ANDREWS AND THE NEW COLONIAL HISTORY

1. See chap. 3, sec. 1.

2. Dixon Ryan Fox, *Herbert Levi Osgood* (New York, 1924), pp. 47–51.

3. *Ibid.*, pp. 67–73.

4. See *ibid.*, pp. 47, 48, 63.

5. Two volumes of Osgood's *American Colonies in the Seventeenth Century* appeared in 1904, the third in 1907. His four-volume study of *The American Colonies in the Eighteenth Century* appeared posthumously, in 1924.

6. *Christian Union,* March 26, 1891.

7. Osgood, "Report of the Conference on Research in American Colonial and Revolutionary History," Amer. Hist. Assn., *Annual Report for 1908* (Washington, 1909), I, 116.

8. Osgood, "The Study of American Colonial History," Amer. Hist. Assn., *Annual Report for 1898* (Washington, 1899), p. 63.

9. *AHR,* XXVIII (1923), 760.

10. "Some Neglected Aspects of Colonial History," N. J. Hist. Soc., *Proceedings,* 3d Ser., IV (1901), 5.

11. Winfred Trexler Root, "American Colonies and the British Empire: Colonial History, Old Style and New," *Hist. Teacher's Mag.,* VI (1915), 282.

12. *Ibid.*

13. Cf. Russell B. Nye, *George Bancroft* (New York, 1944), pp. 284–86.

14. Claude Halstead Van Tyne, *The American Revolution, 1776–1783* (New York, 1905), p. 335. Quotations used by permission of Harper and Bros.

15. Charles Kendall Adams, "Some Neglected Aspects of the Revolutionary War," *Atlantic Monthly,* August, 1898, p. 174.

16. "Study of American Colonial History," p. 63.

17. Sydney George Fisher, "The Legend and Myth-Making Process in Histories of the American Revolution," Amer. Philos. Soc., *Proceedings,* LI (1912), 68.

18. *Colonial Self-Government, 1652–1689* (New York, 1904), p. 337.

19. New York *Evening Post,* May 10, 1905.

20. See illuminating comment by D. R. Fox, *Osgood,* p. 33.

21. "These Forty Years," *AHR,* XXX (1925), 233–34, 236.

22. *AHR,* XIII (1908), 360. 23. *Ibid.*

24. *AHR,* XIV (1909), 830.

25. W. T. Root, *The Relations of Pennsylvania with the British Government, 1696–1765* (New York, 1912), p. i.

26. *Guide to the Study of American History* (Boston, 1896), p. 2.

27. "Report of the Conference on Research," p. 113.

28. "These Forty Years," p. 245. 29. Fox, *Osgood,* pp. 114, 116.

30. *The True History of the American Revolution* (Philadelphia, 1902), p. 8.

31. See Herman Ausubel, *Historians and Their Craft* (New York, 1950), chaps. 1, 2 *passim.*

32. "These Forty Years," p. 247.

33. In George E. Howard, *Preliminaries of the Revolution* (New York, 1905), pp. xiii, xv. Quotations used by permission of Harper and Bros.

34. G. L. Beer, *British Colonial Policy, 1754–1765* (New York, 1907), pp. 315–16.

35. Samuel Eliot Morison, "Edward Channing, a Memoir," Mass. Hist. Soc., *Proceedings,* LXIV (1932), 269.

36. "These Forty Years," pp. 230–31.

37. In Edward Potts Cheyney, *European Background of American History, 1300–1600* (New York, 1904), p. xvi. Quotations used by permission of Harper and Bros.

38. See, for example, Beer, *British Colonial Policy,* p. vi; S. G. Fisher, *True History,* pp. 5, 8, 9; Oliver M. Dickerson, *American Colonial Government, 1696–1765* (Cleveland, 1912), pp. 14–15.

39. *AHR,* XXX (1924), 150; *AHR,* XXXVI (1931), 800–801.

40. *AHR,* XXII (1917), 391; Fox, *Osgood,* pp. 55–59.

41. "The Legend and Myth-Making Process," pp. 59, 69.

42. *The Nation,* August 21, 1913.

43. Unidentified Ms, Andrews MSS, Yale Univ. Lib.

44. *Relations of Pennsylvania,* p. i.

45. *A History of the United States* (6 vols., New York, 1905–25), I, vii.

46. *The Old Colonial System, Part I, 1660–1688* (2 vols., New York, 1912), I, ix.

47. Quoted in E. C. O. Beatty, "Herbert Levi Osgood," in W. T. Hutchinson, ed., *Marcus W. Jernegan Essays in American Historiography* (Chicago, 1937), p. 293.

48. George Louis Beer, *The Commercial Policy of England toward the American Colonies* (New York, 1893), p. 9.

49. "Study of American Colonial History," p. 71.

50. *History,* I, vi; *American Revolution,* p. 20.

51. "These Forty Years," p. 239. 52. *History,* I, v.

53. In E. P. Cheyney, *European Background,* p. xvii.

54. R. H. Fahrney, "Edward Channing," in W. T. Hutchinson, ed., *Marcus W. Jernegan Essays,* p. 301.

55. *AHR,* XVIII (1913), 604.

56. *The American Colonies in the Seventeenth Century* (3 vols., New York, 1904–7), I, xxv.

57. Cited in Fox, *Osgood,* p. 70.

58. *American Colonies in Seventeenth Century,* I, xxv.

59. Cited in Ausubel, *Historians,* p. 190.

60. "Study of American Colonial History," pp. 65–66.

61. In E. P. Cheyney, *European Background,* p. xvi.

62. "History as an Aid to Moral Culture," National Education Assn., *Journal of Proceedings and Addresses* (1894), p. 406.

63. "These Forty Years," p. 232.

64. See W. Stull Holt, "The Idea of Scientific History in America," *Journal of the Hist. of Ideas,* I (1940), 352–53; Andrews, "Some Recent Aspects of Institutional Study," *Yale Review,* I (1893), 381–410 *passim.*

65. *History,* I, v–vi.

66. "Some of the Vagaries and Amenities of History," Assn. of

Hist. Teachers of the Middle States and Md., 4th Annual Convention (March, 1906), *Minutes,* p. 43.

67. *History,* I, v.
68. *European Background,* pp. xxvii–xxviii.
69. Fox, *Osgood,* p. 68.
70. Van Tyne, *American Revolution,* p. 332.
71. *Preliminaries,* pp. 313, 325.
72. *History,* I, vi.
73. *British Colonial Policy,* p. 315.
74. *Ibid.,* p. 316.
75. *Background,* pp. 169, 181, 208.
76. Holt, "Idea of Scientific History in America," pp. 358–59. Perhaps the best expression of this view may be found in G. B. Adams, "History and the Philosophy of History," *AHR,* XIV (1909), 221–36.
77. Holt, "Idea of Scientific History," p. 357.
78. Such enterprise was approved of or encouraged in the presidential messages, to the Amer. Hist. Assn., of Goldwin Smith (1904), Albert Bushnell Hart (1909), Frederick Jackson Turner (1910), and William M. Sloane (1911). See Ausubel, *Historians,* pp. 200–202, 210–19.
79. "History and the Philosophy of History," *AHR,* XIV (1909), 236.
80. "Some Recent Aspects of Institutional Study," pp. 392–93.
81. Beer, *Old Colonial System, 1660–1688,* I, ix.
82. *Pa. Mag. of Hist. and Biog.,* LXI (1937), 332.
83. "Study of American Colonial History," p. 65.
84. See, for example, A. B. Hart, *National Ideals Historically Traced* (New York, 1907), p. 68. Quotations used by permission of Harper and Bros.
85. *History,* I, v.
86. Cited by Fox, *Osgood,* pp. 67–68.
87. *American Colonies in the Seventeenth Century,* I, xxvii.
88. *Ibid.*
89. "Report of the Conference on Research," p. 117.
90. *Background,* p. ix.
91. *AHR,* XIII (1908), 360–61.
92. "Study of American Colonial History," p. 72.
93. Among the more important contributions of the new school on this subject were: chapters in volumes by Andrews and E. B. Greene in American Nation Series; Vol. 3 of Osgood's *American Colonies in the Seventeenth Century* (1907); Beer's *Origins of the Old Colonial System, 1588–1660* (1908), *Old Colonial System, 1660–1688* (2 vols., 1912), and *British Colonial Policy, 1754–1765* (1907); Andrews, *British Committees, Commissions, and Councils of Trade*

and Plantations, 1622–1675 (1908), as well as the introductory descriptions of the English colonial administrative agencies in the *Guides;* Dickerson's *American Colonial Government, 1696–1765* (1912); and, by way of a final summary for the school, Andrews' *England's Commercial and Colonial Policies* (1938), Vol. 4 of his *Colonial Period of American History.*

94. Beer, *Commercial Policy of England,* p. 9.

95. "Study of American Colonial History," p. 70.

96. *History,* II, 8.

97. *American Revolution,* p. 8.

98. For something of Beer's disposition toward English policy, see his *Old Colonial System, 1660–1688,* I, 106–8, 110, 127; II, 108–9, 306–13.

99. E. B. Greene, "The American Revolution and the British Empire," *Hist. Teacher's Mag.,* VIII (1917), 292.

100. "Study of American Colonial History," p. 66; see too, Fox, *Osgood,* p. 68.

101. Greene, *Provincial America,* pp. 67, 69; Root, *Relations of Pennsylvania,* p. 378; Channing, *History,* II, 219; Van Tyne, *Causes of the War of Independence* (New York, 1922), chaps. 2, 3 *passim;* Andrews, *Background,* chaps. 1, 2 *passim.*

102. *Relations of Pennsylvania,* pp. 389–90.

103. *British Colonial Policy,* pp. 287–88.

104. *New Viewpoints in American History* (New York, 1922), p. 164.

105. *Preliminaries,* pp. 47, 64.

106. Channing, *History,* II, 599.

107. "American Colonies and the British Empire," p. 283.

108. Channing to Andrews, February 24, 1910.

109. Osgood: *AHR,* XIV (1909), 830.

110. Root: *AHR,* XX (1915), 419.

111. Jameson to Andrews, May 3, 1914.

112. *AHR,* X (1905), 873–74.

113. *AHR,* XIX (1914), 815–16.

114. New York *Herald Tribune,* February 15, 1925.

115. See, for example, reviews by V. W. Crane, *Miss. Val. Hist. Review,* XII (1925), 426–28; J. T. Adams, *Sat. Review of Lit.,* January 3, 1925.

116. V. W. Crane review, cited in n. 115.

117. *AHR,* XIII (1908), 360.

118. "These Forty Years," p. 245.

119. *Pol. Science Quarterly,* XXXVIII (1923), 143; *AHR,* XXVIII (1923), 761; *Amer. Eco. Review,* III (1913), 633.

120. *The Nation,* August 20, 1924.

121. "The Historian," in *George Louis Beer: A Tribute to His Life and Work* (New York, 1924), p. 37.

122. *Ibid.,* p. 27.

123. *The Nation,* April 9, 1908.

124. *Yale Review,* XXVII (1918), 867.

125. *AHR,* V (1900), 741; "These Forty Years," p. 242.
126. New York *Evening Post,* July 6, 1905.
127. *AHR,* XIV (1909), 364–65; *The Nation,* December 20, 1917.
128. "H. L. Osgood," *Encyclopedia of Social Sciences,* XI, 500.
129. *AHR,* XI (1906), 400.
130. "The Historian," pp. 38–39.
131. *The Nation,* August 21, 1913.
132. *AHR,* XIII (1908), 360.
133. This was the third volume of Osgood's *American Colonies in the Seventeenth Century.*
134. *AHR,* XIII (1908), 361.
135. New York *Evening Post,* July 6, 1905.
136. *AHR,* XIV (1909), 364–65.
137. *AHR,* XVII (1912), 841–43; *Amer. Eco. Review,* III (1913), 633–34; *AHR,* XXIV (1918), 104–5; *AHR,* XXVIII (1923), 760–61.
138. *The Nation,* May 10, 1917.
139. "The Historian," p. 41.
140. *Ibid.,* p. 12.
141. *Ibid.*
142. *The Nation,* August 20, 1924.
143. *AHR,* XXXI (1926), 536.
144. *Ibid.,* p. 537.
145. *The Nation,* August 20, 1924.
146. *AHR,* XXXI (1926), 538.
147. "The Historian," p. 29.
148. *Ibid.,* p. 31.

CHAPTER 8: NEW TIMES, NEW HISTORIES

1. *The English Navigation Laws* (New York, 1939), chap. 19; "The Effect of the Navigation Acts on the Thirteen Colonies," in Richard B. Morris, ed., *The Era of the American Revolution* (New York, 1939).
2. *The Puritan Pronaos* (New York, 1936), p. 265.
3. See, for example, his comments in *Pa. Mag. of Hist. and Biog.,* LXIII (1939), 463–64.
4. *Roots of American Civilization* (New York, 1938), p. xi. Lawrence A. Harper's excellent study of *The English Navigation Laws* (New York, 1939) considered them to have been "a seventeenth-century experiment in social engineering" and suggested, to the age of the New Deal, that "we can profit vicariously from the experience of the past" (p. 5) and that "England's experiment holds forth hope that . . . we can help regulate our own destinies" (p. 384).
5. For two of the most representative statements of the relativist viewpoint see: Charles A. Beard, "Written History as an Act of Faith," *AHR,* XXXIX (1934), 219–31, and Carl L. Becker, "Everyman His Own Historian," *AHR,* XXXVII (1932), 221–36.

6. *AHR,* LV (1950), 280–81. 7. *AHR,* LVI (1951), 262, 268.

8. S. E. Morison in *New Eng. Quarterly,* VII (1934), 729–30.

9. H. S. Commager in New York *Herald Tribune,* December 27, 1936.

10. D. S. Muzzey in *Pol. Science Quarterly,* LIV (1939), 262; S. E. Morison in *New Eng. Quarterly,* VII (1934), 730.

11. *Pa. Mag. of Hist. and Biog.,* LXIII (1939), 464.

12. *New Eng. Quarterly,* X (1937), 793–94; *Pa. Mag. of Hist. and Biog.,* LXI (1937), 334–35; *Yale Review,* XXVII (1938), 646.

13. *New Eng. Quarterly,* X (1937), 795.

14. Amer. Acad. of Pol. and Soc. Science, *Annals,* CCII (1939), 263.

15. *New Eng. Quarterly,* VII (1934), 731.

16. *Pa. Mag. of Hist. and Biog.,* LXI (1937), 335.

17. *New Eng. Quarterly,* X (1937), 794.

18. Louis Hacker in *New Republic,* February 1, 1939.

19. *Ibid.; Science and Society,* IV (1939), 433–36.

20. *Pa. Mag. of Hist. and Biog.,* LXI (1937), 332.

21. *Ibid.*

22. "On the Writing of Colonial History," *William and Mary Quarterly,* 3d Ser., I (1944), 30. The article, it will be noted, appeared after the death of Andrews.

23. *Ibid.,* pp. 33–35.

24. Andrews to C. P. Nettels, January 2, 1938.

25. *Ibid.*

26. "On the Writing of Colonial History," p. 33.

27. Andrews to C. P. Nettels, January 12, 1936.

28. *C.P.A.H.,* IV, 425, note. 29. *Ibid.,* p. 428.

30. Andrews to Hubert Herring, September 22, 1938.

31. "On the Writing of Colonial History," p. 34.

32. *New Eng. Quarterly,* XII (1939), 593.

33. *Pa. Mag. of Hist. and Biog.,* LXIII (1939), 464; *New Eng. Quarterly,* X (1937), 793–95.

34. Andrews to Hubert Hall, November 29, 1938.

35. Statement of Prof. L. W. Labaree of Yale Univ. to author, December 7, 1951.

36. *New Republic,* August 2, 1939.

37. Andrews to C. P. Nettels, January 2, 1938.

38. Andrews to B. A. Konkle, March, 1942; [Spring, 1943].

39. *New Republic,* August 2, 1939.

40. Andrews to C. P. Nettels, January 2, 1938.

41. Andrews to B. A. Konkle [Spring, 1943].

42. *Ibid.*

43. For something of this framework of ideas, see Henry Steele Commager, *The American Mind* (New Haven, 1950), chap. 4;

Vernon Louis Parrington, *Main Currents in American Thought* (3 vols., New York, 1930), III, 189–211; Ralph Henry Gabriel, *Course of American Democratic Thought* (New York, 1940), chaps. 14, 15; and Carlton J. H. Hayes, *A Generation of Materialism* (New York, 1941), pp. 118–22, 328–30.

44. See pp. 138–41.

45. See p. 46.

46. A. B. Hart, *National Ideals Historically Traced* (New York, 1907), p. xiv.

47. See pp. 38, 133–36.

48. See pp. 113–14, 118–19.

49. See W. A. Dunning, *The British Empire and the United States* (New York, 1914), pp. 250 ff.

50. A. C. Coolidge, *The United States as a World Power* (New York, 1908), pp. 239–40.

51. Probably the best single survey of the altered relations between Great Britain and America during this period is Lionel M. Gelber, *The Rise of Anglo-American Friendship: A Study in World Politics, 1898–1906* (London, 1938).

52. R. H. Heindel, *The American Impact on Great Britain, 1898–1914: A Study of the United States in World History* (Philadelphia, 1940), pp. 125–28.

53. R. L. Schuyler, *The Fall of the Old Colonial System* (New York, 1945), pp. 250–51.

54. See pp. 11–12.

55. Heindel, *The American Impact on Great Britain,* p. 128.

56. *Ibid.,* p. 130.

57. *Ibid.*

58. Cited in J. R. Dos Passos, *The Anglo-American Century and the Unification of the English-Speaking People* (New York, 1903), p. 213.

59. John Fiske, *American Political Ideas: Viewed from the Standpoint of Universal History* (Boston, 1911), p. 135.

60. *Ibid.,* p. 6.

61. W. E. Livezey, *Mahan on Sea Power* (Norman, Oklahoma, 1947), pp. 99, 93.

62. Moses Coit Tyler, *The Literary History of the American Revolution, 1763–1783* (2 vols., New York, 1897), I, ix.

63. *Ibid.*

64. *Ibid.,* p. x.

65. "American Colonies and the British Empire," *Hist. Teacher's Mag.,* VI (1915), 282.

66. *New Viewpoints in American History* (New York, 1922), p. 163.

67. C. H. Van Tyne, *The American Revolution* (New York, 1905), p. 351.

68. Dunning, *The British Empire and the United States,* pp. 352, 370.

69. *Ibid.,* p. 371.

70. G. L. Beer, *The English-Speaking Peoples: Their Future Relations and Joint International Obligations* (New York, 1917), p. viii.

71. *Ibid.,* pp. ix, 270.

72. *Ibid.,* pp. 252–53.

73. *Ibid.,* p. 93.

74. *Ibid.,* pp. 164–65.

75. *Ibid.*

76. P. E. Shaw, *The Catholic Apostolic Church* (New York, 1946), chap. 15 *passim.*

77. Statement of Mrs. Charles M. Andrews to author, January 9, 1953.

78. "Present-Day Thoughts on the American Revolution," *Bull. of the Univ. of Ga.,* XIX, No. 11 (1919), 3.

79. See pp. 127–28.

80. See pp. 149, 150, 160, of *Fathers of New England* (New Haven, 1919).

81. "Present-Day Thoughts on the American Revolution," p. 7.

82. *Ibid.,* p. 12.

83. In a speech at the Imperial Conference of 1921, Smuts observed: "America is the nation that is closest to us in all the human ties . . . . She left our circle a long time ago because of a great historic mistake." Cited in A. B. Keith, ed., *Speeches and Documents on the British Dominions, 1918–1931* (London, n. d.), pp. 56–57. Cf. Beer, *British Colonial Policy, 1754–1765* (New York, 1907), p. 316, and his *The English-Speaking Peoples,* pp. vii–x; and Egerton, *The Causes and Character of the American Revolution* (Oxford, 1923), pp. 200–201.

84. "Raleigh's Place in American Colonization," State Lit. and Hist. Assn. of N. C., *Proceedings,* 1918, in Publications of the N. C. Hist. Commission (Bull. No. 25, Raleigh, 1919), p. 75.

85. *Ibid.,* p. 76.

86. "Present-Day Thoughts on the American Revolution," p. 3.

87. *Background,* p. 174.

88. "Present-Day Thoughts on the American Revolution," p. 16.

89. *Yale Alumni Weekly,* December 5, 1919.

90. Washington *Herald,* November 30, 1924.

91. *C.P.A.H.,* I, xii.

92. Minutes of the Committee, April 26, 1933, Andrews MSS., Yale Univ. Lib.

93. Draft of letter, Andrews to George C. F. Williams, January 20, 1930.

BIBLIOGRAPHY

I. THE WRITINGS OF CHARLES MCLEAN ANDREWS

A. *Manuscript Materials*

The two principal collections of Andrews manuscript materials are presently to be found at the home of his widow, Mrs. Charles M. Andrews, 424 St. Ronan Street, New Haven, and at the Yale University Library, New Haven. The first collection consists of some fifteen steel drawers of letters. These letters are of two major categories: those from his correspondents to Andrews, and confined largely to the period of the 1920's and 1930's; and those from Andrews to his mother, Mrs. W. W. Andrews, and written during the period 1886–1906. Mrs. Charles M. Andrews lent her generous cooperation to the present writer in helping complete several files of her husband's letters by obtaining originals or copies of those letters from the people with whom Andrews was in correspondence or from their executors. The Yale University Library collection consists of thirty-seven file boxes and contains, for the larger part, the notes which Andrews took upon the various manuscript collections which he canvassed throughout the course of his life, many no doubt in preparation for his magnum opus on the colonial period. For purposes of distinction, the Andrews materials at the home of Mrs. C. M. Andrews have been cited to as the *Andrews papers* and those at the Yale University Library have been cited as the *Andrews MSS.*

Apart from these two collections, a smaller but very significant collection of Andrews letters is contained in the Jameson correspondence, which is presently to be found at the Carnegie Institution of Washington, Washington, D. C. These letters are concerned principally with the work Andrews did on the *Guides* but touch enough upon other aspects of his work and thought to make them a valuable key to his system of historiography.

B. *Published Writings: Books and Articles*

A complete bibliography of the published writings of Andrews is to be found in *The William and Mary Quarterly,* Third Series, I (1944), 15–26. The bibliography was the product of a joint effort involving his colleagues, G. W. Pierson and L. W. Labaree, and Andrews himself. It has not been deemed necessary, therefore, in the following list, to cite any but the more important of Andrews' published writings or those which reveal the principal components of his system of historiography.

The River Towns of Connecticut. A Study of Wethersfield, Hartford, and Windsor. (Johns Hopkins University Studies in Historical and Political Science, Seventh Series, VII–IX.) Baltimore, 1889.

The Old English Manor. A Study in English Economic History. (Johns Hopkins University Studies in Historical and Political Science, Extra volume XII.) Baltimore, 1892.

"Some Recent Aspects of Institutional Study," *Yale Review,* I (1893), 381–410.

"History as an Aid to Moral Culture," National Education Association, Journal of Proceedings and Addresses, 1894, pp. 397–409. St. Paul, 1895.

"The Connecticut Intestacy Law," *Yale Review,* III (1894), 261–94.

The Historical Development of Modern Europe, from the Congress of Vienna to the Present Time. 2 volumes. New York, 1896–98.

"American Colonial History, 1690–1750," American Historical Association, Annual Report for 1898, pp. 47–60. Washington, 1899.

Colonial Self-Government, 1652–1689. (Volume V of the American Nation: A History, ed. A. B. Hart.) New York, 1904.

"Materials in British Archives for American Colonial History," *American Historical Review,* X (1905), 325–49.

"Some Neglected Aspects of Colonial History," New Jersey Historical Society, Proceedings, Third Series, IV, No. 1 (1901), 1–18. Paterson, 1906.

"Some of the Vagaries and Amenities of History," Association of History Teachers of the Middle States and Maryland, Fourth Annual Convention, Minutes, pp. 42–61. 1906.

Guide to the Manuscript Materials for the History of the United States to 1783, in the British Museum, in Minor London Archives, and in the Libraries of Oxford and Cambridge. (With Frances G. Davenport. Carnegie Institution of Washington Publication No. 90.) Washington, 1908.

The Colonial Period. New York, 1912.

Guide to the Materials for American History, to 1783, in the Public Record Office of Great Britain. (Carnegie Institution of Washington Publication No. 90A.) 2 volumes. Washington, 1912–14. Volume I: The State Papers. 1912. Volume II: Departmental and Miscellaneous Papers. 1914.

"Colonial Commerce," *American Historical Review,* XX (1914), 43–63.

"Anglo-French Commercial Rivalry, 1700–1750: The Western Phase," *American Historical Review,* XX (1915), 539–56, 761–80.

"Some Constructive Aspects of the War," Meredith College, *Quarterly Bulletin,* Series 10, No. 4 (1917), pp. 37–62.

"Present-Day Thoughts on the American Revolution," *Bulletin of the University of Georgia,* XIX, No. 11 (1919).

The Fathers of New England: A Chronicle of the Puritan Commonwealths. (The Chronicles of America Series, Volume VI.) New Haven, 1919.

Colonial Folkways: A Chronicle of American Life in the Reign of the Georges. (The Chronicles of America Series, Volume XI.) New Haven, 1919.

"Remarks on the Writing of American Colonial History," Publications of the Colonial Society of Massachusetts, XX, Transactions, 1917–1919, pp. 159–163. Boston, 1920.

Journal of a Lady of Quality: being the Narrative of a Journey from Scotland to the West Indies, North Carolina, and Portugal, in the Years 1774 to 1776. (Edited, with Evangeline Walker Andrews.) New Haven, 1921. Two subsequent editions appeared, with additional notes and illustrations, in 1934 and 1939.

"The Historian," in George Louis Beer: A Tribute to His Life and Work in the Making of History and the Moulding of Public Opinion, pp. 7–43. New York, 1924.

The Colonial Background of the American Revolution. Four Essays in American Colonial History. New Haven, 1924. Revised edition, 1931.

"These Forty Years," *American Historical Review,* XXX (1925), 225–50.

"The American Revolution: An Interpretation," *American Historical Review,* XXXI (1926), 219–32.

"The Acts of Trade," "The Government of the Empire, 1660–1763," in The Old Empire from the Beginnings to 1783, pp. 268–99, 405–36. (The Cambridge History of the British Empire, Volume I.) Cambridge, 1929.

Our Earliest Colonial Settlements, Their Diversities of Origin and Later Characteristics. New York, 1933.

The Colonial Period of American History. 4 volumes. New Haven, 1934–38.
I: The Settlements. 1934.
II: The Settlements. 1936.
III: The Settlements. 1937.
IV: England's Commercial and Colonial Policy. 1938.
"Historic Doubts Regarding Early Massachusetts History," Publications of the Colonial Society of Massachusetts, XXVIII, Transactions, 1930–33, pp. 280–94. Boston, 1935.
"Vice-Admiralty Courts in the Colonies," an introduction to Records of the Vice-Admiralty Court of Rhode Island, 1716–1752, Dorothy S. Towle, ed., pp. 1–79. (American Legal Records, Volume 3.) Washington, 1936.
"Conservative Factors in Early Colonial History," in Authority and the Individual, pp. 154–69. (Harvard Tercentenary Publications.) Cambridge, 1937.
"On the Writing of Colonial History," *William and Mary Quarterly,* Third Series, I (1944), 27–48. (Posthumous.)

C. *Published Writings: Book Reviews*

Apart from his books and articles, Andrews wrote, according to his own estimate, some three hundred and sixty book reviews. It was the good fortune of the present writer that the reviews were carefully preserved by Andrews in four notebooks. The notebooks are part of the Andrews materials which are still to be found at the home of Mrs. Charles M. Andrews, at 424 St. Ronan Street, New Haven. The periodicals to which Andrews contributed reviews included: *Christian Union, The Nation, Annals of the American Academy, American Historical Review, Political Science Quarterly,* and the *American Economic Review.*

II. OTHER WRITINGS

Adams, Charles Kendall. A Manual of Historical Literature. 3d ed., New York, 1889.
——"Some Neglected Aspects of the Revolutionary War," *Atlantic Monthly,* August, 1898, pp. 174–89.
Adams, George Burton. "History and the Philosophy of History," *American Historical Review,* XIV (1909), 221–36.
Adams, Henry. "The Tendency of History," American Historical Association, Annual Report for 1894, pp. 17-23. Washington, 1895.

Adams, Herbert Baxter. "The Germanic Origin of New England Towns," Johns Hopkins University Studies in Historical and Political Science, First Series, No. II. Baltimore, 1883.

——"Is History Past Politics?" Johns Hopkins University Studies in Historical and Political Science, Thirteenth Series, pp. 189–203. Baltimore, 1895.

——"Leopold von Ranke," American Historical Association, Annual Report for 1896, I, 67–81. Washington, 1897.

——"Norman Constables in America," Johns Hopkins University Studies in Historical and Political Science, First Series, No. VIII. Baltimore, 1883.

——"Special Methods of Historical Study," in Methods of Teaching History, G. Stanley Hall, ed. 2d ed., Boston, 1885.

——The Study and Teaching of History (Phi Beta Kappa Address, William and Mary College). Williamsburg, 1898.

——The Study of History in American Colleges and Universities. Washington, 1887.

Adams, Randolph Greenfield. Political Ideas of the American Revolution. Durham, 1922.

Ausubel, Herman. Historians and Their Craft: A Study of the Presidential Addresses of the American Historical Association, 1884–1945. New York, 1950.

Bancroft, George. History of the United States of America. Author's last revision, 6 volumes. New York, 1883–85.

Barnes, Viola. The Dominion of New England: A Study in British Colonial Policy. New Haven, 1923.

Bassett, John Spencer. "The New School of Historians," *Putnam's Monthly,* II (1907), 250–56.

Bean, Walton. "Revolt Among Historians," *Sewanee Review,* XLVII (1939), 330–41.

Beard, Charles A. The Nature of the Social Sciences. Report of the Commission on Social Studies, Part VII. New York, 1934.

——"That Noble Dream," *American Historical Review,* XLI (1935), 74–87.

——"Written History as an Act of Faith," *American Historical Review,* XXXIX (1934), 219–31.

Becker, Carl. The Beginnings of the American People. Boston, 1915.

——"Everyman His Own Historian," *American Historical Review,* XXXVII (1932), 221–36.

——"Some Aspects of the Influence of Social Problems and Ideas upon the Study and Writing of History," American Sociological Society, Papers and Proceedings, VII (1912), 73–107.

Becker, Carl (*continued*)
——"What is Historiography?" *American Historical Review,* XLIV (1938), 20–28.

Beer, George Louis. British Colonial Policy, 1754–1765. New York, 1907.

——The Commercial Policy of England toward the American Colonies. (Volume III, No. 2 of Studies in History, Economics, and Public Laws, edited by the University Faculty of Political Science of Columbia College.) New York, 1893.

——The English-Speaking Peoples. New York, 1917.

——The Old Colonial System, Part I: 1660–1688. 2 volumes. New York, 1912.

Bellot, H. Hale. American History and American Historians. London, 1952.

Bourne, Edward Gaylord. "Leopold von Ranke," American Historical Association, Annual Report for 1896, I, 67–80. Washington, 1897.

Bridenbaugh, Carl. Cities in the Wilderness. New York, 1938.

Brinton, Crane. "The 'New History' and 'Past Everything,'" *The American Scholar,* VIII (1939), 144–157.

Chamberlain, Mellen. John Adams with Other Essays. Boston, 1898.

Channing, Edward. A History of the United States. 6 volumes. New York, 1905–25.

Channing, Edward, and Albert Bushnell Hart, eds. Guide to the Study of American History. Boston, 1896.

Cheyney, Edward Potts. The European Background of American History, 1300–1600. (Volume I of The American Nation: A History, ed. A. B. Hart.) New York, 1904.

——"Law in History," *American Historical Review,* XXIX (1924), 231–48.

Clark, Dora Mae. British Opinion and the American Revolution. New Haven, 1930.

Commager, Henry Steele. The American Mind. New Haven, 1950.

Coolidge, Archibald Cary. The United States as a World Power. New York, 1908.

Dickerson, Oliver Morton. American Colonial Government, 1696–1765. Cleveland, 1912.

Dos Passos, John R. The Anglo-Saxon Century and the Unification of the English-Speaking People. New York, 1903.

Dunning, William Archibald. The British Empire and the United States: A Review of Their Relations During the Century of Peace Following the Treaty of Ghent. New York, 1914.

——"A Generation of American Historiography," American Histori-

cal Association, Annual Report for 1917, pp. 345–54. Washington, 1920.
——"Truth in History," *American Historical Review,* XIX (1914), 217–29.
Egerton, H. E. The Causes and Character of the American Revolution. Oxford, 1923.
Essays in Colonial History Presented to Charles McLean Andrews by his Students. New Haven, 1931.
Fisher, Sydney George. "The Legend and Myth-Making Process in the Histories of the American Revolution," American Philosophical Society, Proceedings, LI (1912), 53–75.
——The True Story of the American Revolution. Philadelphia, 1902.
Fiske, John. American Political Ideas: Viewed from the Standpoint of Universal History. Boston, 1911.
Fox, Dixon Ryan. Herbert Levi Osgood, an American Scholar. New York, 1924.
Freeman, Edward Augustus. Comparative Politics. London, 1873.
——"An Introduction to American Institutional History," Johns Hopkins University Studies in Historical and Political Science, First Series, No. I. Baltimore, 1883.
Gabriel, Ralph Henry. The Course of American Democratic Thought. New York, 1940.
Gelber, Lionel M. The Rise of Anglo-American Friendship: A Study in World Politics, 1898–1906. London, 1938.
Gipson, Lawrence Henry. "Charles McLean Andrews and the Reorientation of the Study of American Colonial History," *Pennsylvania Magazine of History and Biography,* LIX (1935), 209–22.
——Jared Ingersoll. New Haven, 1920.
Gooch, G. P. History and Historians in the Nineteenth Century. London, 1913.
Greene, Evarts Boutell. "The American Revolution and the British Empire," *History Teacher's Magazine,* VIII (1917), 292–94.
——Foundations of American Nationality. New York, 1922.
——Provincial America, 1690–1740. (Volume VI of The American Nation: A History, ed. A. B. Hart.) New York, 1905.
——The Provincial Governor in the English Colonies of North America. New York, 1898.
Hacker, Louis M. "The First American Revolution," *Columbia University Quarterly,* XXVII (1935), 259–95.
Hall, G. Stanley, ed. Methods of Teaching History. 2d ed., Boston, 1885. A most important volume, containing articles on the theory and practice of historical study and writing by some of the

foremost leaders of the new history, viz., H. B. Adams, J. W. Burgess, A. B. Hart, C. K. Adams, and A. D. White.

Hart, Albert Bushnell. National Ideals Historically Traced, 1607–1907. (Volume XXVI of The American Nation: A History, ed. A. B. Hart.) New York, 1907.

Heindel, Richard Heathcote. The American Impact on Great Britain, 1898–1914: A Study of the United States in World History. Philadelphia, 1940.

Herbert B. Adams: Tributes of Friends. With a bibliography of the Department of History, Politics, and Economics of the Johns Hopkins University, 1876–1901. Baltimore, 1902.

Holt, W. Stull, ed. Historical Scholarship in the United States, 1876–1901: As Revealed in the Correspondence of Herbert Baxter Adams. Baltimore, 1938.

——"The Idea of Scientific History in America," *Journal of the History of Ideas,* I (1940), 352–62.

Howard, George Elliott. Preliminaries of the Revolution, 1763–1775. (Volume VIII of The American Nation: A History, ed. A. B. Hart.) New York, 1905.

Hutchinson, William T., ed. The Marcus W. Jernegan Essays in American Historiography. Chicago, 1937. An important volume, containing appraisals of Osgood, Channing, Beer, and Van Tyne.

Jacobsen, Gertrude Ann. William Blathwayt, a Late Seventeenth Century Administrator. New Haven, 1932.

Jameson, John Franklin. "The American Historical Association, 1884–1909," *American Historical Review,* XV (1909), 1–20.

——The American Revolution Considered as a Social Movement. Princeton, 1926.

——A History of Historical Writing in America. Boston, 1891.

——"The Present State of Historical Writing in America," American Antiquarian Society, Proceedings, XX (1909–10), 408–19. Worcester, 1911.

Johns Hopkins University. Circulars, Volumes VI–VIII. Baltimore, 1886–89.

Kraus, Michael. The Writing of American History. Norman, Oklahoma, 1954.

Labaree, Leonard Woods. "Charles McLean Andrews: Historian, 1863–1943," *William and Mary Quarterly,* Third Series, I (1944), 3–14.

——"The Charles McLean Andrews Memorial," *Yale University Library Gazette,* XVIII (1944), 63–66.

——Royal Government in America. New Haven, 1930.

Morison, Samuel Eliot. "Edward Channing: A Memoir," Massachusetts Historical Society, LXIV, Proceedings, 1930–32, pp. 250–284. Boston, 1932.

——"Faith of a Historian," *American Historical Review,* LVI (1951), 261–75.

Morris, Richard Brandon, ed. The Era of the American Revolution: Studies Inscribed to Evarts Boutell Greene. New York, 1939.

Neds, Ivy Faye. "A Half-Century of American Historiography, 1884–1934." Unpublished Ph.D. dissertation, Ohio State University, 1936.

Neilson, Nellie. "In Memoriam: Charles McLean Andrews," *Bryn Mawr Alumnae Bulletin,* December, 1943, pp. 6–7.

Nettels, Curtis P. The Roots of American Civilization. New York, 1938.

Nye, Russel B. George Bancroft: Brahmin Rebel. New York, 1944.

Osgood, Herbert Levi. The American Colonies in the Eighteenth Century. 4 volumes. New York, 1924.

——The American Colonies in the Seventeenth Century. 3 volumes. New York, 1904–7.

——"Report of the Conference on Research in American Colonial and Revolutionary History," American Historical Association, Annual Report for 1908, I, 111–21. Washington, 1909.

——"The Study of American Colonial History," American Historical Association, Annual Report for 1898, pp. 63–73. Washington, 1899.

Pargellis, Stanley McCrory. Lord Loudoun in North America. New Haven, 1933.

Parrington, Vernon Louis. Main Currents in American Thought. 3 volumes. New York, 1927–30.

Read, Conyers. "The Social Responsibilities of the Historian," *American Historical Review,* LV (1950), 275–85.

Riggs, John. "Charles McLean Andrews and the British Archives." Unpublished thesis, Yale University, 1949.

Robinson, James Harvey. The New History. New York, 1912.

Root, Winfred Trexler. "American Colonies and the British Empire: Colonial History, Old Style and New," *History Teacher's Magazine,* VI (1915), 281–86.

——The Relations of Pennsylvania with the British Government, 1696–1765. New York, 1912.

Root, Winfred Trexler, and Herman Vandenburg Ames. Syllabus of American Colonial History. New York, 1912.

Savelle, Max. "The Imperial School of American Colonial Historians," *Indiana Magazine of History,* XLV (1949), 123–34.
Saveth, Edward N. American Historians and European Immigrants, 1875–1925. New York, 1948.
Schevill, Ferdinand. "Ranke: Rise, Decline, and Persistence of a Reputation," *Journal of Modern History,* XXIV (1952), 219–34.
Schlesinger, Arthur Meier. New Viewpoints in American History. New York, 1922.
Schuyler, Robert Livingston. The Fall of the Old Colonial System. New York, 1945.
Shaw, P. E. The Catholic Apostolic Church. New York, 1946.
Smith, T. C. "The Scientific Historian and the Colonial Period," *Atlantic Monthly,* November, 1906, pp. 702–11.
——"The Writing of American History in America, from 1884 to 1934," *American Historical Review,* XL (1935), 439–49.
Theory and Practice in Historical Study: A Report of the Committee on Historiography. Bulletin No. 54, Social Science Research Council. New York [1945].
Tyler, Moses Coit. The Literary History of the American Revolution, 1763–1783. 2 volumes. New York, 1897.
Van Tyne, Claude Halstead. The American Revolution, 1776–1783. (Volume IX of The American Nation: A History, ed. A. B. Hart.) New York, 1905.
——The Causes of the War of Independence. Boston, 1922.
——Loyalists of the American Revolution. New York, 1902.
Von Laue, Theodore. Leopold Ranke: The Formative Years. Princeton, 1950.
Wills, Elbert V. The Growth of American Higher Education. Philadelphia, 1936.
Winsor, Justin, ed. Narrative and Critical History of America. 8 volumes. Boston, 1884–89.

INDEX

All volumes cited in the following index are by Charles McLean Andrews unless otherwise indicated.